The Evolution of Water Resource Planning and Decision Making

The Evolution of Water Resource Planning and Decision Making

Edited by

Clifford S. Russell

Vanderbilt University, USA, AKF, Institute of Local Government Studies, Denmark and Bowdoin College, USA

and

Duane D. Baumann

Southern Illinois University, USA

In Association with the Institute for Water Resources

Edward Elgar

Cheltenham, UK • Northampton, MA, USA

Published by
Edward Elgar Publishing Limited
The Lypiatts
15 Lansdown Road
Cheltenham
Glos GL50 2JA
UK

Edward Elgar Publishing, Inc.
William Pratt House
9 Dewey Court
Northampton, Massachusetts 01060
USA

A catalog record for this book
is available from the British Library

Library of Congress Control Number: 2009903384

PEFC
PEFC/16-33-111
CATG-PEFC-052
www.pefc.org

ISBN 978 1 84844 047 0 (cased)

Printed and bound by MPG Books Group, UK

Contents

Figures

Tables

Contributors

Baumann, Duane, Professor Emeritus in the Department of Geography, Southern Illinois University, Carbondale.

Boland, John J., Professor Emeritus in the Department of Geography and Environmental Engineering, Johns Hopkins University, Baltimore, MD.

Delli Priscoli, Jerome, Institute for Water Resources, US Army Corps of Engineers.

Flores, Nicholas, Associate Professor of Economics and Research Associate in the Institute of Behavioral Science, University of Colorado, Boulder.

Galloway, Gerald E., Glen L. Martin Institute Professor of Engineering, University of Maryland College Park, former Secretary of the US Section, International Joint Commission; Brigadier General, US Army, retired.

Howe, Charles W., Professor of Economics Emeritus and Research Fellow in the Institute of Behavioral Science, University of Colorado, Boulder.

Loucks, Daniel P., Professor in the School of Civil and Environmental Engineering, Cornell University, Ithaca, NY.

Lydon, Peter, US State Department Officer, retired.

MacDonnell, Lawrence, Counsel, Potzak, Browning and Bushong; former Director of Natural Resources Law Center, University of Colorado School of Law, Boulder.

Moreau, David H., Professor in the Department of City and Regional Planning, University of North Carolina, Chapel Hill.

Rogers, Peter, Professor of Environmental Engineering and City and Regional Planning, Harvard University, Cambridge, MA.

Russell, Clifford S., Professor of Economics Emeritus, Vanderbilt University, Nashville, TN; Visiting Professor, Institute of Local Government, Copenhagen, Denmark; Research Associate, Bowdoin College, Brunswick, ME.

Sagoff, Mark, Senior Research Scholar at the Institute for Philosophy and Public Policy, School of Public Policy, University of Maryland, College Park.

Viessman, Jr, Warren, Professor of Environmental Engineering Sciences Emeritus, College of Engineering, University of Florida, Gainesville.

Abbreviations

ACF	Apalachicola, Chattahoochee and Flint Rivers
ACT	Alabama, Coosa and Tallapoosa Rivers
ADR	Alternative dispute resolution
ASCE	American Society of Civil Engineers
ASFPM	Association of State Floodplain Managers
ATLSS	Across Trophic Level System Simulation
AWRA	American Water Resources Association
BCA	benefit-cost analysis
BOB	US Bureau of the Budget
C&O Canal	Chesapeake and Ohio Canal
C&SF	Central and Southern Florida
CAA	Clean Air Act
CAP	Central Arizona Project
CEQ	Council on Environmental Quality
CERCLA	Comprehensive Environmental Response, Compensation and Liability Act (also known as Superfund)
CERP	Comprehensive Everglades Restoration Plan
COLA	Cost of Living Adjustment
CPI	Consumer Price Index
CPI-U	CPI for all urban consumers
CPI-W	CPI for urban wage earners and clerical workers
CV	Contingent valuation
CWA	Clean Water Act
CWAP	Clean Water Action Plan
DENR	Department of Environment and Natural Resources
DO	Dissolved oxygen
DRBC	Delaware River Basin Commission
DSS	Decision support systems
ECR	Environmental conflict resolution
EMAP	Environmental Monitoring and Assessment Program
ENPC	Ecole National de Ponts et Chaussees
EOP	US Executive Office of the President
EPA	US Environmental Protection Agency
EQ	Environmental quality

ESA	Endangered Species Act
ETP	Economic theory of politics
FEMA	Federal Emergency Management Agency
FERC	Federal Energy Regulatory Commission
FIARBC	Federal Interagency River Basin Committee
FPC	Federal Power Commission
FWPCA	Federal Water Pollution Control Act
FWPCA	Federal Water Pollution Control Administration
GAO	US Government Accountability Office
GIS	Geospatial Information Systems
GPRA	Government Performance and Results Act of 1993
HEC	Hydrologic Engineering Center
HEES	Health and Ecological Effects Subcommittee
HEP	Habitat evaluation procedure
HES	Habitat evaluation system
HQW	High quality waters
HSI	Habitat Suitability Index
HSPF	Hydrological Simulation Program FORTRAN
HUD	Department of Housing and Urban Development
IBI	Index of Biological Integrity
ICCP	Interagency Council on Public Participation
IID	Imperial Irrigation District
IJC	International Joint Commission
INGO	International non-governmental organization
IPCC	Intergovernmental Panel on Climate Change
IPET	Interagency Performance Evaluation Task Force
IUCN	International Union for Conservation and Natural Resources
IWC	Inland Waterways Commission
IWR	Institute for Water Resources
IWRM	Integrated Water Resources Management
MCL	Maximum Containment Level
MCLG	Maximum Containment Level Goals
MS4s	Municipal separate storm sewer systems
MWD	Metropolitan Water District
MWTP	Marginal willingness-to-pay
NAPA	National Academy of Public Administration
NAR	North Atlantic Regional Study
NAST	National Assessment Synthesis Team
NCC	National Conservation Commission
NDWS	National Drinking Water Standards
NED	National Economic Development

NEPA	National Environmental Policy Act
NEWS	Northeast Water Supply Study
NFIP	National Flood Insurance Program
NGO	Non-governmental organization
NOAA	National Oceanic and Atmospheric Administration
NPB	National Planning Board
NPDES	National Pollution Discharge Elimination System
NPL	National Priorities List
NPS	National Park Service
NRB	National Resources Board
NRC	National Research Council
NRCS	Natural Resources Conservation Service
NRD	Natural Resource Districts
NRI	Nationwide Rivers Inventory
NRPB	National Resources Planning Board
NWC	National Water Commission
NWWC	National Waterways Commission
OMB	Office of Management and Budget
ORSANCO	Ohio River Valley Water Sanitation Commission
OSE	Other social effects
P&G	*Economic and Environmental Principles and Guidelines for Water and Related Land Resources Implementation Studies*
P&S	*Principles and Standards for Planning Water and Related Land Resources*
PCSD	President's Council on Sustainable Development
PFI	Per cent of family income
POTW	Publicly owned treatment works
PPI	Producer Price Index
PVID	Palo Verde Irrigation District
QUAL2E	Enhanced Stream Water Quality Model
RBC	River Basin Commission
RCRA	Resource Conservation and Recovery Act
RED	Regional Economic Development
REE	Regional economic effects
RFF	Resources for the Future
ROGEM	River of Grass Evaluation Methodology
SAB	Science Advisory Board
SCS	Soil Conservation Service
SDWA	Safe Drinking Water Act
SFWMD	South Florida Water Management District
SMS	Safe minimum standards

SRBC	Susquehanna River Basin Commission
SWAQ	Subcommittee on Water Availability and Quality
SWAT	Soil and Water Assessment Tool
TMDL	Total maximum daily load
TVA	Tennessee Valley Authority
UCOWR	Universities Council on Water Resources
UNESCO	United Nations Educational, Scientific and Cultural Organization
USACE	US Army Corps of Engineers
USBLM	US Bureau of Land Management
USBR	US Bureau of Reclamation
USDA	US Department of Agriculture
USDA-ARS	US Department of Agriculture, Agricultural Research Service
USDOI	US Department of Interior
USEOP	US Office of President
USFS	US Forest Service
USFWS	US Fish and Wildlife Service
USGS	US Geological Survey
USIACWR	US Interagency Committee on Water Resources
WCED	World Commission on Environment and Development
WEAP	Water Evaluation and Planning System
WET	Wetlands Evaluation Techniques
WMD	Water Management Districts
WMO	World Meteorological Organization
WPCA	Water Pollution Control Act of 1948
WRAS	Watershed Restoration Action Strategies
WRC	Water Resources Council
WRDA	Water Resources Development Act
WRPA	Water Resources Planning Act
WSTB	Water Science and Technology Board
WTA	Willingness-to-accept
WTP	Willingness-to-pay
WWPRAC	Western Water Policy Review Advisory Commission
WWQMTSC	Watershed/Water Quality Modeling Technical Support Center

Foreword

The practice of water resources planning and management within the USA has adapted to keep pace with changes in societal values, advances in technology and scientific knowledge, and emerging water resource needs. Its early origins in nation building focused on the development of water supply, power and transport as the population expanded across the continent during the nineteenth century. It progressed through periods intensively focused on the mitigation of flood losses and later saw the emergence of multi-purpose development of the nation's water resources during the first half of the twentieth century.

The evolution of water resources planning from early single-purpose type projects to subsequent eras emphasizing economic efficiency, multi-purpose planning, and then multi-objective planning and environmental protection continues today as the nation's environmental awaking during the last half-century has advanced beyond environmental protection to embrace the goals of sustainable development, ecological integrity and integrated water resources management.

This transformation has likewise been accompanied by equally significant changes to the nation's water governance framework. The demise of the US Water Resources Council portended a federalism shift in decision-making leadership that continues into the twenty-first century. This paradigm change has been facilitated by reductions in real spending on water resources programs across federal agencies. The resulting devolution of the federal role places increased responsibilities on state and interstate organizations for the planning and financing of solutions which will address the water challenges of today and tomorrow.

Against this dynamic backdrop, it is essential to dissect and understand the implications of the concurrent water resources management changes that have been taken place as a prerequisite for measuring the issues we must face in the future. This book, aptly titled 'The Evolution of Water Resource Planning and Decision Making', was commissioned by the Institute for Water Resources (IWR) to bring together a group of the nation's foremost water experts and academicians to provide their unfettered views on what has brought the nation to this critical juncture. Their collective perspectives on the evolution of thinking on topics such as economic analysis, environmental valuation and the state of US water governance is aimed at informing students and practitioners alike on the nature of the issues looming ahead, while serving to underline the importance of an interdisciplinary approach to water resources planning and management.

Indeed, the development of this book reflects an interdisciplinary approach which mirrors, by design, the breadth of expertise essential to addressing contemporary water resources problems. It is also consistent with the trend in advanced education for multidisciplinary curricula in water resources – such as the advanced degree program developed by several universities as part of a cooperative effort with the Universities Council on Water Resources (UCOWR) and IWR for an interdisciplinary Master's Degree in Integrated Water Resources Planning and Management.

As evidenced by recent events, the USA will continue to face a daunting array of future water resources challenges. Hurricanes Katrina and Rita exposed a surprisingly fragile New Orleans hurricane protection system, while the accompanying flood response and evacuation planning and execution proved unable to deter the tragedy and loss of life that unfolded. Such vulnerabilities are not limited to coastal storms, and while major initiatives across the nation at the federal and state levels are re-evaluating the threats from both coastal and riverine flooding, concerns are accelerating over the nation's aging infrastructure, including dams and bridges and other water resources capital stock.

As this book is being published, portions of the southeastern USA are gripped in a severe drought which has escalated a long simmering interstate dispute over water allocation. The US population continues to grow, with some of the greatest increases occurring in areas already facing increased competition for water, and despite an overall abundance of water in the USA, projections related to global warming and environmental change add to an uncertain future – with some regions facing prospects of more intensive drought while others consider possibilities for more severe inland flooding and/or coastal storms.

As we begin a new century, with a new set of water resources challenges, both within the USA and around the world, this book serves as a reminder that the need for continued infusion of scholarship in water resources practice remains as compelling as ever. In fact, facilitating a continuing intersection of scholarship and practice remains the essence of the purpose of the IWR. Within this context, the Water Resources Development Act of 2007 (P.L.110–114) presents a unique opportunity to further advance the alignment of federal water resources principles with contemporary concepts for integrated water resources management, adaptive management, risk and reliability, system resiliency, improved communication of residual risk and collaborative, transparent decision-making processes.

I am therefore delighted that the IWR had this opportunity to resource and serve as a nexus for supporting the publication of this important book. It will no doubt serve as a scholarly resource for a new generation of practitioners and academicians interested in both the historical context and the future of water resources planning and management.

The IWR is indebted to the esteemed group of authors who poured their passion and knowledge into the various chapters. I wish to thank each of the contributing authors for their tenacity and dedication in seeing this book through to publication. I am certain that the knowledge documented herein will prove invaluable to future decision makers who will have their own distinct set of new water resources challenges to surmount.

Robert A. Pietrowsky
Director, Institute for Water Resources
US Army Corps of Engineers

Preface

Over a half-century ago, Gilbert F. White introduced the concept of flood plain management through his landmark 1942 PhD dissertation, 'Human Adjustment to Floods'.[1] Prior to that time, water resources management strategies were nearly all engineering-based, for example, design and construction of dams and levees. In spite of, or perhaps more accurately because of, our engineering marvels, the actual and potential damages associated with floods continued to rise in the USA, as industrial, commercial and residential development moved in behind the 'safety' of the flood control structures. Professor White argued that the federal government, particularly the US Army Corps of Engineers, needed to broaden its range of flood hazard management alternatives to include social and behavioral adjustments that would address the problem of increasing density and value of flood plain occupancy.

This broader emphasis on the flood plain itself slowly began to capture the attention of planners, economists, political scientists, sociologists and eventually ecologists and biologists. The need for interdisciplinary collaboration came increasingly to be recognized, particularly during the period from the late 1950s through the 1960s. Nevertheless, it was and still is a daunting challenge for engineers, sociologists and biologists to agree on approaches to water resource planning, decision making and management. Through his continuing natural hazard work, and the work of his students, Professor White nurtured the process. His thoughts and actions have taken root in countless ways, perhaps most notably through the work of the University of Colorado's Natural Hazards Center, which he established with support from the National Science Foundation in 1974.

During this period, in response to many social, technical and political stimuli, federal and state water resources planning processes were modified and enhanced. Definitions of benefits were tightened, for example, to rule out counting local economic spillovers resulting from project construction and operation. At the same time, non-market benefits were recognized as legitimate, though reliable methods for their estimation did not yet exist. Tentative efforts to reflect the views of multiple 'stakeholders' outside the bureaucracy began. And more sophisticated ways of exploring the impact of hydrologic and economic uncertainty were developed. During this period Professor White continued to push for change by arguing for a more formalized approach to monitoring the effects of these newly implemented methods in the context of actual projects, to see if the claimed benefits were produced under operating conditions. While there was and continues to be agency resistance to formally auditing programs, numerous studies have been performed along these lines, primarily within the academic field. If one were to try to sum up Gilbert White's principles, the result might be: consider the full range of alternatives in planning; involve all relevant intellectual disciplines; and continually monitor the effects of all initiated projects and programs.

Measuring actual progress in the water resources development and management field against the Whitean principles, it is striking how slowly change has been realized; how tenacious a grip tradition has had in spite of massive changes in knowledge, analytical techniques and computing power, to say nothing of the changes in incomes, tastes, leisure time and travel possibilities the USA has experienced during that period. The new water resource challenges the USA faces today and will face in the future require planners and related professionals to be better informed and more open to innovation than ever before. Informed decision making requires that they not only be skilled in their own specialty areas but also equipped with a broader understanding of related disciplines. As a case in point, one could argue that had the responsible decision makers embraced a more integrated approach in the wake of Hurricane Betsy, which devastated southern Louisiana in 1965, much of the recent damage associated with Hurricanes Katrina and Rita could have been avoided.

In an attempt to address this need, in 2002 the Corps' Chief of Planning, James Johnson, and Mark Dunning, research analyst at the Institute for Water Resources (IWR), proposed and launched a program to train existing and new employees in multi-objective planning and to encourage better collaboration among disciplines in dealing with new environmental problems and approaches. Cooperating with the Universities Council on Water Resources, IWR developed a multidisciplinary curriculum with a practical focus on integrated water resources planning and management. Universities participating in what evolved into the Corps' Advanced Degree Program agreed to develop their own interdisciplinary curricula that balance coursework in economics, engineering, hydrology, ecology, political science, sociology and statistics.

With the launch of the Advanced Degree Program the need was felt for a publication that would summarize and critically appraise the evolution of federal water resource planning over the last half-century. Such a book would, it was thought, benefit not only students enrolled in the program, but water professionals and practitioners more broadly. This volume is the product of that felt need. Great care was exercised in assembling a team of professionals willing to meet this objective. They include eminent scholars with decades of experience, representing the fields of economics, political science, engineering, law, biology/ecology, environmental philosophy and sociology. Their charge in the broadest terms was to describe changes over roughly the last 50 years and to suggest challenges for the future from their points of view. In the initial development of this publication, Professor White was asked for his input and in typical fashion his reaction was immediate and terse, stating: 'I am elated that your efforts are going forward and am fully supportive of the entire program, it is 30 years overdue. Please keep me informed of your progress'. Professor White passed away in 2006 before the final manuscript for this book was completed. Based upon his lifetime achievements, steadfast persistence and clear guidance in water resources planning, we dedicate this book to the late Professor Gilbert F. White.

Duane Baumann and **Paul Bourget**

NOTE

1. G.F. White (1945), 'Human adjustment to floods', University of Chicago Department of Geography, research paper no. 29, Chicago, IL, completed in 1942 and published in 1945.

Acknowledgments

This book grew out of Dr Duane Baumann's vision for an interdisciplinary graduate program in integrated water resources planning and management. He conceived the outline, negotiated with the authors, and organized support for the effort from the Institute for Water Resources of the US Army Corps of Engineers (IWR). Those authors, all notables in the field, put considerable effort into their respective contributions and were extraordinarily cooperative with the editor when he suggested changes to those contributions.

The support from IWR included early face-to-face meetings, which were very helpful in drawing attention to areas that were potentially contentious and therefore worth extra thought. At the end of the writing and editing IWR went through the process of finding and negotiating with a publisher, not the easiest of tasks with a fairly specialized volume, and the authors and editors are grateful to Edward Elgar for persevering. Further, IWR arranged for technical support through CDM, and Ms Eva Opitz and Ms Paula Vukadinovich provided this. Ms Opitz was involved from the earliest stages of the manuscript's development, coordinating with the authors, editors, staff and with IWR and conducting numerous reviews to ensure that the manuscript would meet the exacting standards of the publisher. Ms Vukadinovich demonstrated extreme patience and attention to detail in the development and processing of the several iterations of the manuscript. Those at IWR primarily responsible for the project were Dr Paul Bourget, Mr Robert Pietrowsky and Mr Darrell Nolton, and of these Dr Bourget can fairly lay claim to being the godfather of the final product.

Formally, the book project has been completed under IWR contract with CDM (DACW72-00-D-0001, Task order 56; W912HQ-04-D-0007, Task order 58). However, the views, opinions and findings contained in this publication are those of the authors and should not be construed as an official Department of the Army position, policy or decision, unless so designated by other official documentation.

1. Water resources planning: past, present and future

John J. Boland and Duane Baumann

INTRODUCTION

The chapters that follow describe, from a number of perspectives, the current state of play in the field of water resources planning and management with a heavy emphasis on the United States's experience. In reading this material, it will be helpful to recall that today's planners and managers face very different problems from those of even a few decades ago. Before the middle of the twentieth century, water resources decisions were seen primarily as a matter of finding ways to use the resource to its utmost – to unlock its potential for providing marketable goods and services to human society, even if the results were not always marketed, as recreation typically was not. Water resources planning, in that period, was primarily the province of engineers, with occasional inputs from economists.[1] As this book makes clear, water resources planning and management is a dramatically different enterprise today. Several of the chapters reflect on specific reasons for this difference, but it may be helpful to highlight here three distinct, but interrelated, areas of change that have affected water resources decision making during the past half-century.

- Evolution of demands – Society has changed greatly in 50 years. One major change has been a rising affluence in almost all parts of the economy. Combined with a near doubling of the population since 1950, this has produced very large increases in the use of water resources for recreation, expanded human settlements near formerly pristine lakes and rivers and in flood plains, large municipal and industrial uses in arid and semi-arid regions and expansion of irrigated agriculture. At the same time, a better informed and more affluent society wants better water quality, a better standard of service and more attention to the needs of the future.
- Evolution of governance – As the demands and pressures on water resources development have grown and changed, government has

responded by expanding and transforming water resources policies, regulations and institutions. These changes reflect the changing demands, values and preferences of society, but not perfectly and not quickly. For example, public concern about surface water quality ultimately led to the Clean Water Act (CWA), then to federal and state agencies with the mandate and competence to enforce it and finally to a continuing series of regulations and policies implementing the Act. Yet few would argue, even today, that the Act fully meets the expectations of those who supported it.

- Evolution of analysis – Governance structures (laws, policies, regulations and institutions) are the matrix within which planning and analysis must be done. Thus, the need for predictions of the water quality results from specific policy proposals has led to the development of more numerous, and more sophisticated, mathematical models capable of accepting broader arrays of pollutants as inputs and of predicting larger numbers of quality measures. But, as in the case of the evolution of governance, responses occur only after some lag and then only gradually.

It may be fair to say that today's analytical methods are, in general, appropriate to yesterday's laws and policies; and that those laws and policies reflect in turn the social values of the day before yesterday. Nonetheless, if one understands how water resources planning has developed and where it is today, it may be possible to say useful things about where it is and where it ought to be going. That is the modest goal of this book.

OVERVIEW OF THE BOOK

Chapter 2 addresses the history of water resources planning and development in the United States, describing historical trends from 1800 to 2004. The latter part of this period includes the shift of focus from water resources development to water quality management and ecosystem restoration. It also traces the evolution of state and federal water laws. Contemporary water resources planning processes are described in Chapter 2, along with the planning and management functions of federal, state, regional and non-governmental agencies and organizations. Some observations from history capture the author's views on events relevant to issues of concern in the present. The chapter concludes with a summary and related recommendation for the future.

Historically, many government agencies, political commissions and technical panels have examined and made recommendations for improving water resources planning and decision making. In recent times the public – in general and in the form of a variety of stakeholders – has become much more influential in water resources planning and management processes through a variety of public involvement efforts designed to introduce a greater sense of democratic legitimacy to this process. (These efforts are described briefly in Appendix 2.1.) This evolution, along with the shift from development to environmental protection and restoration, has significantly affected the nature of planning processes and the valuation of proposals for water-related actions. For example, it is recognized that there is a need for broader stakeholder input, for recognition of the spatial and institutional dimensions of 'problem-sheds', for breaking away from the box mentality associated with governments, agencies and interest groups, and for seeking innovative and imaginative solutions to the water resources management issues being faced. History suggests, however, that what can be accomplished in the future will be influenced, even constrained, by agency biases and political boundaries as much as by physical, chemical and biological realities and by the estimated benefits and costs produced by economists.

Nonetheless, economics continues to play a role in water resources planning and Chapter 3 discusses that role, focusing on the conceptual basis for and application of benefit-cost analysis. The logic has always been straightforward: identify and measure the aggregate beneficial and adverse effects of an action and compare them to see if the action is desirable. This has been the basic approach of water resources economic analysis for at least 200 years. During that time, of course, as water resources planning has evolved and changed in form, so has benefit-cost analysis. Benefit-cost analysis has changed to reflect the values and concerns of society and in response to expanded analytical capabilities. In particular, the kinds of effects considered and the sophistication of the methods used to measure them have changed dramatically, especially over the past 50 years.

Among the beneficial effects of water resources development are market goods (electric energy, water supply) and non-market goods (recreation, visual amenity). Similarly, adverse effects include market goods (construction costs) and non-market goods (adverse environmental impacts). The valuation of market goods has long been understood; the ability to value non-market goods has improved greatly in recent decades. Still, benefit-cost analysis cannot yet address all of the economic issues of concern to decision makers or the public. For example, despite much progress, the treatment of uncertainty still leaves much to be desired and the application of economic analysis to new activities, such as ecosystem restoration or dam removal, poses new challenges for analysis.

The emergence of environmental values and enactment of policies to preserve or enhance the environment have affected water resources planning and management in a variety of ways, four of which are discussed in Chapter 4. First, following the massive disposition of federal lands in the nineteenth century, an influential minority began working to preserve some of the nation's unique natural areas, many of which were closely related to water resources. Second, in the early twentieth century it was recognized that some species of flora and fauna were being substantially reduced in number, some even to the point of extinction, as a result of land and water resources development. Third, as growth in urban centers far outpaced development of public water supplies, fire protection, storm water facilities and disposal of sewage and garbage, the protection of public health became a larger issue for governments at all levels. In particular, without adequate treatment, discharged waste water was seriously degrading streams and interfering with a number of beneficial uses. Fourth, in the twentieth century, as the federal government became a dominant force in water resources development, concern arose about the effects of the projects themselves on water and related land resources.

The period from 1965 to 1980 was one of especially rapid growth in public concern about the environment and saw the formulation of many of the protective policies which still exist today. While it is true that a number of initiatives to address pollution problems and preserve natural areas were taken prior to 1965, the flurry of activity in the years after 1965 was unprecedented and that year may be taken as a convenient historical divide. Programs were enacted to preserve wild and scenic rivers; to protect threatened and endangered species; to accelerate improvement in ambient water quality; to establish national drinking water quality standards; to attack contaminated sites, especially those threatening groundwater; to require that environmental values were given consideration in all federal and many state actions; and to put in place processes to ensure that environmental quality values would be reflected in the formulation and evaluation of water resources projects. Some adjustments to these policies have occurred over the intervening decades, but the basic structure remains largely intact.

While many of these initiatives were long overdue, they created a highly fragmented system for managing water resources. Although comprehensive and multiple purpose planning had long been promoted, if never fully realized, the proliferation of programs and management agencies led us away from that ideal. Single purpose regulatory programs that tended to freeze existing uses supplanted planning for the multiplicity of future water-related needs and alternative uses of the resource.

Increased attention to environmental values in water management has in turn led to an increased demand for analytical techniques to predict the beneficial or adverse environmental outcomes of large investments. The combination of increased demand for the outputs of predictive models, increased funding for research and phenomenal advances in computing capability has led to significant advances in methods for predicting spatial and temporal flow patterns and chemical and biological quality of surface and groundwater systems. In many cases, advances in predictive models have outpaced monitoring systems necessary to calibrate and evaluate them. One particular problem – predicting outcomes for complex water-dependent ecological systems – remains an elusive goal. That problem is well illustrated by the difficulty of determining instream flow requirements to sustain aquatic ecosystems. Recent research has shown how difficult that problem is and the extent to which the current generation of models fails to provide a solution.

The concept of sustainability or sustainable development has attracted widespread attention over the past 15 to 20 years. Although the terms 'sustainable development', 'sustainable use' and 'sustainability' do not appear in any federal water resources regulations or statutes, many of the concepts of water quality and water resources management that emerged in the late nineteenth and twentieth centuries would fit comfortably under those broad concepts. Policies based on safe yield, wise use, maximum contaminant levels, maximum daily loads, protection of endangered species and preservation of wild and scenic rivers are clearly compatible with the principle of meeting the needs of the present without compromising the needs of future generations.

Two questions that flow from this review are, first, whether a dramatically more comprehensive environmental planning structure is needed and, second, to what extent should management of water resources be subsumed within that structure? Is the goal of integrating all aspects of water management under a comprehensive program reachable? Should an effort be made to reach it? Or, given concerns that any reopening of environmental policies in the present political climate could lead to loss of much that has been gained, should we continue to seek only marginal changes to existing policies?

Chapter 5 investigates the long problematic attempts to achieve collaboration between ecologists and economists. As noted at the beginning of this chapter, in 1962, when Maas et al. and the Harvard Water Program tried, with some considerable success, to report on and advance the state-of-the-art in water resources project analysis and planning, the game was largely the province of engineers and economists and the most important chips in play were water quantity and activities dependent on quantity.

The growth of citizen demands for outdoor recreation and for the protection of the natural environment more broadly, as reflected in new laws and institutional arrangements, have brought water quality into the game in a central way. Indeed, it seems safe to say that there is no longer such an animal as the purely quantity-related water project or plan. One of the several implications of this change has been the discovery of the need for ecological expertise alongside the skills brought to the table by the traditional players. However, efforts to fit the ecologists around the same table have not often been successful. Frequently, collaboration has taken a back seat to bickering about the point of the collaboration, which sometimes leads on to bickering about the worth of what each discipline brings to the table.

Why this should be so is not immediately obvious as commentators on and participants in these efforts have often observed, the very words 'ecologist' and 'economist' share the Greek root *oikos*, house. So why can they not share more and bicker less? Chapter 5 offers an explanation based on contrasting perceptions of the nature of the uncertainty we face in making policy or making plans and developing projects involving the natural world and the resulting positions on the appropriate definition and measurement of the 'value' of what is at stake. Put very briefly, ecologists tend to believe that our ignorance of the myriad processes and interconnections that characterize the natural world is so pervasive that even an apparently small intervention could lead to ecological disaster, with profound negative implications for human life. Thus, total values of systems are always relevant and should be sought. By contrast, economists may be said to have faith that the results of small interventions will be small changes in the state of the natural world, so that only the values of those small changes are relevant to policy discussions.

Determining what to do about these mismatched perspectives is harder than noting the mismatch. But the chapter argues for starting with quite specific questions posed to multidisciplinary teams that can expect to stay and work together for years rather than weeks or months. It dismisses efforts at grand philosophical resolutions via blue-ribbon panels as unlikely to lead beyond platitudes.

Chapter 6, returning to matters of analytical techniques, examines political decision making about water development and management in the USA, in particular, the federal role in achieving wise and sustainable uses of the resource for the public interest. In this connection, two hypotheses regarding the mode of governance are explored in a fairly general way:

- That the process and outcomes of water decisions are controlled by considerations of rationality applied to the administration of the resource by the federal system paying attention to state's and citizen's rights and also to the needs and demands of stakeholders and interest groups.

- That the outcomes result from the contention and struggle among a wide variety of stakeholders and interest groups, only lightly controlled by the federal institutions except when egregious situations arise demanding federal intervention.

The chapter starts by examining the great misunderstandings of what is encompassed by the concept of governance. In the eyes of many technical persons (engineers, economists, development planners and so on) governance is just about laws, regulations and institutions that are typically exogenously given. The common belief is that there is an 'ideal' set of laws, regulations and institutions that will result in good governance of water resources regardless of what else is happening in the country. Practical experiences, however, are quite different.

The role of the US federal government related to water derives indirectly from its authority to regulate interstate commerce and to manage federally-owned lands. Exercise of these constitutionally delegated powers may at times take precedence over inconsistent state actions. Individual and collective uses of water are determined initially as a matter of the property law of the one of the 50 states in which the water is found. In general, water is regarded as a common resource until it is applied to some legally protected use, after which a variety of federal, state and local rules come into play. Under the legal fiction that water belongs to everyone, states started developing more specific rules respecting uses of water. Today states are likely to directly supervise the process of establishing rights to use water, requiring a user to apply for permission. In sum, while the water resource itself is regarded as public property, individuals may establish legal rights to the use of some portion of water – subject to public regulation.

The driving force in any area of governance is politics. The conventional view of the relationship of politics to governance portrays an orderly world where politicians act as rational legislators in formulating laws for the general welfare, which in turn are implemented by institutions, which carry out the legislated water policies through rules and regulations. Real politics, however, is not so neat. Governance is now not seen to be a simple linear process, but rather a discursive and a highly complex set of interactions between laws and institutions and personal and group interests as well as the general interest: '. . . policy is more like an endless game of monopoly than sewing machine repair' (Stone, 1988, p.261). Water as a public resource is especially susceptible to political influences, substantial individual and public entity rights to sue over water acts as a brake on change, but this is opposed by the need for redefinition of rights to claim water. Such redefined rights must both reflect the core individual benefits which water rights carry and separate out and preserve their public good dimensions. The tension between these very divergent paths leads directly to political impasses.

The literature on politics and political theory leads to at least three different pathways for explaining political decision making. First, and a priori the most attractive to professional planners, is in the direction of the Economic Theory of Politics (ETP). This theory, referred to here as the rational model, aims at a synthesis of the ethics of Rawls with the political theories of Lasswell (1936) and Dahl and Lindblom (1953) and the welfare economics of Pareto, Hicks and Bergson. The second approach assesses institutions and sees how well they are meeting their stated goals, as Arthur Maass did in his analysis of the relationships between Congress and the US Army Corps of Engineers (USACE) (Maass, 1951). Call this the institutional model. A third path derives from the Polis Model of Stone (1988, 2001), who argues that rational behavior models (usually the ETP) miss the point of politics. Stone outlines how a model of political reasoning should perform:

> . . . a model of political reasoning ought to account for the possibilities of changing one's objectives, of pursuing contradictory objects simultaneously, of winning by appearing to lose and turning loss into victory, and most unusual, of attaining objectives by portraying oneself as having attained them. . . Political reasoning is reasoning by metaphor and analogy. (Stone, 2001, p. 9)

Two radically different perceptions of the nature of society emerge from this literature. The unit of analysis shifts from the individual to the community. Self-interest is extended also to include public interest. The conflicts now change from those between self-interests to those between self-interests and the public interest. The nature of collective activity moves from competition to a mixture of cooperation and competition. Most importantly, the criteria for decision making change from maximizing self-interest to the promotion of the public interest and loyalty to people and places. The nature of the information used tends to move from objective to ambiguous, interpretive, incomplete and strategically manipulated. Ultimately, what matters under the Polis Model are ideas, the pursuit of power and the maintenance of alliances.

The chapter uses the case of the Colorado River and examines the outcomes through the lenses of these different political models. The evolution of the governance problems on the Colorado River has been well documented. The conflicts among water users in the Colorado Basin have arisen in part due to the de facto assignment by the US Constitution of control over allocation of water to the states. Other complicating factors are the international nature of the basin geography, the presence of an interstate compact that is effectively from another era, in addition to expectable water conflicts among users in arid country. All of these conflicts have become more intense in recent times as real increases in water demands are now being felt throughout the basin. Using Stone's metaphor; it has been a 75-year monopoly game – and the game is not over yet!

In the long and rich history of the Colorado Basin, there is arguably strong support for the rational model. But future political behaviors connected to implementation of the current agreements are likely to be better explained under the Polis Model. In going from the rational to the Polis Model, the Laws of Nature are replaced by Laws of Passion and the currency of exchange is seen to be ideas, persuasion and alliances rather than material exchanges (traditional 'log rolling' style trading of economic benefits).

Using specifically 'political' models of water governance, as suggested in this chapter, rather than clinging only to 'rational' methods, could have major implications for how the federal government does business in the water arena. Since what emerges is that the control exercised and protection of the public interest achieved comes from actions taken at all levels down the chain from federal to state to river basin to county, to city and even neighborhood, what is the appropriate role for the federal water bureaucracy? Certainly there should at least be more explicit federal recognition of the role of politics in determining what is, or should be, good policy for water in the USA.

Chapters 2 through 6 all have at least a trace of historical flavor, be it of policy evolution or analytical methods development. Observing this, the casual reader, if such a person actually exists, might conclude that the water resources management 'system' is through evolving and that analytical methods have been developed to the point that further progress is unlikely. But this would, indeed, be a casual reading, for there is no shortage of new ideas and further challenges cataloged in those chapters. Chapter 7 makes all this clear and explicit by bringing together past and future and putting both in the context of broader national and international events; concerns newly recognized as urgent, such as global climate change; and the shifting sands of governance. The chapter emphasizes how large are the tasks facing the next generation of policy makers, analysts and variously interested stakeholders, calling for increased research efforts in everything from benefit-cost analysis, through ecological modeling, to the philosophy and mechanics of public involvement. The next section anticipates some of this material and, it is hoped, primes the reader to see beyond the background provided to the nature of the existing challenges or, what amounts to the same thing, the nature of the opportunities available.

A LOOK AT THE FUTURE

Here are five challenges or opportunities depending on the reader's taste in rhetoric that are likely to continue to be important for decades, if not generations.

As society's values and preferences continue to evolve, so will water resources policies, practices and management. The next two chapters document, for the past 50 or more years, major changes in law, regulation and policy (Chapter 2) as well as the mode of economic analysis (Chapter 3). These changes reflect trends in the ways in which water resources are used and the values that society places on those uses. These drivers are, in turn, affected by rising population and increasing affluence. The connections are not perfect: analytical capabilities tend to lag policies and regulations; policies and regulations tend to lag recognition of changed demands being placed on the resource. However, the evolution is continuous and will doubtless continue: first to catch up to demand, preferences and resource conflicts already apparent; and next to address the rising demand, altered preferences and increased conflicts expected for the future.

There is a strong argument for the re-establishment of a single set of federal standards and practices for water resources project evaluation; it is not clear that this will happen in the near future. Improvements in analytical capabilities are of little avail unless they are consistently applied and actually result in better analysis. The last attempt by the federal government to set uniform practices for water project evaluation ended with the publication of the *Economic and Environmental Principles and Guidelines for Water and Related Land Resources Implementation Studies* (P&G) in 1983. At that point, the P&G was voluntary guidance. Since then, individual agencies have drafted their own procedures (the USACE efforts have been based on the P&G); Office of Management and Budget (OMB) has another, though skeletal, set of standards and procedures. Among the numerous inconsistencies across the agencies is the existence of several different discount rates to be applied to federal projects (see Chapter 3). Many have called for the updating and repromulgation of the P&G. But there is no federal agency with authority or direction to do this. Some argue for an interagency body with the power to promulgate standards and procedures, to update them from time to time and to monitor their application by the various agencies. However it is done, improvement and rationalization of the methods for project evaluation would surely be helpful, but such a change depends on the will of Congress.

Environmental quality, including water quality, will continue to suffer from fragmentation in laws, agencies and enforcement, but some improvement is likely. As noted in Chapter 4, a major deficiency is the lack of an accepted and operational overall concept of ecosystem health and services. Yet improvements in models and computational ability allow planners to take 'problem-shed' approaches, producing plans that are effectively integrated despite regulatory and operational fragmentation. As this approach becomes more widespread, it will inevitably be reflected in institutional arrangements and management policies. Eventually, laws and regulations may evolve to a more integrated state, with resulting improvements in the effectiveness and efficiency of environmental policy.

Water resources conflicts will increasingly be resolved at the local and state level, with little or no role for the federal government. For much of the twentieth century, the federal government maintained a hierarchy of federal agencies and federally-sponsored river basin commissions (RBCs) which were expected to resolve most conflicts over access to or use of water resources. But when major conflicts arose, this system was unable to resolve them. This was true for the Colorado River Compact (see Chapter 6) and is currently the case for the Apalachicola-Chattahoochee-Flint (ACF) River Basin in the Southeast United States, to cite two very prominent multi-state disputes. When solutions, or partial solutions, or accommodations have been found, they have resulted from negotiations among local or state agencies, with substantial participation by stakeholder groups. Such negotiations may or may not yield efficient strategies, but the results are effective and sustainable. We can expect to see much less 'top-down' direction and much more 'bottom-up' planning and implementation – simply because it solves problems.

Despite considerable ongoing debate in the water resources community, there is no general agreement on the best roles for federal government, versus state and local government, versus the private sector. As outlined in Chapters 2 and 3, the water resources sector has been marked by steady enlargement of the federal role, at least up until the latter half of the twentieth century. Since the 1980s, there has been a trend toward devolution of project planning and financing responsibilities to state and local government. More recently, there has been much talk about the presumed advantages of private sector participation. Advocates argue that the original rationale for government action (very large-scale projects which could not be financed by the private sector) is no longer valid and that for-profit firms can deliver projects that are both more effective and less costly. Opponents argue that given the many non-market benefits associated with water projects, for-profit firms will underproduce services that produce no cash flow, thus resulting in less beneficial projects. This volume does not tackle this issue directly, but it does fill in many details of the current situation. It is left to the reader to draw conclusions.

CONCLUDING REMARKS

From the above brief descriptions, it should be clear that this book attempts both to describe the changes that have occurred in the world – in preferences, politics, policies and analysis – and to provide frameworks for thinking about those changes, their interrelations and how those frameworks do, and to some extent how they should, affect the world. This is perhaps most obvious in the case of the discussion of benefit-cost analysis (Chapter 3), for this technique, in the eyes of many economists at least, is an explicitly normative tool that ought to be used for assessing the social desirability of alternative policies, plans and projects. But the point also applies to the discussions of the growing role of environmental understanding in water resources management (Chapter 4) and of water politics (Chapter 6). Particularly in the case of politics the search for models that aid our understanding takes center stage, for the reality of politics is even messier than familiar, traditional models have admitted. A new and still somewhat unfamiliar framework represents an attempt to deal with the messiness without throwing out the notion of an overarching framework within which predictions and prescriptions might become possible. Even Chapter 5, dealing with the difficulties of collaboration between ecologists and economists, represents a search for a framework to help us make sense of actual case histories.

This book, then, does not aspire to make its readers experts in any of the subjects covered, to teach them how to do a benefit-cost analysis or run a water quality model, for example. Rather, it will have succeeded if its readers see concepts, connections and explanations for events that they had not seen before and, perhaps even more important, if they have their own ideas about where the gaps in our understanding lurk . . . where effort should be directed in the future.

NOTE

1. Introduction, in Maass et al. (1962), pp. 1–11.

REFERENCES

Dahl, R.A. and C.E. Lindblom (1953), *Politics, Economics and Welfare*, Chicago, IL: University of Chicago Press.

Lasswell, H.D. (1936), *Politics: Who Gets What, When and How?*, New York, NY: McGraw-Hill.

Maass, A. (1951), *Muddy Waters: The Army Engineers and the Nation's Rivers*, Cambridge, MA: Harvard University Press.

Maass, A., M. Hufschmidt, R. Dorfman, H.A. Thomas, Jr, S.A. Marglin and G.M. Fair (1962), *The Design of Water-Resource Systems: New Techniques for Relating Economic Objectives, Engineering Analysis and Governmental Planning*, Cambridge, MA: Harvard University Press.

Stone, D.A. (1988), *Policy Paradox and Political Reason*, Glenview, IL: Scott Foresman and Co.

Stone, D.A. (2001), *Policy Paradox: The Art of Political Decision Making*, 3rd edn, New York, NY: Norton.

2. A history of the United States water resources planning and development

Warren Viessman, Jr

INTRODUCTION

The objectives of this chapter are to acquaint the reader with historical trends in water resources planning and development from 1800 to the first decade of the twenty-first century, including:

- The evolution of supporting legislation.
- The changes in analytical requirements for project analysis.
- The shift in focus from water resources development to water quality management and ecosystems restoration.
- Contemporary federal, state, regional and international water resources planning processes.
- Recommendations for future actions and policies.

Many agencies, organizations, commissions and panels have been active and influential in planning, designing, constructing and managing facilities for the development and use of water resources. An understanding of how the US water policy evolved over time will help us understand how what we do in the future will be influenced, and sometimes constrained, by historical events and current agency biases. Indeed, the future effectiveness of initiatives in water management will depend on the extent to which attention is paid to lessons learned from past successes and failures.

This evolution is summarized in the following sections. A more complete accounting of the period 1800 to 1970 may be found in Holmes (1972, 1979).

WATER RESOURCES PLANNING AND DEVELOPMENT FROM 1800 TO THE EARLY TWENTY-FIRST CENTURY

1800 to 1900: The Emergence of Water Resources Planning

Much of the water resources development occurring in the earliest part of the nineteenth century resulted from private sector initiatives aimed at harnessing the water power of rivers in the Northeast of the new United States and improving the transport of people and materials both within this region and toward the western frontier. In Massachusetts (and its territories that were to become Maine), New Hampshire, Rhode Island, Connecticut and New York dams were built and large industrial enterprises were located along major streams and rivers to take advantage of the energy available from the falling water. Many of the dams constructed during this period still exist even if not still in use for power production and their futures are often the subject of lively, even bitter, debate. Another dimension of this era of largely privately financed developments was the construction of canals. Thus, digging of the Erie Canal began in Rome, NY, in 1817, with the objectives of opening the country west of the Appalachian Mountains to settlers and to providing inexpensive transportation of market products in both directions. It helped to establish New York City as a global trading center and Buffalo as a regional powerhouse and was considered to be the engineering marvel of the day. Construction on the Chesapeake (Bay) and Ohio (River) (or 'C&O') Canal began in 1828 and for nearly a century the C&O was the lifeline for towns and businesses along its 184-mile route between the nation's capital and Cumberland, MD.

During this era, the federal government's concern with the nation's waters focused on navigation. Thus, the Gallatin Report of 1808 proposed, in part, an extensive system of canal and river improvements (Holmes, 1972), justifying federal involvement on the basis of economic development of the west, encouragement of political unity and enhancement of the national defense. One outcome of the report was the creation of the US Army Corps of Engineers (USACE) in 1802, the first major water construction agency in the USA and the only organization in the USA at that time with the technical capabilities to engage in the water projects envisioned. Congress established the responsibilities of USACE for planning river and harbor improvements in 1824; in 1826 the Omnibus Rivers and Harbors Act was passed authorizing specific waterway improvements and surveys. For several years, authorizations (providing the authority to act) and appropriations (providing the funds for authorized actions) for river and harbor improvements were made in the same bill. Later, however, the Omnibus Rivers and Harbors Act, separately authorizing the planning stages of some projects and construction phases of others, became the standard form of legislation for ongoing USACE navigation and flood control programs.

Originally flood control was a local responsibility. However, as the lower Mississippi River Basin was settled, interest in federal intervention intensified. In 1874 Congress appointed a commission to report on a permanent plan for reclaiming a portion of the Mississippi River subject to heavy flooding. This led to the establishment of the Mississippi River Commission, authorized to survey the river and prepare plans to improve navigation and prevent flooding in 1879.

With flood control and navigation programs established, the federal government turned its attention to irrigation. The 1877 Desert Land Act authorized the sale of 640-acre tracts of land in four states and eight territories to persons who would agree to irrigate them within three years. Later, in 1890, the federal government received statutory authority to reserve a right-of-way for ditches and canals that it might later construct on public lands west of the 100th meridian (roughly the beginning of the High Plains, or in current terms, the middle of the Dakotas and Nebraska and the eastern edge of the Texas Panhandle). The reservation was valid as long as such ditches and canals were patented under any of the land laws of the USA. This action paved the way for the Reclamation Act of 1902, which supported most of the major irrigation developments that exist today.

In the late nineteenth century the federal government also took an interest in water power. Beginning in 1879, Congress enacted numerous statutes that provided for the leasing of water power or surplus water to private companies and authorized the construction of private dams to generate power. An 1890 act prohibited building dams on navigable waters without permission from the Secretary of War.

Table 2.1 summarizes the above-mentioned projects.

1900 to 1933: The Era of Multiple Purpose Projects

During the first decades of the twentieth century, the functions of the USACE were expanded to include construction of flood control works and the development of water power, while the US Bureau of Reclamation (USBR) was established in 1902 and authorized to engage in irrigation works. At the same time that single-purpose project responsibilities were being parceled out, the concept of multi-purpose water resources planning emerged. The aim was to promote more efficient use of the resource by

Table 2.1 1800 to 1900: emergence of water resources planning

Legislation	
1826	Omnibus Rivers and Harbors Act
1877	Desert Land Act (set stage for 1902 Reclamation Act)
Institutions	
1802	US Army Corps of Engineers
1871	US Commission on Fish and Fisheries
1879	Mississippi River Commission
Analysis	
1808	Gallatin Report (economic development as justification for projects)
Other events	
1817	Erie Canal begun
1828	Chesapeake and Ohio Canal begun

recognizing the value of serving more than one purpose when planning new developments (Krutilla and Eckstein, 1958). Constituencies that would reap the benefits of proposed water projects generated the motivation for water resources planning. The views associated with Theodore Roosevelt, President from 1901 to 1909, are reflected in many features of this era. These included prominently: conservation of natural resources, especially those in the public domain; encouragement of small independent enterprises such as the family farm, and expansion of the federal government's authority to affect the nation's economic life.

The National Board of Engineers for Rivers and Harbors was created in 1902 within USACE to review all reports on preliminary examinations, surveys, projects or changes in projects. The board was required to evaluate the commercial potential of proposed projects and compare them with construction and maintenance costs, with the goal of eliminating economically questionable projects and was empowered to make recommendations to the Chief of Engineers based on its findings. Also in that year, the Reclamation Act directed the Secretary of the Interior to make examinations and surveys and to locate and build works needed for irrigation. It also required that the Secretary estimate the costs of proposed works and determine the quantity and location of lands to be irrigated. All facts related to the practicability of each irrigation project were to be included in the examinations. As noted previously, this Act was a key piece of the federal policy of providing water for opening the West to settlement.

Reports, such as those published by the National Conservation Commission (NCC, 1909) and the National Waterways Commission 'NWWC' (US Senate, 1912) provided the foundation for actions taken by the federal government during this era and later on. For example, the NWWC report urged specific navigation improvements, prevention of deforestation of land bordering mountain streams and promotion of water power development. It also advocated a federal reservoir system for flood control, noting that the costs could be justified by multiple-purpose benefits.

During this same era, new water resources planning agencies were created, including the US Forest Service (USFS) and the Federal Power Commission (FPC, now the Federal Energy Regulatory Commission, FERC). Existing agencies, such as USACE, again had their authorities expanded. Thus, in 1912, Congress granted discretionary authority to the Secretary of War to include (in permanent facilities for navigation) civil works that might be desirable for the development of water power. Follow-up legislation in 1913 required that reports on examinations and surveys of waterways include information regarding the development and use of water power.

In 1916, President Wilson signed an act creating the National Park Service (NPS) within the US Department of Interior (USDOI). It was given the primary mission of managing the then new national parks. However, since many of these parks contained potentially valuable water resources, NPS became a stakeholder in many water-related deliberations.

In 1917 the first Flood Control Act was passed. It gave USACE responsibility for planning and building flood control works, such as levees, on the Mississippi and Sacramento Rivers, but not for the construction of reservoirs. This Act provided for watershed surveys when planning flood control projects and established the principle of cost sharing for flood control. It also provided for comprehensive studies of watersheds including consideration of the economical development of water power.

Other legislation affecting USACE during this era showed considerable support for multi-purpose planning (Holmes, 1972). For example, legislation in 1910 provided that each survey of a navigable stream include measurements and investigations necessary for planning and proper consideration of all uses of a stream affecting navigation.

The USBR also acquired regional multi-purpose planning functions during the 1920s when the 1920 Kincaid Act directed the Secretary of the Interior to investigate the Imperial Valley of California and consider the potential for irrigating it by diverting water from the lower Colorado River. The report, resulting from this investigation, recommended construction of several facilities and suggested that the federal government undertake all future developments along the Colorado River. In 1928 the Boulder Canyon Project Act provided authority to study the feasibility of multi-purpose projects in six other Colorado River Basin states. The objective of these studies was to formulate a comprehensive plan for development and control of the Colorado River and its tributaries. And, as though to make sure that there would always be too many cooks in the kitchen, the Federal Water Power Act of 1920 gave the FPC authority to conduct continuing surveys of water power potential and development across the USA. The Act also required determination of whether power derived from federal dams could be used for public purposes. As if to emphasize the possibility for agency conflict, in 1925 Congress directed USACE and FPC to jointly prepare a list and estimate the cost of determining where power development might be practicable on navigable streams. The idea was to produce general plans for the improvement of those streams for navigation in combination with the development of power, flood control and irrigation. Potential surveys were listed in House Document 308 (US House of Representatives, 1926) and authorized in the 1927 Rivers and Harbors Act. A list of streams was submitted to Congress in 1927 and the resulting surveys became known as the 308 Reports. The general authority implied by the required 308 Reports permitted USACE to make general plans for all river basins in the USA except the Colorado, which was assigned to the jurisdiction of the USBR. These 308 Reports, which took over 20 years to complete, formed the basis for the water resources developments that took place from the early 1930s until the late 1960s.

Following a series of major floods on the Mississippi River in 1928, Congress adopted a sweeping program for flood control on that river and directed that the federal government bear the entire cost of the program. Although the 1928 Act only provided for levees and diversion floodways, one section did call for studies of the impact of a reservoir system on the Mississippi River tributaries on lowering floods. Studies made pursuant to that section of the Act showed that USACE believed reservoirs would reduce flood heights and should be recommended. USACE also believed there should be local participation in the planning and financing of reservoir construction.

Although the principle of multi-purpose planning received much rhetorical support during this period, it was not widely evident in practice (Holmes, 1972). Single-purpose developments focusing on irrigation, navigation, water power generation and flood control were still the norm. Most of the water project construction during the multi-purpose projects era occurred in the West, Midwest and South. The Reclamation Program focused on providing irrigation benefits to the 17 western states. Most waterway improvements were for the benefit of Midwestern farmers and businesses on the Ohio, Missouri and Mississippi Rivers. Flood control programs focused mainly on the Mississippi Valley and water power developments tended to support industries and the public in the West, Midwest and South.

Table 2.2 summarizes the above-mentioned events.

Table 2.2 1900 to 1933: multiple-purpose projects

Legislation	
1902	Reclamation Act
1917	(first) Flood Control Act
1920	Federal Water Power Act
1927	Rivers and Harbors Act
1928	Boulder Canyon Project Act
Institutions	
1902	National Board of Engineers for Rivers and Harbors
1902	Reclamation Service (to become Bureau of Reclamation)
1905	US Forest Service
1909	National Conservation Commission
1912	National Waterways Commission
1916	National Park Service
1920	Federal Power Commission (to become Federal Energy Regulatory Commission)
Other events	
1927	308 Reports on navigation and power development

1933 to 1943: Economic Efficiency and Economic Stimulation

The Flood Control Act of 1936 formalized economic evaluation of water projects. Since this was the middle of the Great Depression, water and other public works projects were viewed as a means of stimulating the nation's economy by providing jobs. However, the Roosevelt administration feared that public works activities might be looked upon as pure pork barrel, so all water projects were to be related to and coordinated with plans for comprehensive river basin development. Furthermore, federal-planning agencies were to follow the principle that they should deal with all national resources, defined as including human resources and institutions as well as the traditional elements of land, water and minerals (ibid).

Several significant institutions were launched during this period. Perhaps most dramatically, the Tennessee Valley Authority (TVA) was created in 1933. This organization, unique in the USA, is empowered to exercise all federal functions related to the development and management of land and water resources within the Tennessee River Basin, which includes parts of seven states. This includes authority to plan, construct and operate dam and reservoir projects for purposes of navigation, flood control and generation of hydroelectric power.

Four national resource planning organizations and several emergency planning agencies also emerged and subsequently played roles in the development or management of the nation's waters. Created in 1933, the National Planning Board's (NPBs) most important accomplishment relative to water was coordinating the work of the President's Committee on Water Flow (ibid.). That committee's report included multi-purpose plans for ten river basins. Many of the projects suggested by the report were later authorized for development. In June 1934 the National Planning Board was reorganized as the National Resources Board (NRB) and under that name recommended that studies of water projects for consideration by Congress be based on drainage basins as comprehensive units and that a wide variety of water uses and controls be considered in the plans. The NRB, however, enjoyed only a brief life and was itself replaced by the National Resources Committee in 1935. The new committee's most significant achievement was a nationwide study of drainage basin problems and programs. The study included recommendations for both federal and state actions and was undertaken in cooperation with newly formed state planning boards. In 1939, the US Executive Office of the President (EOP) was created and the National Resources Committee reconstituted as the National Resources Planning Board (NRPB), authorized to undertake research and analyse problems involving water and other resources and to report its plans and programs to the President and Congress. The NRPB was also assigned joint responsibility with the US Bureau of the Budget (BOB, now the Office of Management and Budget, OMB) for the review of studies and plans of the construction agencies and for all construction agency reports to Congress. This may be said to mark the beginning of formal economic analysis of water projects. Two emergency (in the economic sense relevant to the Depression concerns for employment and incomes) planning agencies with relevance to water resources were also established: the Public Works Administration and the Works Progress Administration. These agencies were responsible for the financial support of state and local planning and of public works projects constructed by state, local and federal agencies.

During the 1930s, a number of new water-related agencies emerged and the functions of several existing agencies, principally the USACE and the US Department of Agriculture (USDA), expanded. In 1935 Congress authorized USACE to supplement its completed 308 Reports with additional studies as needed 'to take into account important changes in economic factors as they occur and additional stream-flow records or other factual data' (Section 6, 49 stat. 1028, 1048). This provided the foundation for a nationwide river basin planning program. The USDA was involved in coordinating water resources planning sponsored by the national resources planning organizations. In addition, the USDA became active in investigating certain agricultural aspects of the USBR projects.

The Soil Conservation Service (SCS) within the USDA (now the Natural Resources Conservation Service, NRCS) was created in 1935. Its mission was to protect soil resources for agricultural purposes. Currently, the NRCS supports small watershed projects and on-farm improvements to protect soils and reduce water quality degradation.

The 1930s brought a milestone in water resources planning and evaluation: the formalization of economic evaluation of water projects. The routine use of benefit-cost analysis to test a project's worth is generally taken to have been foreshadowed by the language introduced by the Flood Control Act of 1936, which provided that 'the Federal Government should improve or participate in the improvement of navigable waters or their tributaries, including watersheds thereof, for flood-control purposes if the benefits to whomsoever they may accrue are in excess of the estimated costs' (49 stat. 1570, 33 U.S.C. 701a). Although this provision applied only to flood control works of the USACE and the USDA, other water planning agencies soon adopted it for all purposes (ibid.). Unfortunately, the agencies were not always consistent in the way they defined terms or went about their analyses, a fact that led to controversy over benefit-cost analysis over the years. Another issue of concern was who should pay the cost of water projects and the question of cost sharing is still a topic of debate in and between Congress and the Executive Branch. The question is one of subsidy: how much of the cost of a project function, such as flood control, should be borne by the federal government and how much by state and local beneficiaries? The earliest notions were that major works for purposes such as flood control were in the national interest and that therefore the federal government should assume the cost. As time passed, attitudes of citizens and members of Congress have shifted and today the general attitude is that the user (beneficiary) pays the costs.

In 1940 the US Fish and Wildlife Service (USFWS) emerged within the USDOI, but it had originated as the US Commission on Fish and Fisheries in the Department of Commerce in 1871. The USFWS's goal is to conserve, protect and enhance fish, wildlife and plants and their habitats. In carrying out its mission, the agency has often been in conflict with USACE and other construction agencies.

Cooperation with local governments and encouragement of local participation in water programs were given lip service during this period. The policies espoused by the resources planning organizations usually centered on national concerns, including the provision of low-cost electricity and water for 160-acre western farms. Though the attempt was made to foster local cooperation, intense local opposition to water proposals sometimes arose. The broadening of focus away from single-purpose projects,

Table 2.3 1933 to 1943: economic efficiency

Legislation	
1936	Flood Control Act
1938	Flood Control Act
Institutions	
1933	Tennessee Valley Authority
1933	National Planning Board
1934	NPB becomes National Resources Board
1935	National Resources Committee
1939	Executive Office of the President (Bureau of the Budget)
1939	NRC becomes National Resources Planning Board
1939	Public Works Administration
1939	Works Progress Administration
1940	US Fish and Wildlife Service
Analysis	
1933	NPBs multi-purpose plans for ten rivers
1935	Authorization to supplement 308 Reports on economy
1936	Flood Control Act, benefit-cost language
1942	Human adjustment to floods, Gilbert White
Other events	
1939	World War II begins for Europe
1941	World War II begins for USA

attractive to local constituencies and toward multi-purpose projects with conflicting purposes became a contentious issue.

Table 2.3 summarizes the above-mentioned events.

1943 to 1969: Emergence of Multiple-Objective Focus and Analyses

After 1943, the focus in water resource planning and management began to shift from achieving multiple purposes, such as flood control and water supply, to achieving multiple objectives, such as economic development and environmental protection. Emphasis on economic evaluation of water projects increased (see Chapter 3). Numerous commissions, including the National Water Commission (NWC), were formed to assess water issues confronting the nation and to make recommendations regarding options for solving these problems. These bodies were consistent in their recommendations that river basin planning be carried out comprehensively as opposed to being oriented towards single purposes or projects. A book on water management strategies by the late Gilbert White is relevant to these developments (White, 1969).

During the 1940s and 1950s, the construction agencies expanded their

Table 2.4 1943 to 1969: multiple-objective analysis

Legislation	
1944	Flood Control Act
1948	Water Pollution Control Act
1956	Water Pollution Control Act
1956	Flood Control Act
1955	Rivers and Harbors Act
1965	Water Resources Planning Act
1965	Rivers and Harbors Act
1965	Flood Control Act
1966	Clean Rivers Restoration Act
1968	Wild and Scenic Rivers Act
1968	Flood Insurance Act
Institutions	
1949	US Commission on Organization of the Executive Branch
1950	Presidential Water Resources Policy Commission
1952	House Subcommittee to Study Civil Works
1955	Presidential Advisory Commission on Water Resources Policy
1959	Senate Select Committee Water Resources
1965	Water Resources Council
1967	North East Water Supply Study
Analysis	
1950	Green Book (revised 1958)
1952	Circular A-47
1958	Multiple-Purpose River Development (Krutilla and Eckstein, 1958)
1962	Senate Document 97
1962	Design of Water Resource Systems (Maass et al., 1962)
Other events	
1945	World War II ends
1950	Korean War begins
1953	Korean War ends

programs significantly, even with little national interest in water programs other than the continuing concern for improving flood protection. But, by the end of the 1950s, some water resources issues, especially protection and improvement of environmental quality began to capture wide national interest (Table 2.4). At the same time, after abolition of the NRPB in 1943, federal water resources planning became fragmented and of narrower scope. The Executive Branch of the government lost the capability to develop comprehensive water resources plans or to evaluate the plans prepared by the construction agencies. New water resources programs were mostly the work of the congressional committees responsible for individual agency programs. Not surprisingly, each of the construction agencies developed close ties with their congressional supporters and the subsequent programs were heavily oriented to agency missions and geographical areas of responsibility. Thus, the USACE focused on the desires of local communities seeking flood protection, the USBR on stimulating economic development in the west through irrigation development and the SCS on protecting the nation's soil and water through watershed conservation programs. Congressional sponsorship was based more on serving local constituencies than on furthering national objectives.

After World War II, USACE continued as the principal water resources construction agency, with more than 50 per cent of federal water resource-related authorizations and appropriations going to its programs. Flood control issues dominated, but navigation ran a close second. The Flood Control Act of 1944 was USACE's main governing policy during this period. It authorized the introduction of recreation facilities at USACE sites, but not, until 1965, the inclusion of recreation benefits in benefit-cost ratios. The 1944 Act also authorized the USBR to participate in the Pick-Sloan plan (Missouri River Basin development plan), the largest project of its type in which the USBR had participated up to that time. With this law, Congress took responsibility for coordinating efforts between the USACE and the USBR.

As already noted, the use of benefit-cost analysis in the evaluation of alternative public projects had its roots in the Flood Control Act of 1936. The great challenge for application lies in estimating the benefits and costs and in establishing a conceptually defensible discount rate to allow transforming long future time streams of both benefits and costs into comparable single numbers (generally 'present values', that is, values as of the time of analysis before the project is actually built). To provide guidance, a series of increasingly sophisticated documents were published. The first of these was a report by the Subcommittee on Benefits and Costs of the US Interagency Committee on Water Resources (USIACWR) entitled *Proposed Practices for Economic Analysis of River Basin Projects*, commonly known as 'The Green Book' (USIACWR, 1950). First published in 1950, then revised in 1958, it was widely used through the early 1960s. In 1952 the BOB issued Circular A-47 (US Bureau of the Budget, 1952), which set out standards for evaluating water resources projects and contained the provision that total project benefits must exceed the costs, as well as the proviso that the benefit of each individual purpose within multi-purpose projects must exceed its portion of costs. It also included several cost-sharing provisions and set a maximum period of 50 years for repayment of federal investments in water resources projects. These guidelines were adopted by the Eisenhower Administration. In 1962 a new set of guidelines was issued entitled *Policies, Standards and Procedures in the Formulation, Evaluation and Review of Plans for Use and Development of Water and Related Land Resources*, known as Senate Document 97 (US Senate, 1962). In 1964 President Kennedy rescinded Circular A-47, giving preference to Senate Document 97 (Rogers, 1993). Two classic Harvard University studies published during this period also addressed issues related to economic analysis of water resources projects and suggested analytical approaches (Krutilla and Eckstein, 1958; Maass et al., 1962). The latter, titled *Design of Water Resource Systems*, encouraged development and application of mathematical models to support planning and decision-making processes. The advent of high-speed digital computers facilitated implementation of the techniques contained in the publication and thus supported formal, numerical analysis of large-scale water resources systems over long periods of time (see also Chapters 3 and 4).

During the same years that analytical guidelines were being sharpened, efforts were underway to increase coordination of planning efforts across federal agencies and to broaden the viewpoints of the planners themselves, especially where it came to matters of environmental quality. Thus, beginning in the late 1940s a series of commissions and committees was created focused on coordination within the Executive Branch broadly and on water resource coordination more narrowly. The most prominent of these efforts were: the US Commission on the Organization of the Executive Branch of the Government, 1949; the President's Water Resources Policy Commission, 1950; the Subcommittee to Study Civil Works of the House Committee on Public Works, 82nd Congress, 2nd Session, 1952; and the Presidential Advisory Committee on Water Resources Policy, 1955 (Holmes, 1972). All four produced work carefully considered by the legislative and executive branches, and although the details of the recommendations varied, the studies were in agreement with a general approach to water resources planning.

All of the bodies favored comprehensive planning for river basins rather than an individual purpose or project basis. They also favored integration of planning by federal, state and local participants and the establishment of uniform policies for economic evaluation of projects and repayment of costs. These recommendations drove many of the reforms in water resources organizational structure and management that eventually emerged in the late 1960s.

On 20 April 1959 the Senate Select Committee on Water Resources had been established. A decade later, it made five broad recommendations (US Congress, 1969). First, it called for the federal government, in cooperation with the states, to prepare comprehensive water development and management plans for all major river basins in the USA. Second, it recommended that the federal government encourage the states to more actively participate in planning and implementing water resources development and management activities. Third, it called for a periodic assessment of water-supply and demand relations to be made for each water resource region of the nation. Fourth, the committee proposed a federal program of coordinated scientific research on water. Fifth, it recommended a specific program to encourage efficiency in water development and use. The recommendations of the Select Committee are often considered the starting point of a new era in water resources planning and development in the USA. The report gave the Executive Branch approval to initiate radically new policy directions (Holmes, 1979; US Congress, 1969). The role of existing construction agencies expanded to include emphasis on objectives such as storage for in-stream quality, municipal and industrial water supply, recreation, fish and wildlife protection and the regulation of floods. It was also recognized by Congress that the traditional focus of water programs was in need of revision to ensure proper handling of the most urgent water problems identified in the 1960s. Although the committee made no legislative proposals, the Water Resources Planning Act (WRPA) of 1965 was an outgrowth of its work. The Act was designed to encourage conservation, development and use of the nation's water and related land resources on a comprehensive and coordinated basis and it established the Water Resources Council (WRC), provided for River Basin Commissions (RBCs) and authorized financial assistance to the states for comprehensive water resources planning.

Where the environment was concerned, the following actions were taken:

- The 1946 Fish and Wildlife Coordination Act initiated cooperative efforts among water agencies to prevent harm to or loss of wildlife as a result of federal actions to impound, divert or control water. The Act also mandated that the cost of planning, construction and maintenance of facilities for protection of wildlife should be part of the total cost of the water resource project. In 1958 Congress amended the Act to add wildlife enhancement to the planning purposes. This forced federal agencies to consult with the USFWS on water resource construction projects.
- The 1948 Water Pollution Control Act authorized the US Surgeon General of the Public Health Service to work with federal, state, interstate and local government agencies to prepare comprehensive pollution control plans for interstate rivers. The legislation included a pollution abatement procedure, but did not provide for enforcement action without approval of the state involved. The 1948 Act

also provided grants and loans to local governments for construction of sewage treatment works, yet no funds were appropriated for this purpose. In 1956 a much stronger pollution control bill passed. This Act authorized a program of 30 per cent incentive grants to subsidize municipal wastewater treatment plant construction. The federal abatement procedure was also strengthened.

- After two years of debate over federal water quality standards by Congress, the Water Quality Act of 1965 was passed. It provided a timetable for the states to create water quality standards for their interstate receiving waters. The standards were then enforceable by the federal government. The 1965 Act was a turning point in the federal government's enforcement role because the Act gave the government authority to make basic water quality policy and permitted it to take direct action against water polluters.

Related developments included the strengthening of the role of the SCS in 1953, when it was given full administrative responsibility for watershed programs. In 1954 Public Law 566 authorized the USDA to help local organizations conduct improvement works for flood prevention and agricultural aspects of water use and conservation for watersheds not exceeding 250000 acres. The help authorized included studies, plans and financial assistance for appropriate programs. Under the SCS's small watershed program, the construction of large dams, such as those permitted under the authority of USACE, USBR and TVA, was not allowed. However, SCS engaged in many projects nationwide related to the needs of rural areas. In addition, in the 1940s, the National Park Service (NPS) had begun reporting to USBR on the recreational potential of reservoir sites and river basins and in 1945 it began recreation planning for USACE projects, but only when requested to do so. While NPS did not always share the views of the USACE or the USBR relative to water development projects, indeed it often opposed them, in 1947 it became responsible for recreation planning at USBR projects. This was probably not the best idea for promoting interagency coordination.

Another significant development was the growing respectability of non-structural alternatives in the control of flood damages. The first movement away from a structural-only approach began in the 1950s and gained momentum with circulation of work by Gilbert F. White and his colleagues at the University of Chicago detailing changes in urban occupancy of flood plains and advocating land use control and zoning as an alternative to levees and floodwalls for reducing the damages from floods (White, 1945; Kates, 1962; White, 1964). As a result of mounting flood losses nationally, even construction agency attention in the 1960s began to shift from structural to non-structural approaches. Consideration began to be given to measures such as zoning, flood insurance, relocation, flood forecasting and alternative types of storage, despite the bias inherent in the guidelines for Benefit-cost analysis (BCA) toward structural alternatives, for which both costs incurred and damages avoided are likely to be more easily estimated. The 1960 Flood Control Act officially launched this effort and authorized USACE to provide flood plain information. In 1966 the Johnson Administration submitted 'A unified national program for managing flood losses', House Document 465, (US House of Representatives, 1966) to Congress including recommendations for federal agencies, including research and administration (Grigg, 1996). A consequence of House Document 465 was the Flood Insurance Act of 1968. Even TVA felt the pressure, for after a spate of dam building, many communities in the TVA region were still subject to damaging floods and structural solutions seemed likely to be economically unjustifiable. As a result, the TVA began a cooperative program with state and local governments that involved land use planning to help communities avoid or minimize flood damage where floods could not be prevented. This was one of the earliest on-the-ground efforts at non-structural flood control.

At least in part because Senate Document 97 had amended the benefit-cost analysis standards, allowing more projects to meet the test of economic efficiency and thus be eligible for authorization, many new projects were authorized and initiated during the brief Kennedy years. These included a wide array of projects that would substantially affect the environment, such as the USBR's Fryingpan-Arkansas trans-mountain diversion and new canals that greatly increased the length of the nation's inland waterways system (Holmes, 1979).

However, the 1960s were not just about building. During the later years of the decade, several significant regional and basin-wide, water-related studies were implemented. For example, Title I of the Rivers and Harbors Act and Flood Control Act of 1965 authorized USACE to undertake the Northeast Water Supply Study (NEWS) in cooperation with other federal, state and local government agencies and to develop plans to meet the long-range water supply needs of the northeast megalopolis. It was further authorized to construct, operate and maintain relevant water supply works, including reservoirs and inter-basin transfer facilities. The study was funded in 1967 and completed in the 1970s.

The USACE also participated in several Type I regional framework studies provided for by the WRPA of 1965. These studies were to incorporate the most recent developments in planning theory and methods. One such effort was the North Atlantic Regional Study (NAR) in which needs for water and related land resources were projected to the year 2020, considering the following three objectives: regional development, national income and the environmental quality. A major finding was that water quality maintenance was the highest priority need throughout the region (ibid.).

While President Johnson continued most of Kennedy's initiatives for water resources planning, research and development, when elected president in 1964, he made the preservation of nature a keystone of his domestic policy. In 1966 Johnson began to focus his attention on water quality, and it was his position that the entire river basin, rather than a locality, should be the focus of pollution control efforts. He proposed a clean rivers demonstration program in which the federal government provided funds to interstate and/or regional water pollution control authorities on a first-ready, first-served basis. Those participating in the program would be required to have permanent water quality planning organizations, water quality standards and implementation plans in effect for all waters of the basin designated.

When the Clean Rivers Restoration Act passed in 1966, it contained no provision for Johnson's demonstration program, though it did acknowledge his river basin planning concept. But the greatest effect of the 1966 Act was its substantial increase in the level of funding that could be appropriated to subsidize the construction of wastewater treatment facilities. Unfortunately, because of the increasing costs of the Vietnam War, the construction grant program was not funded at the levels authorized in the 1966 Act. But the Wild and Scenic Rivers Act, passed in 1968, did provide for a national system of rivers to be protected from federal water development, symbolizing the interest of Congress in protecting the environmental attributes of special water bodies.

An excellent example that brought together the themes of sophisticated planning methods, the use of non-structural approaches and the consideration of multiple objectives is the study of Washington, DC's metropolitan area water supply problems, reported in Palmer et al. (1979). A unique amalgam of institutional cooperation and analytical expertise involving simulation and optimization models, the Potomac River Basin study produced a system management rather than structural solution to the problem. The principal features of the approach included:

- Combination of simulation and optimization techniques to provide practical rules for operation of the water supply system.
- Use of the National Weather Service River Forecast System based on a soil moisture accounting model and its direct integration with reservoir operation.
- Development of a technique to predict water demand and application of it to water resources system design and operation.

- Combination of distribution analysis and hydrologic modeling to develop operating procedures for a complex water supply system.
- Use of risk analysis to identify the start of potential droughts and to quantify the risks of continued drought.
- Use of drought games to test and improve water supply operating procedures and to illustrate the use of those procedures to decision makers.

The benefits of coordinated water management were substantial (estimated in excess of one quarter billion dollars based on costs of implementing proposed reservoir development alternatives at that time) (Sheer, 1981). The environmental impact was minimal since major reservoir construction was not involved.

Despite such advances in technique, shifts toward more subtle views of available policy tools, such as multi-objective decision-making aids and non-structural flood damage mitigation approaches, and heightened interest in environmental, especially water, quality, the focus of water resources programs during the 1960s remained one of rather traditional development via new construction projects.

1969 to 1980: The Environmental Era

During this period, emphasis shifted from water resources development to water quality protection and management, with the passage of the National Environmental Policy Act (NEPA) of 1969, the Water Pollution Control Act Amendments of 1972, the Safe Drinking Water Act (SDWA) of 1974, the Resource Conservation and Recovery Act (RCRA) of 1976 and Amendments in 1977 to what had come to be known as the Clean Water Act (CWA) (Table 2.5). Reflecting this same shift in emphasis, new guidelines explicitly required the consideration of an 'Environmental Quality Account' in the analysis of proposed projects.

In 1969 the Nixon Administration took office with good conservation intentions. And while Congress prodded his administration to take action in the areas of water pollution control and environmental policy more broadly, budgetary restraints imposed by the Vietnam War (Holmes, 1979) limited his efforts. Nevertheless, the environmental movement, which had been strengthening during the last part of the 1960s, supported this prodding. By 1970 the Nixon Administration became convinced of a need for massive federal investment in the wastewater treatment plant construction program and in his February 1970 Message on environmental quality, President Nixon proposed a four-year, $10 billion program of state, federal and local investment in wastewater treatment facilities.

Table 2.5 1969 to 1980: environmental era

Legislation	
1969	National Environmental Policy Act
1972	Federal Water Pollution Control Act (Amendments) (Clean Water Act)
1973	Endangered Species Act
1974	Safe Drinking Water Act
1976	Resource Conservation and Recovery Act
1977	Clean Water Act (amended)
1980	Comprehensive Environmental Response, Compensation and Liability Act
Institutions	
1970	Council on Environmental Quality
1972	National Commission on Water Quality
1973	Principles and Standards
1973	National Water Commission Report
1978	Water Policy Initiatives (President Carter)
Other events	
1964	USA becomes seriously involved in the Vietnam War
1975	USA withdraws from Vietnam

The federal share of this proposed authorization was $1 billion per year. Although the actual authorized funding level was less than many environmental advocates desired, it was much more than any previous presidential request (ibid.).

In 1970 NEPA became law, with the President praising the Act and proclaiming the three-member Council on Environmental Quality (CEQ) a great asset in informing him on important environmental issues. The Administration promptly put the provisions of NEPA into effect and in March 1970 the President issued an Executive Order instructing all federal agencies to report on possible inconsistencies between their authorities and policies and those codified in NEPA. Then, in April 1970 the CEQ issued interim guidelines for the preparation of environmental impact statements.

In December of 1970 President Nixon's environmental interests led to the creation of a new independent regulatory agency, the US Environmental Protection Agency (EPA). He based his action on the recommendations of his Advisory Council on Executive Organization (the Ash Council). The EPA assumed the environmental management functions of several existing agencies and brought together all of the federal pollution control programs related to water, air, solid wastes, pesticides and radiation. The Administration viewed the EPA as the most effective way of reorganizing multiple agencies into a single, interrelated system. However, creation of the EPA made even more pronounced the separation of water quality from other water programs. It appears sentiment at the time was that water resources development and water pollution control were at best unrelated and at worst antagonistic concerns (ibid.).

Even with the enactment of the NEPA and the creation of the EPA, comprehensive response to water pollution issues was still lacking. During congressional hearings in 1971, it became evident the existing program was underfunded and lacked the ability to create enforceable restrictions on pollution discharges from either public or private sources. In an ambitious effort to fix things, including the unenforceability of the water quality standards provisions of earlier legislation, Congress passed the Water Pollution Control Act Amendments of 1972 (Public Law 92-500), which became the CWA. The law ended two years of intense debate, negotiation and compromise and resulted in the most assertive step yet taken in the history of national water pollution control activities. The Act departed in several ways from previous water pollution control legislation, expanding the federal role, increasing the level of funding for subsidizing construction of publicly owned waste treatment works, elevating planning to a higher level of significance, opening new avenues for public participation and creating a regulatory mechanism with technology-based effluent standards and a national permit system for all point-source dischargers as the basis for enforcement. Two goals and eight policies were articulated and, as part of the strategy for their implementation, Congress set deadlines for achievement of specific goals and objectives. The grand objective of the Act was to restore and maintain the chemical, physical and biological integrity of the nation's waters. Beneath this overarching target, the more specific goals were: first, to reach, wherever attainable, a level of water quality that would provide for the protection and propagation of fish, shellfish and wildlife and for recreation in and on the water; and, second, to eliminate the discharge of pollutants to the navigable waters of the USA.

The policies aimed at achieving the objective and goals were:

- To prohibit the discharge of toxic pollutants in toxic amounts.
- To provide federal financial assistance for construction of publicly owned treatment works. In particular, the law committed the federal government to provide subsidies amounting to up to 75 per cent of the capital costs of new public treatment works and authorized $18 billion of funding for this purpose.
- To develop and implement area-wide waste treatment management planning.
- To mount a major research and demonstration effort in wastewater treatment technology.

- To recognize, preserve and protect the primary responsibilities and roles of the states to prevent, reduce and eliminate pollution.
- To ensure, where possible, that foreign nations act to prevent, reduce and eliminate pollution in international waters.
- To provide for, encourage and assist public participation in executing the Act.
- To pursue procedures that reduce paperwork and interagency decisions on procedures and prevent needless duplication and unnecessary delays at all levels of government.

Congress intended the Act be more than a general mandate for point-source discharge control. It embodied a new approach to dealing with water resources. For example, the construction grants for publicly owned treatment works (POTW) made available to encourage meeting of permit terms, provided not just for standard treatment processes, but also for:

- The recycling of potential sewage pollutants through the production of agriculture, silviculture and aquaculture products or any combination thereof.
- The confined and contained disposal of pollutants not recycled.
- The reclamation of wastewater.
- The ultimate disposal of sludge in a manner that would not result in environmental hazards.

The statute also outlined a long-term program to reduce water use, reduce the generation of wastes and establish financially self-sustaining, public-owned pollution control facilities.

Reinforcing this movement toward a serious federal role in environmental quality protection and restoration, in September 1973 the WRC published *Principles and Standards for Planning Water and Related Land Resources* (P&S) (WRC, 1973). This document and its revisions recognized and required the use in planning and evaluation of four major accounting stances: National Economic Development (NED, the 'efficiency' stance), Environmental Quality (EQ), Regional Economic Development (RED) and Other Social Effects (OSE). Although the EPA was included in the Federal Register for review of the P&S, the agency was excluded from their provisions when evaluating its own proposed rules and standards.

Also in 1973 the NWC released its landmark report *New Directions in U.S. Water Policy* (NWC, 1973). The report's recommendations still may be seen as a model statement of goals for water policy refinement in the long run. The report's seven recurring themes were:

- Future water demands are not inevitable but are in large part the result of policy decisions within the control of society. Good planning should be based on a range of plausible alternative futures.
- National priorities are shifting from water resources development to restoring and enhancing water quality.
- Water resources planning must be tied more closely to land use planning.
- Water use efficiency should be emphasized and policies to encourage wise water use and conservation practices should be promoted.
- Sound economic principles should be incorporated in decisions about whether or not to build water projects. Beneficiaries should pay for the costs of the services they receive and unjustified subsidies that distort allocation of scarce resources should be eliminated.
- Laws and legal institutions should be re-examined in the light of contemporary water problems.
- Development, management and protection of water resources should be controlled at that level of government nearest the problem and most capable of effectively representing the vital interests involved.

Extending the march of environmental legislative victories, in 1973 Congress passed the Endangered Species Act (ESA), recognizing the human impact on extinction of plants and animals (Public Law 90-542). The initial focus of the Act was on protecting habitats for terrestrial species, but water-related conflicts began to emerge almost immediately. And in the same year the National Commission on Water Quality (mandated by the 1972 Act) began considering mid-course corrections because the mandates for fishable-swimmable waters by 1977 and for zero discharge of pollutants by 1985 were clearly not going to be met. The Commission generally recommended deadline extensions on a case-by-case basis, but for the 1985 deadline, it recommended a five- to ten-year blanket extension. It also requested appointment of a new commission to oversee progress. Recommendations were also made regarding non-point pollution, shortfalls in funding and assigning states regulatory authority.

In December 1974 the SDWA became law, with the purpose of ensuring that water supply systems serving the public met minimum standards for the protection of public health by identifying contaminants and establishing maximum acceptable levels for them. Prior to the SDWA, only water supplies used by interstate carriers were governed by federal drinking water standards. After the Act passed, EPA established federal standards to control the levels of contaminants in drinking water supplied by all public water systems. It also established a federal–state system for ensuring compliance with these standards. The major provisions of the SDWA were:

- Establishment of primary regulations for the protection of the public health.
- Establishment of secondary regulations related to taste, odor and appearance of drinking water.
- Establishment of regulations to protect underground drinking water sources by the control of surface injection.
- Initiation of research on health, economic and technological problems related to drinking water supplies.
- Initiation of a survey of rural water supplies.
- Allocation of funds to states for improving their drinking water programs through technical assistance, training of personnel and grant support.

Two further laws relevant to the protection of water quality came into force before the end of the decade: the RCRA in 1976 and the Comprehensive Environmental Response, Compensation and Liability Act (CERCLA), also known as the Superfund Act, in 1980. Their connections to water quality were potentially dramatic if physically somewhat indirect, involving protection, especially of groundwater, from the leaching of toxic and other pollutants from operating and defunct landfills and other on-land disposal sites.

In 1977 the CWA was revised in an attempt to correct identified shortcomings. The salient points of the revision were:

- States were specifically mandated primacy over water quality and water use issues.
- Municipalities were given evidence of an increased federal commitment in the form of construction grants and training assistance.
- The public received assurances of the priority of water quality in the form of effective enforcement and incentive provisions for governments and industries to achieve the goal of fishable and swimmable waters.
- Industry received the necessary extensions of compliance deadlines under the National Pollution Discharge Elimination System (NPDES).
- Environmental groups witnessed the incorporation of a Natural Resources Defense Council/EPA consent decree into the law that established the principle of toxic effluent standards and set forth a process to implement effluent limitations.

In 1978 President Carter developed his *Federal Water Policy Initiatives* (President Jimmy Carter, 1978). They were designed to improve water resources planning and management, to permit construction of sound water projects, to emphasize water conservation, to enhance federal-state cooperation and to increase the focus on environmental quality. On 5 June 1979 he signed Executive Order 12141 authorizing development of an Independent Water Project review process. Under the proposed rules, it was generally believed many western water projects would no longer meet the test of authorization. This did not sit well with Congress and appears to be one of the reasons the WRC was eliminated in 1982 by being given a zero budget.

The tide of pollution turned in many localities during the environmental era. Aside from water quality improvement and protection, most other water resources initiatives (particularly development-oriented ones) slowed considerably after about 1970. During the Carter years, the executive and legislative branches of the government debated many issues, but the outcomes were generally stalemates. Every energy and water appropriations bill before Congress after 1976 was a major source of conflict. President Carter's 1977 hit list of what his administration felt to be unsound water projects was a major symbol of the antagonism between the President and many pro-water development members of Congress.

1980 to Present: Devolution and Environmental Restoration

During this period, one of the most dramatic changes in water policy was the introduction of project cost-sharing rules that gave state and local sponsors clear incentives to be careful what they wished (or asked) for and gave the federal construction agencies matching incentives to pay more attention to those wishes and requests. Water quality, both in the ambient setting and when captured as drinking water, continued to be a major concern, but new on the policy horizon was the protection and especially the restoration of natural systems such as the Florida Everglades. Projects aimed at restoration were seen by some as the modern substitutes for dams and canals in the budgets of the construction agencies.

From its first days in early 1981, the Reagan Administration's approach to water project planning and implementation reflected a philosophy of transferring responsibility for some water programs to the states, increasing the level of non-federal cost sharing for water projects and programs and encouraging full recovery of project costs. This was accompanied by an intention to decrease the relevant federal regulatory burden and eliminate the backlog of project authorizations. As another facet of this campaign, in 1981 the Administration encouraged passage of the 1981 Municipal Wastewater Treatment Construction Grant Amendments with key provisions that included reducing grant-funding levels, shifting construction costs to municipalities and limiting eligible categories for funding. This reduced funding commitment at the federal level reflected both a desire to reduce federal spending levels generally and a decision that the environment was an area in which this could be done with little pain. The second part of this decision was perhaps not the wisest one the Administration made, for during the eight years of Reagan stewardship public support for environmental programs increased markedly.

In 1982 the Reagan Administration eliminated the budget for WRC, leaving it still authorized but no longer funded. The Administration's view was that the Cabinet Council on Natural Resources and the Environment and the Office of Water Policy in the USDOI, both created in 1981, early in the term, would fill the void created by the demise of WRC. This action has left the federal government without any national-level mechanism for coordinating state, federal and regional water resources planning processes, with no broad water resources assessment process and without any protocol for dialogue with the states on national water resources management issues. Then in 1983, as part of its more general attack on environmental regulations, the Administration replaced the P&S with *Economic and Environmental Principles and Guidelines for Water and Related Land Resources Implementation Studies* (P&G) (WRC, 1983) based on a single NED objective rather than the four accounting 'stances' of the earlier document (for more detail, see Chapter 3).

The year 1986 was a very busy one on the water resources front (Table 2.6):

- Congress amended the SDWA, providing federal grants to states for establishing wellhead protection programs. The EPA guidelines for the programs were somewhat unusual in that they allowed regional flexibility, rather than prescribing uniform national standards. The Act also provided for protection of aquifer recharge areas that were primary sources of drinking water. Drinking water standards would apply to these areas and underground injection of effluent was regulated. Enforcement provisions of the Act were strong and in 1987 the first criminal conviction under the Act was obtained (*United States* vs *Jay Woods 1987*).
- Congress also amended the Federal Power Act to require that issuance (or renewal) of licenses for hydroelectric power facilities give equal consideration to energy conservation; to protection of, mitigation of damage to and enhancement of, fish and wildlife; and to

Table 2.6 1980 to present: devolution and environmental restoration

Legislation	
1986	Safe Drinking Water Act (amended)
1986	Federal Power Act (amended)
1986	Water Resources Development Act (WRDA)
1990	WRDA (reauthorized)
1992	Western Water Policy Review Act
1996	Safe Drinking Water Act (reauthorized)
Institutions	
1981	Cabinet Council on Natural Resources and the Environment
1981	Office of Water Policy (in USDOI)
1982	WRC budget zeroed out
Other events	
1983	WRC publishes *Economic and Environmental Principles and Guidelines for Water and Related Land Resources Implementation Studies* (P&G)
1986	FEMA takes over Interagency Flood Management Task Force
1989	Beginning of heavy federal involvement in Everglades restoration

protection of recreational opportunities and preservation of other attributes of environmental quality when considering licensing of power generating facilities.

- The passage of WRDA 1986 came after years of effort by both the Carter and Reagan Administrations to require greater levels of non-federal cost sharing for water projects and programs. Prior to this fairly dramatic shift, the federal government had borne most of the construction costs of water projects, although, since 1936 project sponsors had been required to provide lands, easements and rights-of-way needed for the projects and to commit, in some cases, to operate and maintain the projects after completion. (Table 2.7 shows different cost-sharing levels for different project purposes.) That change significantly affected federal and state roles in water management. It increased the likelihood that states would be more discriminating in their pursuit of water projects and suggested that they play a more significant role in identifying alternative strategies for meeting their long-term water supply, flood control and water quality control desires. The Act authorized over 270 water projects and many studies.
- Finally, in the same year, the Federal Emergency Management Agency (FEMA) assumed responsibility for the Federal Interagency Flood Management Task Force and submitted a revision to the Unified National Program for Managing Flood Losses. The revisions included a federal disaster mitigation strategy, increased

Table 2.7 Project cost-sharing for different purposes

Purpose	Non-federal share (%)
Reconnaissance Study	0
Feasibility Study	50
Navigation – Harbors	20: depth < 20 ft 35: depth 21–45 ft 60: depth > 45 ft
Navigation – Inland	50 from fuel tax
Flood Control	
Structural	Min. 35 to max. 50
Non-structural	25
Hydroelectric Power	100
M&I Water Supply	100
Agricultural Water Supply	35
Recreation	50
Navigation	50
Other	50 of separable cost
Hurricane and Storm Damage	35
Aquatic Plant Control	50

Source: USACE (2002).

research and a focus on coastal zone flooding (Grigg, 1996). The non-structural thrust of flood management has remained the standard for the remainder of this era.

Congress reauthorized the CWA in 1987 as the Water Quality Act of 1987 (Public Law 100-4). One focus of the 1987 Act was the beginning of an effort to control non-point sources of pollution, an effort that could be traced back to Section 202 of the 1972 CWA, but the 1987 Act (Section 319) required the states to prepare non-point source management plans. Agricultural fields, animal feedlots and urban areas, including streets, were to be targeted. Significantly, however, the new law did not authorize mandatory controls. A total of $400 million in federal funds was authorized for use by the states to implement cleanup programs and there was provision for state creation of revolving funds to facilitate low-interest loans to local governments for sewage treatment improvements. It also provided more options for state and federal sharing of programs under the NPDES. The EPA and the states now divide the categories of discharges regulated within each state.

During his first two years as President, the first George Bush adopted a more positive environmental agenda than had Reagan, but the White House was itself divided on environmental issues for economic and ideological reasons. Nonetheless an important piece of water resources legislation was passed in 1990, a new version of the WRDA, which provided USACE with a specific environmental protection mission and represented a significant expansion in the breadth of USACE activities. Thus, Public Law 101-540, Section 306 of the Act states: 'The Secretary [of the Army] shall include environmental protection as one of the primary missions of USACE in planning, designing, constructing, operating and maintaining water resources projects.'

Although the environmental movement to protect the Florida Everglades, the largest single marsh system in the nation and the habitat for numerous species of birds, mammals, amphibians and reptiles, some of which are endangered or threatened, had begun in the 1960s, it was the early 1980s before the state of Florida initiated the 'Save Our Everglades' program to address the widespread concern of its citizens for the protection of this unique ecosystem. This program aimed to restore the Everglades to a state more closely resembling that existing at the turn of the twentieth century, before South Florida development significantly altered the water flow patterns and amounts by creating an elaborate system of drainage canals and flow control structures aimed at draining land for agriculture and urban development and protecting those lands from subsequent flooding. In 1989 the federal government became heavily involved in Everglades restoration when the Everglades National Park Protection and Expansion Act passed in Congress. (Only about 15 to 20 per cent of the original Everglades lands were contained in the Everglades National Park; see Dzurik, 2002.) The Act authorized the purchase of over 107 000 acres east of the existing park. In 1992 Congress authorized the Central and Southern Florida (C&SF) Project Comprehensive Review Study. The study included representatives from the South Florida Water Management District (SFWMD), the USACE, the Everglades National Park and other state and local government agencies and not surprisingly, adopted a multi-agency cooperative approach to planning the restoration effort. A major focus was on restoration of flows of fresh water from Lake Okeechobee through the Everglades to Florida Bay. The Reconnaissance Report was completed in 1994. In 1996 the WRDA, in Section 528, entitled Everglades and South Florida Ecosystem Restoration, directed the restudy to propose a comprehensive plan for the purpose of restoring, preserving and protecting the South Florida ecosystem and in 1998 USACE released a draft of its Comprehensive Everglades Restoration Plan (CERP). The estimated price tag was $7.8 billion, half to be provided by the State of Florida. The WRDA of 2000, signed by President Clinton, approved the CERP and authorized $1.4 billion for ten restoration projects that were to serve as the foundation for future actions.

In 1996 the SDWA was again reauthorized. This was the first major revision to the Act in ten years and the amendments focused on funding related to contaminants that were thought to pose the greatest risk to human health and those most likely to occur in a given water system. Rather than prescribe those contaminants, EPA was given latitude to select which contaminants to regulate, but required to use the best available scientific information and objective practices when proposing drinking water standards. The Act established Maximum Contaminant Level Goals (MCLG) and Maximum Contaminant Level (MCL) standards. The MCLGs are desirable minimums (often zero), while the MCLs are practicable standards based on costs, laboratory capabilities and physical/chemical feasibility. The Act also established a revolving trust fund for drinking water system upgrade loans, required that water system operators be certified, maintained requirements for setting both a MCL and a MCLG for regulated contaminants based on health risk reduction and benefit-cost analyses and required EPA to establish a database reflecting the presence of unregulated contaminants in water.

The Western Water Policy Review Act of 1992 had directed the President to undertake a comprehensive review of federal activities in the 19 western states that directly or indirectly affected the allocation and use of water resources and to submit a report of findings and recommendations to the Congressional committees having jurisdiction over federal water programs. A Western Water Policy Review Advisory Commission (WWPRAC) was appointed to carry out the charge and the Commission's report, *Water in the West: Challenge for the Next Century*, was published in 1998 (Western Water Policy Review Advisory Commission, 1998). The major topics addressed were:

- Principles of water management for the twenty-first century
- New governance of watersheds and river basins
- Tribal water rights
- Water quality
- Management of water and water facilities
- Flood plain management
- Maintaining the water infrastructure
- Protecting productive agricultural communities
- Improving decision making, reducing conflict.

The Commissioners hoped that the many diverse recommendations they made would help guide Congressional actions in the coming years.

It should be noted, however, that funding problems and a change in the control of Congress constrained the Commission's achievements from the start.

While the Clinton Administration supported a broad agenda of environmental policy reform, its sporadic political leadership in that field disappointed environmentalists. There is scant record on water related actions by the second Bush Administration, but it appears that the economic impact of environmental policy has once again become important and that the President has leaned toward development.

The terrorist attacks of September 11, 2001 generated concern about the security of the nation's water sources and water supply infrastructure. In response, public and private organizations have formed partnerships to determine effective preventive measures and counter-measures to improve water supply security. EPA is working with water utilities, water associations, state and federal agencies to develop strategies to strengthen their security capabilities. The Public Health Prevention and Bioterrorism Preparedness Act of 2002 includes provisions for funding security initiatives. Since September 11, water utilities have made considerable expenditures on security measures and they have improved their emergency response capabilities. It is expected that these efforts will continue to expand. In 2002 the Aspen Institute raised the question: 'Should removing a dam be an option in managing river systems in the United States?' (Aspen Institute, 2002). This reflected the decay of the condition of many dams, the obsolescence of others, the environmental impacts of these structures and the tension between such positive possibilities as water power generation and negative effects such as the interference of dams with anadromous fish runs. The Aspen Institute study team noted that dam removal had usually not been adequately considered as an option in decision-making processes and their recommendations focused on this deficiency. As a follow-up to the Aspen report, the Environmental and Water Resources Institute of the American Society of Civil Engineers (ASCE) has conducted a number of nationwide dam removal workshops and a Dam Removal Clearinghouse has been established at the University of California, Berkeley (www.lib.berkeley.edu/WRCA/damremoval/).

It appears that water resources development and management in the twenty-first century will continue to depart from the historic structural orientation and focus more on high priority outputs, such as ecosystem protection and restoration, flood damage reduction and navigation. It is also expected that water resources planning will take on a more integrated approach, capturing the true spatial and temporal dimensions of water problems and recognizing the interactions of components of natural systems (air, water, land, plants and animals) with the relevant, social, political, legal and economic attributes of the problem-shed. The Water Resources Development Act of 2000, for example, authorized ten regional/watershed restoration programs, the most notable is Florida's Everglades ($7.8 billion). That Act also authorized the use of adaptive management techniques in the planning process.

A survey of State Water Planning in 2005 by the ASCE (Viessman and Feather, 2006) disclosed several major occurrences since Earth Day, 1970 which affected the focus of water resources development and management: (1) devolution of federal water resources obligations to the states; (2) emergence of sustained public support for environmental protection and restoration; (3) elimination of funding for the Water Resources Planning Act of 1965 which had supported comprehensive state and river basin water plans; and (4) the emergence of direct and widespread stakeholder involvement in water resources planning as a result of social dynamics and changes in federal cost sharing policy resulting from the Water Resources Development Act of 1986. These events fostered the development of plans that embodied concepts of sustainability, integration and climate change. The notion of 'watershed focus' was rekindled and there was an adoption of new techniques, such as adaptive management, outcomes assessment and shared vision planning.

EVOLUTION AND ELEMENTS OF PLANNING PROCESSES, FOCUSING ON THE US ARMY CORPS OF ENGINEERS

Over the last half of the twentieth century, planning processes within federal agencies changed in response to changes in national values, adjustments in the guidance issued to agencies by Congress and the administration and shifting attention within the agencies to the facets of planning itself. Figure 2.1 schematically illustrates trends in the evolution of USACE responsibilities and their degree of complexity and the variety of influences on those responsibilities. These same influences were mirrored in other agencies. Prior to the 1950s, internal regulations developed over time primarily guided the development of agencies' reports. The issuance of OMB Circular A-47 in 1952, the circulation of the 'Green Book' and the influence of the early publications of the Harvard Water Program brought water resources planning into a new era. Several later documents increased the professionalization of planning activities within the agencies and broadened the disciplines represented in the process: (1) Senate Document 97 of 1962, endorsing water resources development as a means of increasing economic growth; (2) the 1965 WRDA that required the establishment of broad-based principles for the evaluation of proposed projects; (3) the 1973 P&S published by the then new WRC; (4) NEPA and related environmental legislation of the early 1970s; and (5) the P&G of 1983.

The USACE Institute for Water Resources (IWR) was established in 1969 to guide that agency's efforts to keep up with changing requirements. Increased attention was focused on education and training of USACE planners in new techniques for economic analysis, public participation and planning in general. The focus shifted from planning for specific projects to planning that took the broader view required by today's society.

Passage of the WRDA of 1986 established serious cost sharing as part of USACE project planning. Especially important for planning was the requirement for project sponsors to cost-share feasibility studies. Planning efforts of the sort previously led by USACE became joint efforts with local sponsors. At a minimum, the views of local sponsors regarding the need for environmental aspects of projects had to be taken more seriously and sometimes resulted in the blending of primary project purposes (flood control, navigation and so on) with environmental enhancements. Legislation in the early 1990s gave USACE new authorities for taking a broad-based planning approach, but failure of administrations to push for funding of such programs left this something of a dead letter. Further, efforts to improve the business management of USACE shifted focus away from innovative planning and the development of planners so that by the turn of the new century, it was apparent major steps would be needed to restore the strength of the planning program.

ELEMENTS OF THE PLANNING PROCESS

At a very general level, water resources planning involves processes and goals. Processes are the methodologies and goals define the purpose of the plan. Water resources plans address water availability (all sources); water uses (purpose, amount and timing); impacts of water development and use on water quality and the environment; deficits and surpluses in water supply; population trends; constraints on water development and use; relevant laws and regulations; economic conditions; and the political climate of the planning region. The trends discussed previously and the preferences of society have influenced the evolution and attributes of water resources planning protocols (Dzurik, 2002; Grigg, 1996; Rogers, 1993).

Planning processes generally include the following elements: identifying problems, defining goals and objectives, establishing a database, obtaining stakeholder input, managing conflicts, coordinating planning efforts, identifying and evaluating alternatives, making recommendations, developing implementation plans and establishing monitoring programs (Dzurik, 2002; USACE, 1997). Planning frameworks have evolved from single-purpose, to multi-objective, to integrated. This transition reflects: (1) increased awareness and understanding of water-environment interactions; (2) increasing stakeholder involvement; (3) improvements in analytical capability; and (4) the globalization of water-related issues (Elgin et al., 1975; US Government Accountability Office (GAO), 1978; Hanke, 1981; James and Lee, 1971; US Congress, 1975; USACE, 1997).

Figure 2.1 depicts an expansion over time of the scope of water resources planning. (The vertical axis simply represents changes in relative responsibilities, it is not quantitative.)

It should be noted that the breadth of focus of water resources planning discussed here is not the same as that conducted by the EPA (Schad, 1998). For the most part, EPA's water quality plans focus on compliance with EPA regulations and solving water quality problems, whereas water resources planning practices of the construction agencies embrace a broader spectrum of issues, such as allocation of water resources, flood damage reduction, navigation, hydroelectric power generation and environmental protection and restoration. Dealing with this dichotomy is a continuing challenge for water resources planners and managers.

Identifying Issues and Problems

Planning is the framework for dealing with water management problems. Contemporary water management issues are the foundation for establishing planning objectives. As new issues emerge, adjustments in planning strategies must be made to keep them current. Issue identification deals with the broad conceptual picture, while problem identification translates issues into specifics for watershed or other water management plans.

Defining Goals and Objectives

Water resources plans must address the goals and preferences of society. The goals are broad generalizations such as restoration of environmental attributes. Society's preferences are illustrated by contemporary views of the public such as opposition to structural measures for water management. Objectives are achievable targets that address the prevailing goals. In the USA the principal water resources planning objectives have been to maximize the NED and maintain the integrity of the environment. Once goals are established, a plan is developed to achieve them.

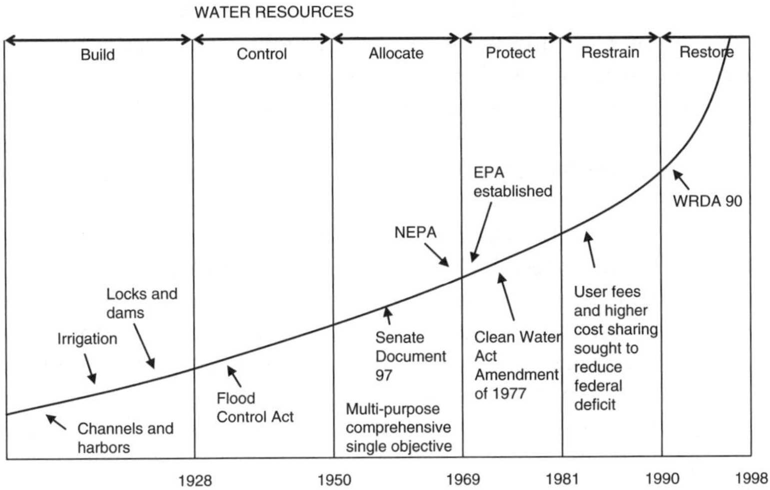

Source: National Research Council (1999). Reprinted with permission from the National Academies Press, Washington, DC.

Figure 2.1 Trends in the evolution of the US Army Corps of Engineers responsibilities and approaches

Social and environmental goals and objectives may be used to shape contemporary water resources plans via several possible routes: they may be considered explicitly if not mathematically from the beginning in framing the setting; or they may be introduced as constraints on actions; or a multi-objective approach may incorporate these goals in the objective function so that outcomes of evaluations of alternatives may be compared in terms of the implied costs of pursuing each such objective in terms of economic efficiency and other objectives.

Establishing a Database

There is a need for a continuing assessment of the quantity, quality and uses of water. Such assessments should be considered an integral part of the planning process for they provide the database for identification of emerging issues and information on the ability of existing institutions to deal with identified problems. Data collection and analysis can be expensive, however, and it is important that care be taken to acquire the right data and to use the data in the most productive manner. Prerequisites include determining the type and format of data needed and the types of anticipated analyses. Assessment processes should be designed to fit the level of planning envisioned. Statewide assessments, for example, are likely to be oriented toward issue identification and review of relevant policies and programs; while regional and local level assessments would more likely focus on operational and management needs.

Obtaining Stakeholder Input

Stakeholder interest in water resources management has increased significantly in the last three decades. Individuals and interest groups have become active in bringing their views to the attention of decision makers by way of attempting to influence the outcomes of proposals for the expenditure of public funds. Without stakeholder acceptance, plan acceptance is unlikely, so planners have developed various approaches for bringing stakeholders to the table. The effectiveness of these efforts has varied from success to failure depending largely on the stage at which involvement occurs, the willingness of stakeholders to negotiate and the skill of the planning agency and even of the individuals most directly involved. There does not appear to be a general formula for getting stakeholders to the table and keeping them there or of assuring positive results, but in Appendix 2.1 the history of efforts is briefly reviewed and some lessons drawn.

Managing Conflicts

Stakeholder input will often reveal conflicts, at which point negotiation, rather than confrontation, is the most productive path to follow. The alternative is litigation and this is costly and time-consuming. Conflict resolution strategies employed by planners include: informal gatherings to air views and discuss differences; introduction of third-party facilitators, mediators or arbitrators; and public education, sometimes in the form of cooperative (shared vision) model building. Which approach is the right one depends on the circumstances and the prevailing political climate. Efforts to manage conflict should, in any case, begin when the conflict is discovered.

Coordinating Planning Efforts

Effective coordination of the agencies involved in water resources planning has long been a goal at all levels of government. It has never been easy because of differing agency missions, traditions and authorities; and the turf-protection attitude that usually accompanies these. Dealing with such problems requires a willingness on the part of agency heads to reach a negotiated solution to their common problems. Short of legislative action to consolidate agencies and their missions, the next best approach is to develop effective linkages among the agencies that reduce, if they do not eliminate, the barriers to cooperative efforts. Coordinating mechanisms include interagency agreements and mandates by Congress, the latter often being the most effective arrangement.

Identifying and Evaluating Alternatives

Because of uncertainties surrounding forecasts and disagreements about particular choices independent of forecast results, planners commonly explore several plausible, but different alternatives for consideration by decision makers. This permits considering and comparing plans for a breadth of future conditions and gives decision makers a better basis for deciding on a plan to support. Although an infinite number of futures might be envisioned, the human mind can deal effectively with only a few of them. Thus, it is common for planners to consider futures reflecting predicted high, low and median conditions. It is also good practice to formulate one or more strategies for meeting the objectives of a plan in the context of each projected future (Elgin et al., 1975).

Once formulated, plans must be evaluated according to measures of worth. Such measures are usually economic, environmental and social in character. The evaluations determine: whether a proposed plan will have a positive or negative effect on the national economy, usually based on Benefit-cost analysis; what the environmental impacts will be; whether the social costs are reasonable; what the specifically regional costs and benefits will be; whether the stakeholders likely will accept the plan; and whether funding will be available to ensure implementation.

At the federal level, there are well-established criteria for evaluating water resources plans. For actions proposed by state and local governments or by the private sector, the criteria may deviate from those of the federal government, but generally there will be some prescribed standards of judgment.

The current USACE evaluation process, similar to the NEPA process, is guided by the P&G of 1983 (WRC, 1983) which are intended to ensure conceptually consistent evaluation of planning proposals involving water and related land resources. (For further detail see Chapter 3; Caulfield, 2000; WRC, 1973; Gardner, 2000; Hufschmidt, 2000; Loucks, 1998; Schilling, 1998; WRC, 1983; Viessman, 2000; Young, 2000.)

Making Recommendations

While planners should not make the ultimate decision regarding choice among the plans they develop, they should be expected to draw attention to the important differences among the options they consider and to make their own recommendations, based on their analyses, regarding the choice among the alternative plans. Options considered to be less favorable, but feasible, should be explained in the context of the planning objectives. The planners' recommendations should be designed to aid decision makers in understanding the merits of the choices available, thus enabling them to reach better-informed decisions.

Developing Implementation Plans

The *sine qua non* for plan implementation is the authorization and appropriation of funds. But continued stakeholder support is also vital to success. Good information, presented in understandable terms, can go a long way toward convincing both stakeholders and those making decisions that the proposed plans are in their best interests. When plans are not successfully implemented the reasons may include: failure of planners to develop economically, politically or socially acceptable alternatives, leading to lack of public support; failure of coordination among planning and development agencies; or ineffective linkages between planning and implementing agencies.

Establishing Monitoring Programs

The ultimate test of the effectiveness of planning is found in plan implementation and the achievement of planning objectives, but the outcomes of plan implementation can only be determined by monitoring project or program performance over time. Programs required for this assessment purpose may also serve as a source of information for making adjustments to operating policies or construction schedules when deficiencies are found. Unfortunately, this important element is all too often overlooked or poorly funded.

OTHER AGENCIES AND ORGANIZATIONS RELEVANT TO WATER RESOURCES PLANNING

Many agencies, levels of government and non-governmental organizations (NGOs) are either directly involved in water resources planning or at least capable of influencing plans or planning processes. At a minimum, therefore, the planning roles these institutions play should be understood. But the NWC, in its 1973 report, *New Directions in U.S. Water Policy*, set out a broader normative view of institutional responsibility, stating

'. . . development, management and protection of water resources should be controlled by that level of government nearest the problem and most capable of effectively representing the vital interest involved' (NWC, 1973 p. 10). The commission envisioned a continuing federal role in planning and financing, but believed it should gradually diminish, proposing that, 'Regional and State entities, as well as local units of government, should assume increasing roles in the control of water resources use and preservation' (ibid.). President Carter's water policy reforms of 1978 included emphasis on an increasing role for the states and the administrations that have followed Carter's have continued to move in that direction.

Federal Agencies

Many federal agencies play significant roles in planning for the development and management of water resources in the USA. The principal construction agencies, USACE, USBR and NRCS, are very influential, but their roles have changed with the shifting of concern from water quantity to water quality and environmental protection. The principal regulatory agency, EPA, became an important player in the early 1970s, in terms of its budget share and regulatory programs. While the federal role in water resources planning and management in the USA is broad, it is not dominant in many areas. For example, major expenditures for public water supply development, treatment and distribution and for sewers and wastewater treatment are largely borne by local governments.

State Agencies

Most states have water resources agencies that are counterparts of federal ones. Some of these are quite venerable but others have resulted from requirements for states to manage or participate in federal water-related programs. All states have agencies with responsibility for one or more aspects of water resources planning and management. There is usually a Department of Natural Resources (or something similar) responsible for water resources planning and development and a Department of Environmental Protection (or something similar) responsible for water quality planning and protection. Few states combine the two dimensions in a single agency, though Virginia has a water supply and water quality planning program designed to look ahead to the year 2030. Most states have an explicit goal related to water resources development and management, and water resources planning processes are often project- or purpose-oriented and tend to be organized around surface water, groundwater, water quality or water quantity issues, but may also be comprehensive. State water planning may or may not include regional plans, but consideration of sub-basins or regions is becoming more prevalent (as in California, Florida, Nebraska, Ohio, Pennsylvania, Texas, Virginia and Wisconsin, for example). There has not been widespread concern with addressing consistency of water-related plans at local, regional and state levels.

The water management agencies of some states (Texas and California, for example) have large expert staffs, but others depend on federal agencies for assistance on technical matters. States with water right or water permit systems commonly have agencies charged with administering these. While state, federal and local government agencies and organizations may have broad authority including functions such as planning, constructing, regulating and managing, they also have narrow functions such as issuing permits. Agencies with wide-ranging powers offer the attraction for those concerned of minimizing the number of entities that must be dealt with, but the very comprehensiveness of their powers can be an invitation to abuse.

Local Governments

Local governments are involved in water resources planning, usually focused on local water issues such as drinking water supply and wastewater treatment. Sometimes special districts, covering more than one political jurisdiction have been established to deal with a particular issue such as storm water. Public and private water and wastewater utilities are actors in this arena. Plans are often project- or purpose-oriented rather than comprehensive, but they do incorporate many of the planning components referred to earlier in this chapter. For major metropolitan areas, the planning staffs may be sizable and highly qualified. Partnerships with local and regional water and wastewater utilities are common and stakeholder input is sought. Local governments may also be players in regional or state water resources planning processes. In Florida, for example, a state statute requires that local government comprehensive plans be consistent with the state's regional versions and with the state's comprehensive plan. And in California cities must prepare water plans that coordinate growth with water supply.

Regional Institutions

Regional institutions involved in water management have been established in the USA over the years as outlined in the historical section above. Their functions have varied from forums aimed at facilitating discussion and modest coordination to institutions with broad authorities to plan, construct and operate water management systems. They have been defined on a variety of bases and on varying scales. Thus, some have involved entire large, multi-state river basins, while others have been focused on small watersheds or groups of local political jurisdictions such as counties with only an imperfect match to hydrologic boundaries. Since the early 1900s, many councils and commissions have considered the merits of regional or river basin organizations, recognizing that regional, in addition to state and local, perspectives are often useful in coordinating with federal water resource investment planning. Large regional institutions such as those dealing with major river basins generally follow planning protocols similar to those of federal agencies and they tend to be comprehensive in their goals. Institutions focused on small watersheds tend to have fewer objectives and often focus heavily on water quality problems.

As discussed above, the first, and probably best known, water-oriented regional organization is the TVA. The TVA is unique and has had a long, generally successful, though occasionally contentious history (Hargrove, 1994). It is not likely to be duplicated, being to some large extent a child of the special circumstances of the Great Depression.

In 1943 a Federal Interagency River Basin Committee (FIARBC) program was established to encourage the creation of informal, voluntary interagency committees organized around basins or groups of basins. The Arkansas-White-Red, the Southeast Basins and the Pacific Southwest committees were among those formed. The interagency committees have little power and their principal achievement has been the provision of forums for communication among state and federal agencies and the other units of government involved.

In 1948 the Ohio River Valley Water Sanitation Commission (ORSANCO) was established. This interstate commission, representing eight states and the federal government, develops programs to improve water quality in the Ohio River and its tributaries. Activities include setting wastewater discharge standards, conducting biological assessments, monitoring the chemical and physical properties of the waterways and conducting special surveys and studies.

In 1961 the states of New York, New Jersey, Pennsylvania and Delaware joined the federal government in creating the Delaware River Basin Commission (DRBC). Like the TVA, the DRBC has broad powers, including project planning, implementation and operation and has settled disputes over water allocation among the participating states. It is perhaps best known in the field of water resources for its pioneering study of the cost-effectiveness of various alternatives for improving water quality in the Delaware Estuary and Bay, where effectiveness was defined in terms of dissolved oxygen (DO) levels at critical times for shad migration (DRBC, 1970).

Another RBC, the Susquehanna River Basin Commission (SRBC), designed along the lines of the DRBC, was established in 1973. The DRBC and SRBC are state-federal compact commissions and their creation required a consensus of the states participating. Other compact commissions have been proposed, but a lack of consensus stifled all efforts other than those for the Delaware and Susquehanna.

The WRPA of 1965 developed the Pacific Northwest, Missouri River, Upper Mississippi River, Great Lakes Basin, Ohio River and New England River Basin Commissions designed as planning and coordinating entities and forums, where representatives of states and federal agencies could coordinate activities and jointly develop river basin or regional plans for water and related land resources. Since they had no management or operating authority they did not replace the functions of the federal agencies. An independent chairperson, appointed by the President, coordinated the activities of the RBCs. Each federal agency with an interest in the river basin was entitled to membership, as was each state lying totally or partially within the basin or basins where more than one was involved. The act provided that every reasonable effort be made to arrive at a consensus on all issues. Creation of an independent chairperson and staff, divorced from federal and state agencies, was an important departure from the rotating chairmanships of predecessor interagency committees and encouraged loyalty to the institution and an opportunity for focusing on regional goals rather than on the narrower objectives of the member states and federal agencies. However, the performance of the RBCs was hampered by budgetary constraints, problems of coordination, lack of authority to enforce decisions and the necessity to act by consensus. Obligations of members to their parent organizations, the voluntary nature of the coordination process and the limited capacity of members to speak for their organizations added to the difficulties. The result was that the RBCs fell short of expectations and, in 1981, were abolished. The former RBCs were later reshaped into various forms of interstate institutions charged with coordination of interstate water resources planning, but they were generally not successful. After the demise of the RBCs, interest in such organizations declined. An anomaly was the formation of new interstate compacts for the Apalachicola, Chattahoochee and Flint (ACF) Rivers and for the Alabama, Coosa and Tallapoosa (ACT) Rivers by the states of Georgia, Alabama and Florida. The driver for this action was a decade-long dispute over the allocation of water in the ACF River Basin, which continues to be a contentious issue. Indeed, failure to resolve differences among the states resulted in litigation yet to reach conclusion.

The problems of fragmented interests in water problems within states and the extension of problems beyond the jurisdictions of governmental units led to the consolidation of some organizations and the emergence of new authorities with the ability to manage water resources in a multi-jurisdictional region. Two such organizations are the consolidated Natural Resource Districts (NRD) in Nebraska and the Water Management Districts (WMD) in Florida. These regional models merit a more detailed description and one is provided for the NRDs in Appendix 2.2.

Non-Governmental Organizations

NGOs are private organizations that may be involved in advocacy, litigation, lobbying, research, public education or some combination of these activities, relative to public issues of concern to them. They may be supported by individual contributions, by foundations, by corporate gifts and even by grants from governmental units at federal, state or local levels. International non-governmental organizations (INGOs) have the same general functions, but their focus is on international problems. NGOs are almost always designed to influence public opinion and governmental action and those interested in water resource issues can have significant effects on the formulation of water management policies, plans and projects. Many of the national versions, such as the Natural Resources Defense Council, Environmental Defense, the Sierra Club and the Wilderness Society, have the expertise and political influence to get official consideration, if not always endorsement, of their views. The likelihood of success in a planning effort may well depend upon bringing these stakeholders to the table as partners in plan development rather than as opponents.

SOME OBSERVATIONS SUGGESTED BY THE HISTORY OF POLICY AND PLANNING

Since the turn of the twentieth century, interest in water resources has shifted from development for traditional purposes to more efficient management and the protection and restoration of water quality and water environment systems. The history of water resources planning and development summarized previously reveals some important continuing themes and issues warranting consideration in establishing future plans and policies:

- Local political pressures, along with broad national interests and crises have heavily influenced US water resources development, being the drivers for legislative action.

- The need to address regional interests has been recognized for years, but regional or river basin planning efforts fit awkwardly within the federal system and have often been of limited scope or ineffectual.
- Although not written explicitly, a national water policy exists in the form of a dense network of statutes, rules and traditions that has evolved over time. Occasionally efforts are made to provide a sharper focus, but this always proves difficult, in large part because of the vast differences in regional interests where water is concerned.
- The WRPA of 1965 was a milestone in water management. It established the WRC and RBCs; recognized the several levels of planning; fostered coordination and collaboration; involved the states; and provided a much-needed assessment process. The demise of the WRC in 1982 left a void.
- The NEPA of 1969 signaled a substantial increase in federal support for environmental protection. This had significant implications for water policy because the requirement for environmental impact statements indirectly initiated a movement toward more holistic water planning and management.
- The 1973 report *New Directions in U.S. Water Policy* by the NWC explored the status of the nation's waters and recommended new directions for water policy. Although more than 30 years old, the report's seven recurring themes still stand as useful guidelines for the future.
- The WRC's 1975 assessment included an attempt to identify and quantify water needs for environmental protection. It also projected a future water use trend that indicated water use could be decreased in the future even though the population and economic activity levels were increasing. The WRC's projections have been borne out by the US Geological Survey (USGS) water use statistics through the year 2000.
- The solution to water supply problems in the Washington, DC metropolitan area suggested by research demonstrated that creative, holistic approaches to water management have much to recommend them and that they can be implemented without the need for massive institutional reforms. Effective forums in which to seek solutions to problems that transcend normal political or agency boundaries are, however, needed.
- Contemporary trends in water management include:
  - making more conservative use of water
  - aiming at low impact development
  - embracing environmental protection and restoration as equal partners in water-allocation decision making

- taking stakeholder involvement seriously
- educating the public for a broader understanding of water and environment issues
- recognizing that water management is best practiced within the problem-shed of concern
- embracing integrated water resources planning and management
- utilizing consensus-based decision making
- recognizing the importance of risk management and risk communication
- expanding research in areas such as ecosystem needs for water and the valuation of water dedicated to environmental purposes

RECOMMENDATIONS FOR THE FUTURE

Water policy development for the new century must embrace both resource-related and institutional issues. The physical properties and distribution of water are keystones, but legal, political, social, economic and environmental building blocks must be crafted into these policies as well. Dimensions of uncertainty, public perception and political sensitivity must be addressed. Hard-line technical approaches may be, and often are, socially unacceptable and compromise is usually required; but, even so, settlements should be based on the best information available. Unfortunately, institutional and social configurations and attitudes often impede objective analyses and encourage narrowly focused or inefficient policy designs. Generally, integrated water management should be the goal at all levels of government for the twenty-first century. This means that the full spatial, environmental and institutional dimensions of problems must be recognized and the component interactions addressed. Complete integration is probably an impossible dream, but it is practical to move incrementally towards it. This implies the desirability of:

- Establishing a new federal water policy coordinating institution (Viessman, 2000). A format with some of the attributes of the former WRC would: (1) provide guidance in designing federal water policy, (2) coordinate federal water programs and agencies, (3) assess the status of the nation's and the world's water environment, (4) provide foresight capability, (5) facilitate research and (6) coordinate and support state water resources planning and management programs. The new institution should also have the authority to stimulate and facilitate, but not to direct, regional water resources initiatives for appropriate problem-sheds. It should have representation from state and NGOs, as well as federal agencies. There is a sound rationale for having this council attached to the White House, thereby setting it somewhat apart from interagency politics.

- Restoring the focus on regions or problem-sheds as platforms for water resources planning and management. Planning and management institutions should be designed bottom-up to reflect the needs and character of the area to be served. Participants would include concerned citizens, local governments, appropriate representatives of federal and state agencies and NGOs. These regional institutions would be charged with making assessments, suggesting regional policies and identifying paths that should be taken to deal with plausible future scenarios.
- Bringing the single-objective regulatory approach used by the EPA into conformance with the multi-purpose, multi-objective planning system that for many years has provided guidance for federal planning. Requiring that all federal water-related programs be subject to the P&G could facilitate reconciliation of the two approaches (Schad, 1998).
- Providing the resources needed to plan for meeting potential global climate change and related challenges. It is likely that many of the most vexing water management problems to be faced in the future will be global in nature. Dealing with major water issues in a single nation is difficult, but when the problem transcends national boundaries, necessary institutional arrangements are generally nonexistent or not backed up by sufficient authority to be effective. The time for developing plausible climate change scenarios and exploring alternatives for dealing with them is now.
- Supporting analytical and database initiatives. Good decision making is heavily dependent upon the quality of available data and the ability to analyse this data so that information can be presented regarding the outcomes to be expected from exercising the options proposed. The value of interactive simulation models in aiding decision makers is well documented. Resources are needed to further develop and promulgate these decision-support tools and to develop and maintain the databases needed to assure that they can be used effectively.
- Incorporating environmental values into the economics of water allocation. Protocols for making trade-offs and establishing relative values for making water-allocation decisions for environmental purposes are needed. Casting the value of a constructed waterway in

monetary terms is relatively easy to do, but problems abound when it comes to establishing a value for wetlands, a natural habitat or an in-stream flow to support fish and wildlife. This is a challenge in need of additional research.

ACKNOWLEDGMENTS

Many sources have been drawn upon in preparing this chapter. The author hopes that suitable acknowledgment has been given to them. In particular, the outstanding historical works of Beatrice H. Holmes provided a wealth of information. The author also wishes to acknowledge the contributions made by the following reviewers: Kyle E. Schilling, Mark Dunning, Larry MacDonnell, David H. Moreau, Mark Sagoff, Paul Bourget, Daniel P. Loucks and Duane Baumann.

REFERENCES

Aspen Institute (2002), *Dam Removal: A New Option for a New Century*, Washington, DC: The Aspen Institute.

Caulfield, Jr., H.P. (2000), 'Early federal guidelines for water resource evaluation', *Water Resources Update*, **116**, 14–17.

Delaware River Basin Commission (DRBC) (1970), *Final Progress Report on Delaware Estuary and Bay Water Quality Sampling and Mathematical Modeling Project*, report to the Federal Water Pollution Control Administration, US Department of Interior, Trenton, NJ: DRBC.

Dzurik, A.A. (2002), *Water Resources Planning*, 3rd edn, Savage, MD: Rowman and Littlefield.

Elgin, D.S., D.C. MacMichael and P. Schwartz (1975) *Alternative Futures for Environmental Policy Planning: 1975–2000*, Washington, DC: Center for Study of Social Policy, Stanford Research Institute.

Gardner, B.D. (March 2000), 'The importance of property rights in water', *Water Resources Update*, **116**, 31–5.

Grigg, N.S. (1996), *Water Resources Management*, New York, NY: McGraw-Hill.

Hanke, S.H. (1981), 'On the feasibility of benefit/cost analysis', *Public Policy*, **29** (2), 147–57.

Hargrove, E.C. (1994), *Prisoner of Myth: The Leadership of the TVA, 1993–1990*, Princeton, NJ: Princeton University Press.

Holmes, B.H. (June 1972), 'A history of federal water resources programs 1800–1960', miscellaneous publication no. 1233, Washington, DC: US Department of Agriculture.

Holmes, B.H. (September 1979), 'History of federal water resources programs and policies 1961–1970', miscellaneous publication no. 1379, Washington, DC: US Department of Agriculture.

Hufschmidt, M.M. (2000), 'Benefit/cost analysis: 1933–1985', *Water Resources Update*, **116**, 42–9.
James, L.D. and R.R. Lee (1971), *Economics of Water Resources Planning*, New York, NY: McGraw-Hill.
Kates, R.W. (1962), 'Hazard and choice perception in flood plain management', University of Chicago Department of Geography research paper 78, Chicago, IL.
Krutilla, J.V. and O. Eckstein (1958), *Multiple Purpose River Development: The Economics of Project Evaluation*, Baltimore, MD: The Johns Hopkins Press.
Loucks, D.P. (1998), 'Watershed planning: changing issues, processes and expectations', *Water Resources Update*, **111**, 38–46.
Maass, A., M.M. Hufschmidt, R. Dorfman, H.A. Thomas, Jr., S.A. Marglin and G.M. Fair (1962), *Design of Water Resource Systems: New Techniques for Relating Economic Objectives, Engineering Analysis and Governmental Planning*, Cambridge, MA: Harvard University Press.
National Conservation Commission (1909), Senate Document 676, 60th Congress, 2nd Session, 1, 24–7.
National Research Council (1999), *New Directions in Water Resources Planning for the US Army Corps of Engineers*, Washington, DC: National Academies Press.
National Water Commission (NWC) (1973), *New Directions in U.S. Water Policy – Summary, Conclusions and Recommendations*, Washington, DC: US Government Printing Office.
Palmer, R.N., J.R. Wright, J.A. Smith, J.L. Cohon and C.S. ReVelle (1979), *Policy Analysis of Reservoir Operation in the Potomac River Basin*, vols I–III, College Park, MD: Water Resources Research Center.
President Jimmy Carter (1978), *Federal Water Policy Initiatives*, House Document 95-347, Washington, DC: US Government Printing Office.
Rogers, P. (1993), *America's Water: Federal Roles and Responsibilities*, Cambridge, MA: MIT Press.
Schad, T.D. (1998), 'Water policy: who should do what?', *Water Resources Update*, **111**, 51–61.
Schilling, K.E. (1998), 'The future for water resources planning and decision-making models', *Water Resources Update*, **111**, 62–8.
Sheer, D.P. (12 November 1981), *Assuring Water Supply for the Washington Metropolitan Area – Twenty-Five Years of Progress, in a 1980s View of Water Management in the Potomac River Basin*, report of the Committee on Government Affairs, US Senate, 97th Congress, 2nd Session, Washington, DC: US Government Printing Office.
United States vs *Jay Woods Oil Co., Inc.* (5 June 1987), 'ED Mich. Number 87 CR20012 BC', unreported opinion, cited in *Environmental Reporter*, **18** (6), 502.
US Army Corps of Engineers (USACE) (2002), *Summary of Water Resources Project Cost Sharing: Non-Federal Representatives*, Washington, DC: Civil Works Program Development and Executive Course.
US Army Corps of Engineers (USACE), Institute for Water Resources (November 1997), *Planning Primer*, Institute for Water Resources report 97-R-15, Fort Belvoir, VA: US Army Corps of Engineers.
US Bureau of the Budget (1952), *Budget Circular A-47*, Washington, DC: US Government Printing Office.

US Congress (1969), *History of the Implementation of the Recommendations of the Senate Select Committee on National Water Resources*, Senate Committee on Interior and Insular Affairs, 90th Congress, 2nd Session, Washington, DC: US Government Printing Office.
US Congress (1975), *Alternative Futures for US Agriculture*, Part L, Senate Committee on Agriculture and Forestry, 94th Congress, 1st Session, Washington, DC: US Government Printing Office.
US Government Accountability Office (1978), *An Overview of Benefit/Cost Analysis for Water Resources Projects: Improvements Still Needed*, CED-78-127, Washington, DC: US Government Accountability Office.
US House of Representatives (1926), *USA Grand Coullee Study – Scoping Report*, House Document 308, 69th Congress, 1st Session, Washington, DC: US Government Printing Office.
US House of Representatives (1966), *A Unified National Program for Managing Flood Losses*, communication from the President of the United States, transmitting a report by the Task Force on Federal Flood Control Policy, House Document 465, 89th Congress, 2nd Session, Washington, DC: US Government Printing Office.
US Interagency Committee on Water Resources (USIACWR) (1950), *Proposed Practices for Economic Analysis of River Basin Projects*, The Green Book (revised 1958), Washington, DC: US Government Printing Office.
US Senate (1912), *Final Report of the National Waterways Commission*, Senate Document 440, Washington, DC: US Government Printing Office.
US Senate (1962), *Policies, Standards and Procedures in the Formulation, Evaluation and Review of Plans for Use and Development of Water and Related Land Resources*, Senate Document 97, 87th Congress, 2nd Session, Washington, DC: US Government Printing Office.
Viessman, Jr, W. (2000), 'Are we still on the wrong road?', Water Resources Update, **116**, 74–9.
Viessman, Jr, W. and Timothy D. Feather (eds) (2006), *State Water Resources Planning in the United States*, Reston, VA: American Society of Civil Engineers.
Water Resources Council (WRC) (1973), *Establishment of Principles and Standards for Planning Water and Related Land Resources*, Federal Register, Part III, 38 (174), Washington, DC: US Government Printing Office.
Water Resources Council (WRC) (1983), *Economic and Environmental Principles and Guidelines for Water and Related Land Resources Implementation Studies*, Washington, DC: US Government Printing Office.
Western Water Policy Review Advisory Commission (1998), *Water in the West: Challenge for the Next Century*, Washington, DC: Western Water Policy Review Advisory Commission.
White, G.F. (1945), 'Human adjustment to floods: a geographic approach to the flood problem in the United States', University of Chicago Department of Geography research paper no. 29, 225, Chicago, IL.
White, G.F. (1964), 'Choice of adjustment to floods', University of Chicago Department of Geography research paper 93, Chicago, IL.
White, G.F. (1969), *Strategies of American Water Management*, Ann Arbor, MI: University of Michigan Press.
Young, R.A. (2000), 'Thoughts on economic evaluation and western water policy', *Water Resources Update*, **116**, 85–90.

APPENDIX 2.1 EVOLUTION OF PUBLIC INVOLVEMENT IN WATER PLANNING

Jerome Delli Priscoli

Introduction: What is Public Participation in Water Resources Management and Why Should Decision Makers be Interested in It?

As we know, the control of water is the control of life and livelihood. Thus, how we exercise this control reveals what we value, who we are and what type of society we seek to become. Not surprisingly, water resources planning has evolved along with our evolving understanding of how we control and manage water. The past decades have brought fundamental changes in key dimensions of water management including the objectives sought, evaluation criteria and procedures employed. Perhaps the greatest change has been in the role of the public in the planning process.

Public participation (or involvement) in water resources management can mean many things to many people. The approaches used in the US Army Corps of Engineers (USACE) to help water resources have been pragmatic and have not dogmatically advocated a definitive definition of participation. However, USACE experiences do reveal areas of growing concern to the water field within which to discuss what participation is and why it is important. These are:

1. Ethical dimensions of water management.
2. Water management and civic culture.
3. Tension between the technical and political.
4. Reconciling the discontinuities between geographic and jurisdictional boundaries.
5. Need for better and more conflict management.

Ethical dimensions of water management

We can see profound ethical implications in all aspects of the traditional water uses such as: flood control and management; drought contingency planning and management; irrigation, hydroelectric power and agriculture; water supply and sanitation; navigation; ecological maintenance and health; and public health and disease control. Ethical considerations around these uses concern the distribution of benefits and costs of the services; who gets how much of the water and who pays; the distribution of risks, who is vulnerable and to what degree. Today, this includes service for the nature and ecology as well as people.

Ethical implications are also clear in all aspects of water management decision making such as: planning, regulating, operating, financing and investing, designing and implementing and others. They concern who participates and what are their sources of legitimacy; what are the decisions they participate in; do they have access to formulating options or only to reacting to options already formulated; how and what type of opportunity costs are considered; the valuing, implicit or explicit, in trade-off decisions; level and type of information open to the public; disclosure and characterization of impacts; the way professionals interact with non-professionals and the use, as well as misuse, of technical and professional information.

The public engineers must move beyond just standards to guidelines to principles. In philosophical terms, this means moving more to utilitarianism perspectives as the basis of policy making. We should be moving to blending water management's public health, preservationist and our conservative utilitarian traditions. Accountability, performance and power sharing will become part of the public ethic we must foster. As engineers, we must move even further to blending and mixing quality and quantification in our approaches.

It is not that engineers, scientists and technical professionals have become irrelevant. The public need them more than ever. However, for their expertise to be put in service, a new model of relationships must be built with those whom they would serve.

This new model, often called 'informed consent', demands broader understanding, by all stakeholders, of the special ethical demands faced by decision makers. For example, when is the decision not to decide a greater evil than to decide and to possibly incur unexpected negative effects? Meaningful participation often brings both decision makers and participants into a new awareness of this ethical reality. Lack of participation or non-meaningful participation allows stakeholders the luxury of negative 'nay-saying' without confronting the reality of decision-making pressures; and that is dangerous. Admittedly, getting the public in touch with such realities, which are often described in obscure and esoteric language, is difficult. But we must. And participation is one of our main tools to do so.

Today's ecology and water disputes must overcome the syndrome of advocacy science if we are to preserve the legitimacy of the scientific enterprise, which is so necessary for water management. We must ask what are the ethics of using science to persuade publics, especially under conditions where there is fundamental disagreement among scientists and where even the models and data themselves are weak.

Participatory processes force all of us to confront these questions.

Water management and civic culture

Building the physical water infrastructure in a collaborative and participatory way is now an important means for building the civic infrastructure and the civil society or what many call the governance environment. However, this is not new. Water, governance and civic culture have always been connected (Delli Priscoli and Hassan, 1998). Fountains of ancient Rome, like standpipes in small villages today or in medieval cities of Europe, have played roles in building civic culture as well as quenching thirst. They were occasions for civic dialogue and meeting places central to creating a sense of civic belonging and responsibility. We should not forget that civil society, civic culture and civil engineering share common roots. Whether it is irrigation associations, community water and sewage and even large-scale multi-purpose river operations, water management forces us to connect and to balance rights to water with responsibilities for managing water. Most democratic theorists see the experience of such balancing as central to development of civic society (Kettering Foundation, 1991).

Such balancing moves publics away from passive acceptance to active choice of decisions that directly affect our lives. It is the heart of democratic civic culture. There is little place here for the old paternalism of engineering design that says, 'I will take care of everything for you.' So too there is little place for the new regulatory paternalism that says the state will protect you based on some obscure and nonexistent holistic wisdom; a wisdom, like engineering of the past, which is often achieved among experts usually bound together in joint missionary zeal by unwritten ideological consensus. The movement is exercising freedom to choose activities and responsibilities – no matter how frightening or overwhelming. It is not a freedom from interference, inconvenience or action. It means taking responsibility for choosing a design (destiny) and actively pursuing it.

Participation, especially in the civic works of water, is central to this process.

Tensions between the political and technical

Traditionally we have come to view the separation between the political, usually seen as legislative voting, and the technical, usually seen as implementing the executive agencies. When confronted with complex water management decisions, this distinction breaks down (Delli Priscoli, 1974). Often it is with the implementation or administration of general laws that the distribution of impacts becomes clear. Politics is 'Who gets What, When and How' (Lasswell, 1958). Often the what, when and how become apparent only during implementation. Thus, administrators of technical agencies begin to appear as the bestowers or deniers of political benefits. And this is becoming truer and truer as we become more complex.

To manage this gray area, scholars and commentators, from Habermas to Robert Reich, have been calling for a new paradigm of public dialogue, which leads to civic discovery (Reich, 1996). This call reflects the chief goals of participatory processes: to foster deliberation, to encourage social learning, to create new alternatives and to build or enhance through empowering experiences the civic infrastructure.

In his book *Degrees of Belief: Subjective Probability and Engineering Judgment*, Vick notes the essential features of informed consent. It is interesting to look how closely these professional ethics from hard engineering parallel those that would be espoused by participation and collaboration advocates and how they strongly suggest a democratic civic culture as we confront the dilemma of technical versus political (Vick, 2002). The elements are:

1. The decision rests with the decision maker.
2. Probabilities communicate information to inform the decision.
3. Judgment is expected to be incorporated in probability estimates.
4. Probability estimates incorporate ranges where appropriate.
5. Probabilities for adverse consequences are accompanied by means to reduce either or both.
6. The decision maker is encouraged to seek other opinions.
7. Motivational bias in probability estimates is not tolerated.

Participation means much to both water management and to our civic cultures.

Discontinuities between geography and jurisdictions

Our water problems are integrated around watersheds and river basins. However, our administrative units to deal with them are fragmented. Participatory processes are essentially tools to help us bridge the discontinuity between geographical and jurisdictional boundaries found in water resources management.

Ultimately, participation is a bottom-up phenomena. Participation becomes a driving force for the vertical (state, local and regional) as well as the horizontal (across agency) negotiations vital to decisions, which rarely fit traditional jurisdictional boundaries. And both are central pieces of the current advocacy for integrated water resources management (IWRM) found throughout the world water community (GWP, 2000).

Participation and conflict management

Our modern participation experience was born of multi-party, multi-issue disputes usually precipitated by new ecological value challenges. By contrast, participation's associated movement, conflict management or alternative dispute resolution (ADR), began by focusing on mediation and various forms of non-binding arbitration. This movement was born of the more traditional model of labor-management disputes, which involved limited numbers of parties and more discernable interests. Practitioners in both of these traditions have come together in a variety of professional forums and societies. The growth of environmental mediation in the USA during the 1990s is one major example. Many of the same 'process' tools and techniques are used in each field.

But beyond these convergences, important differences between participation and ADR exist. Participation has been driven primarily by values of empowerment, creativity and open access to government. ADR, while not ignoring such values, has been sold more on the values of efficiency, timeliness and cost effectiveness of decision-making processes. These values of empowerment, open system access, efficiency and timeliness can and do often conflict. In the end, some people may just not agree among themselves nor with water managers or other decisions but we will all have to learn to live together while we disagree. In this sense, participation is far more then conflict resolution. Participation seeks to help us discern public interest, community will and to articulate preferred futures. Political philosopher Ben Barber puts it best when he says, 'participation teaches us the arts of Democracy' (Barber, 1997).

Both are critical to water resources managers but should not be confused.

Brief Chronology of Changes in Public Involvement in Water Resources Planning

Public participation (or involvement) in water resources management has moved from a focus on legalistic and formal public hearings in the pre-1960s to US government leadership in alternative process tools in the 1970s, to de-emphasis on participation and more focus on selected cost-sharing partners in the 1980s and to negotiations and dispute resolution in the 1980s, and currently to renewed concerns with both dispute resolution and participation in the late 1990s and early 2000s. Today USACE is in a period of merging lessons learned from the fields of dispute resolution and participation along with new tools for interactive modeling among stakeholders. Changing values toward our ecology are calling for new consensus tools to reach agreements among non-commensurate values. Rapidly moving technology has produced inexpensive new means for stakeholders to actually jointly model and jointly create technical visions of water resources to provide the basis for trade-off and negotiations.

Pre-1960s

In this time period, planning was an activity reserved for experts. The public was seen as lacking technical understanding and, therefore, as having little to offer the planning process. Interaction with the public was confined to public hearings to present already-created plans. The public had little influence on the planning process and that only if able to mobilize political support sufficient to impress elected representatives.

1960s

The public consciousness-raising that lay behind the civil rights and the anti-war movements resulted in a general growth of activism and protest in support of social goals. When organized opposition to water resources projects, often based on environmental concerns, emerged at roughly the same time, water resources planners began to adopt open planning models such as that of the Susquehanna River and the Northwest Fishbowl Planning approach (Borton et al., 1970; Widditsch, 1972) that emphasized a two-way flow of communication with the public. The National Environmental Policy Act (NEPA) legislation in 1969 provided a statutory basis for a more in-depth and proactive involvement of the public, especially in the project scoping process.

1970s and early 1980s

Additional legislation and executive orders mandated public involvement. The concept of public involvement as a planned effort to involve citizens in decision making through mutual two-way communication became a specific part of the planning process. The USACE contracted with Synergy training services for a landmark training program introducing the importance of consulting with the public during the planning process and focusing on the use of interactive workshops as an alternative to formal public hearings. Hanchey's publication, *Public Involvement in the Corps of Engineers Planning Process* (Hanchey, 1975), laid out a systematic approach using interactive workshops. One of the first applications occurred in the St Louis District in 1975 and employed interactive workshops using the Nominal Group Technique to elicit public expressions of water resources 'needs' and potential preferred solutions to flooding problems in the community. Throughout the 1970s and early 1980s, water resources agencies experimented with innovative public involvement methods and broadened their use to encompass all aspects of water resources planning and management, including regulatory decision making (Creighton et al., 1982).

In the 1970s USACE Public Participation (involvement) led by the Corps' Institute for Water Resources (IWR) focused primarily on civil works water resources planning. It is fair to say that USACE became a US government leader in the field culminating in collaboration with the White House to create the Interagency Council on Public Participation (ICCP). The centerpiece of the USACE strategy was to build capacity of its professional mangers to assure participatory processes were used in water resources management. It did this through training programs in public participation and involvement. Some of these set standards for training throughout the US government.

1980s

During the late 1980s, after passage of the Water Resources Development Act (WRDA) of 1986 and the introduction of substantial cost sharing by project beneficiaries, a fundamental change in the motivation for public involvement occurred. The role of the cost-share partner – the local sponsor – became critical and planning and public involvement became considerably more streamlined to focus primarily on meeting local sponsor needs. The use of structured public involvement programs to interact with diverse publics was significantly reduced, except for larger, more complex studies. The focus on cost sharing and reduced emphasis on planning meant reduced interest and use of public involvement processes. The USACE field focused more and more on the cost-shared partner as the important public and negotiations with them as the key to projects.

As USACE interests in water resources planning and in public participation waned, interest in alternative dispute resolution and conflict management grew rapidly in areas of civil works operations, engineering and construction, clean up of hazardous sights and even within areas of the USACE bureaucracy such as personnel. This interest was spawned in great part by the support for these new process programs by USACE legal council. The greatest interest was shown in contract management. Many of the process tools from public involvement were then applied to these growing areas of interest in USACE with considerable success. For example, through the new ADR program USACE achieved a 50 per cent per year reduction in claims or about $500 million per year. New USACE training, which built on older public involvement training programs, once again set some standards in the field for all of the US government, and the programs won the Hammer Award presented by Vice President Al Gore. The greatest successes were registered in contract management and what has come to be called partnering; which really seemed a variant of collaborative problems solving found in public involvement.

With a general decline in water resources investments for new, large projects, planning attention broadened to include issues of managing projects already constructed and addressing conflicts about the operation or modification of existing projects. Alternative dispute resolution processes, borrowing heavily from the general concepts of interactive public involvement, introduced new process tools into USACE; mini-trials, mediation, conciliation and fact finding were examples of processes that adopted the same consultative and facilitative approach to interacting with the public that earlier public involvement processes emphasized (Creighton et al., 1998).

1990s

In the late 1990s, concern grew in many areas of water management, from regulatory functions to planning and to operations. The fields began to converge as the US government, through the Office of Management and Budget (OMB) and the Council on Environmental Quality (CEQ) initiated new programs called environmental conflict resolution (ECR), and directed agencies to report on how ECR techniques were being used. Essentially ECR combined the tools found in both the dispute resolution field and the public involvement field and focused them on all aspects of environmental conflict.

Today: Early 2000s and the Future

Since the middle of the twentieth century, water resources planning has shifted its focus from multiple-purpose projects to IWRM systems that emphasize a more holistic consideration of water resources issues and collaborative partnerships among stakeholders, often at a watershed or problemshed scale. In this emerging framework, agency roles move from top-down planner to convener/facilitator of a joint sponsor/agency/stakeholder forum, which is designed to seek balanced, sustainable and implementable solutions. Planning in such a framework has become more a process of encouraging learning among stakeholders than directing a series of steps in which others have an ability to influence and interact at specific intervals.

Today ECR is a centerpiece to achieving promised goals of the USACE – Civil Works Program: 'We will broaden our collaboration with others to enhance the chances of balancing water uses and making wise investments and trade-offs decisions' (JP Woodley and Chief USACE, March 2004, Civil Works Strategic Plan).

Two of the five identified national water challenges used as baseline in the USACE Civil Works Strategic Plan are based on ECR, to:

- Achieve greater balance between traditional water resources demands and environmental/ecosystem objectives.
- Minimize institutional barriers to efficient and effective water resources planning, decision making and management.

Two of the four key Corps principles of IWRM which the Corps seeks to adopt are ECR:

- Balance across multiple uses or functions. The objective is to seek greater balance across objectives. Interdisciplinary views and collaboration become germane to identifying how best to achieve multiple objectives.
- Collaborative approach. Collaboration can involve several federal agencies (for example, Environmental Protection Agency, US Fish and Wildlife Service, Natural Resources Conservation Service, Bureau of Reclamation, US Geological Survey and land management agencies), state and local agencies, the private sector and interest groups, and can take many forms.

The Corps watershed approach contains nine methods of which at least four are directly ECR:

- coordinating planning and management
- promoting cooperation among government agencies at all levels
- encouraging public participation
- establishing interdisciplinary teams.

Consequently, the USACE capacity to integrate the water uses among its business programs systematically in river basins and watersheds now depends on ECR or public involvement and conflict resolution tools. While the salience of these process tools has grown and while USACE had maintained considerable leadership and investment in them, current surveys show that the capacity to use process tools within USACE had become weak. For example, USACE field surveys showed:

- An uneven use of ECR and process tools.
- Little systematic knowledge of what USACE is actually doing in the area.
- Only anecdotal evidence of their use but limited understanding of ECR and process approaches, especially as applied to civil works.

In fact, with the atrophying of public involvement interest, there seemed to be a digression in public image to pre-1970s level of competence in interactive processes. Few process training programs still exist and none of the current District Engineers and few Senior Leaders have training in the process areas, despite their grown salience to USACE missions.

With this in mind and with uneven knowledge, USACE has begun new ECR programs, once again using training as a centerpiece for rapidly building capacity with the field. The USACE Civil Works Regulatory program seemed to be mentioned most frequently as needing more process tools. In addition, a number of suggestions have been emerging:

- improve training
- setting up one-stop help centers
- disseminating more cases studies from the Corps as examples
- updating regulations
- providing guidelines on how to fund the process.

Lessons Learned Over Four Decades

Public involvement tools are necessary to water resources managers as they must manage multiple demands by multiple stakeholders, some of which conflict. USACE must manage watershed stakeholders so they can jointly define problems and generate solution alternatives. Indeed USACE seems to be moving in these directions when one looks at programs such as:

- coastal America
- regional sediment management
- Section 729 of the Water Resources Development Act of 1986; Congress authorized the Corps to study water resources needs of river basins and regions in coordination with stakeholders
- increased use of general and area-wide permitting
- need for negotiated operating plans
- new models that have emerged in the Everglades, CalFed and coastal Louisiana.

Dealing with and trading off among the benefits accruing from different, and often conflicting, values is the key for water resources managers. Over the years USACE has found that:

- When agencies are confused about the difference between technical and values choices, stakeholders often begin to second-guess the agency technically.
- Most significant decisions made by agencies are not really technical decisions, but values choices, informed by technical information.
- Agencies still have to make decisions that involve values choices; but values choices are prime candidates for ECR and participation.
- Stakeholders view decisions about values as 'political'.

- Technical training does not make us more qualified than others to decide what is good for society.
- When there are big values differences, the other side will always appear 'over-emotional' and 'irrational'.
- People of a similar point of view will cluster together.

The driving philosophy behind public involvement and process approaches is that they are a means to: improving the way water resources managers makes decisions; helping USACE to deal with a changing mission (which means dealing with changing or new values); building capacity of the Corps in key areas of collaboration skills; and to externally help USACE deal with changed public images.

Key Competencies, Tools and Processes

Over time USACE has come to see that water resources managers need to understand and have competence to work with the following challenges:

- why conduct participation?
- who is the public?
- what is involvement?
- designing programs
- techniques and applications
- communication – facilitation
- designing workshops – meetings
- teaming
- language of consensus and negotiations
- identifying and breaking conflict escalation patterns
- beyond extremes getting to middle ground
- principles of consensus building.

The primary public involvement tools to help them do so can be seen in Figure A2.1. Likewise the conflict resolution tools to help them do so can be seen in Figure A2.2. Figure A2.3 shows the link to tools describing how to integrate the process tools with analytical tools into one jointly owned shared vision.

Conclusions and Issues for the Future

Early efforts at involving the public in agency-led water resources planning were criticized for being little more than sales pitches – attempts to build support for predetermined decisions. Public involvement often took

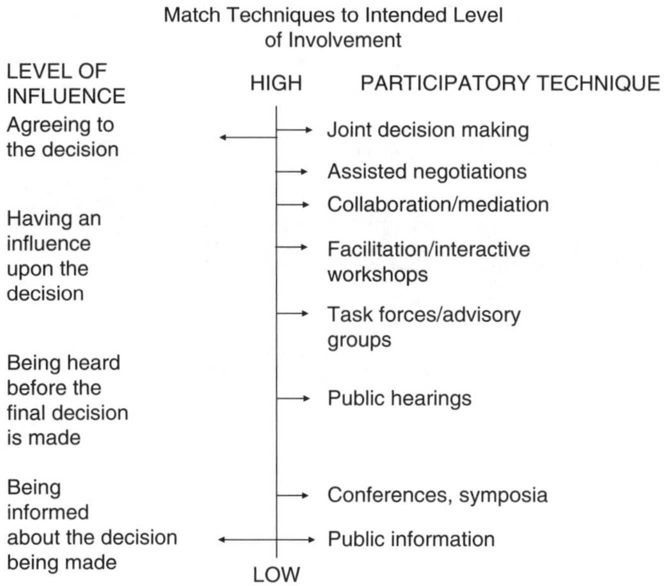

Figure A2.1 Matching level of influence expected and participation tools

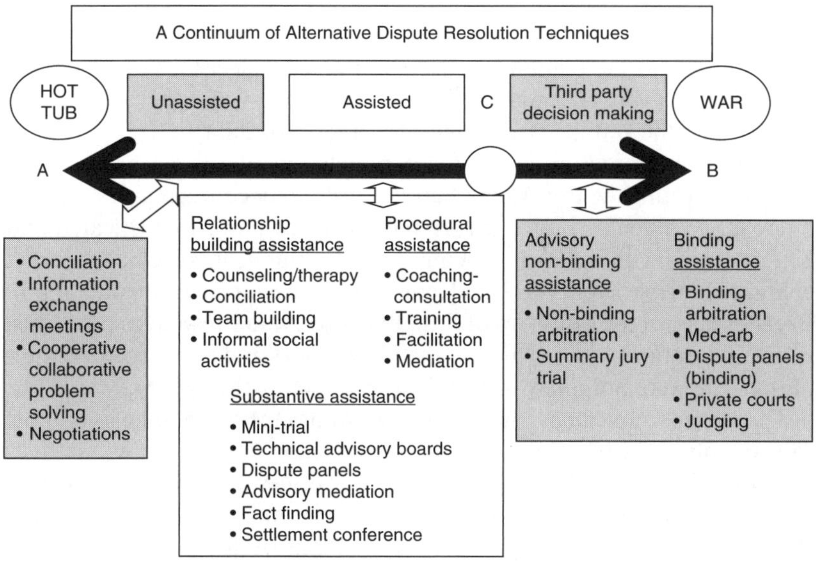

Source: From Delli Priscoli and Moore (1985).

Figure A2.2 Continuum of dispute/conflict management tools

Note: Printed with permission.

Figure A2.3 *Shared vision planning: integrating interactive modeling and participation*

place too late in the planning process to influence decisions; much of the ostensible two-way communication was really one-way agency education to convince the public of the rightness and desirability of agency positions. Public interaction was often conducted using formal public hearings and meetings with formats that did little to encourage give and take interchange. Even as public involvement became more sophisticated and better aligned with decision-making steps, the public involvement process continued to be agency-led and constructed as an instrumental input. Broader perspectives or ways of thinking about water resources problems, issues and options beyond agency mandates, rules and even accepted ways of thinking were not likely to be taken seriously by the agency.

The current movement toward the IWRM has resifted emphasis to: how can we solve this problem together? From: how do we follow our rules and procedures? It is likely that the past critiques of public involvement will become less and less relevant. However, in building coalitions among stakeholders, the planning process may become too focused on particular stakeholders and lose touch with the interests of the broader but unrepresented public. Solutions developed in such circumstances may be more costly than necessary and at variance with broader points of view.

The foundational skills of public involvement are growing in salience. These include the abilities to design interactive workshops, conduct small group facilitation and to utilize a thought process to map out design objectives and the flow of information among stakeholders during the planning process. Similarly, skills in interest-based negotiation will remain central for helping diverse groups of stakeholders to work productively toward balanced solutions to water resources problems. Low-tech procedures employing flip charts, markers and dots remain the standard tools for those practicing public involvement. Beyond foundational skills, new techniques and technology hold great promise for advancing public involvement. Simulation models, some stakeholder built (with expert assistance), allow stakeholders to learn about the sensitivity of outcomes to assumptions about the future and about preferences. These shared vision models can be quite useful in helping to keep the focus on assumptions with big effects. Similarly, computer-assisted voting enables groups to rapidly show preferences and where key disagreements exist.

The demands for participation in water management and ecological decision making are both indicators and symptoms of problems in water management and democratic institutions. The values held by those whom administrators and executives serve are changing. Older administrative organizations and institutions, which themselves are the embodiment of values from previous times, have often lagged behind their publics. New publics bring new demands. At the same time, the complexity of decisions increasingly raises the question of how to achieve democratic accountability. Our water resources demands do not conform to traditional jurisdictional boundaries. The ethical basis of professionalism is now moving from paternalistic to informed consent. Participation is a means to adapt and to make our democratic institutions work better in this context. But participation is also helping to reinvent our civic cultures. Participation is a means to achieve important psychological transference within our publics: that is, from passive victims of, or reactors to, risk toward active choosers of levels of risk (Delli Priscoli, 1989). In this way, water management reform becomes a major tool for providing experiences for building democratic civic cultures on which democratic systems depend.

In classical political theory, democracy is defended because citizens participate in decisions that affect their lives and this experience will educate and build responsibility among citizens – and better citizens (Thucydides, Peloponnesian Wars). What issues could be more important and affect us more than the purposeful designing of our ecological future? And our water resources life support system? Our technology and experts tell us that we have enough water – if we cooperate!

Two hundred years ago, Thomas Jefferson, himself steeped deeply in both the technical and political worlds, once said about making the technical/administrative accountable (Peden, 1954):

> I know of no safe depository of the ultimate powers of the society but the people themselves and if we think them not enlightened to exercise their control with wholesome discretion, the remedy is not to take it from them, but to inform their discretion.

Two hundred years later, reflecting on the same problem, one of America's leading theorists, Robert Dahl, said (Reich, 1996):

> Complexity threatens to cut the policy elites loose from effective control by the demos. The result could be . . . a kind of quasi-guardianship of the policy elites . . . indeed specialization, which is the grounds for the influence of policy elites, may itself impair their capacity for moral judgment . . . If democratic process is not firmly anchored to the judgments of the demos, then the system will continue to drift over to quasi-guardianship.

BIBLIOGRAPHY

Barber, Benjamin (1997), keynote speech to the International Association of Public Participation Practice (IAP2) Conference.

Borton, T.E., K. Warner and J.W. Wenrich (1970), *The Susquehanna Communication – Participation Study*, report 70-6, Fort Belvoir, VA: US Army Corps of Engineers, Institute for Water Resources.

Broome, Taft (1986), 'The slippery ethics of engineering', *Washington Post*, December, Section D3.

Carpenter, Susan (1995), 'The blurring of roles between public participation and conflict resolution practitioners', *Interact*, **1** (1) (Fall), 37–53.

Creighton, J., J. Delli Priscoli and C.M. Dunning (eds) (1982), *Public Involvement Techniques: A Reader of Ten Years Experience at the Institute for Water Resources*, report 82-R1, Fort Belvoir, VA: US Army Corps of Engineers, Institute for Water Resources.

Creighton, J., J. Delli Priscoli and C.M. Dunning (eds) (1998), *Public Involvement and Dispute Resolution: A Reader of the Second Decade of Experience at the Institute for Water Resources*, report 98-R-5, Fort Belvoir, VA: US Army Corps of Engineers, Institute for Water Resources.

Dahl, Robert A. (1989), *Democracy and Its Critics*, New Haven, NJ: Yale University Press, p. 340.

Delli Priscoli, Jerome (1975), 'Public participation in regional-intergovernmental water resources planning: conceptual frameworks and comparative case studies', PhD dissertation, Georgetown University, p. 549. For a review of the debate over representativeness of administration, see also: Carl J. Friedrich (1966), 'Public policy and the nature of administration responsibility', in Peter Wol (ed.), *Public Administration and Policy*, New York, NY: Harper, pp. 236–9;

and Herman Finer, 'Administrative responsibility in democratic government', in Peter Wol (ed.), *Public Administration and Policy*, New York, NY: Harper, pp. 257–9.
Delli Priscoli, Jerome (1984), 'Public involvement in risk assessment', keynote speech at workshop, University of Southern California, Los Angeles, 10 December.
Delli Priscoli, Jerome (1989), 'Public involvement, conflict management: means to EQ, and social objectives', *Journal of Water Resources Planning and Management*, **113** (1), 31–42.
Delli Priscoli, Jerome (1998), 'Water and civilization: using history to reframe water policy debates and to build a new ecological realism', *Water Policy*, **1**, 623–36.
Delli Priscoli, Jerome and M.R. Lamas (2001), 'International perspective on ethical dilemmas in the water industry', in Cheryl K. Davis and Robert E. McGinn (eds), *Navigating Rough Waters: Ethical Issues in the Water Industry*, Denver, CO: American Water Works Association, pp. 58–9.
Delli Priscoli, Jerome and C. Moore (1985), *Executive Training Course in Conflict Resolution*, Alexandria, VA: Institute for Water Resources.
Fisher, D. and C. Davis (1992), 'Civil society and the environment in Central and Eastern Europe', Ecological Studies Institute, London, May.
Global Water Partnership (GWP) (2000), 'Integrated water resources management (IWRM)', Technical Advisory Committee (TAC), background paper no. 4, Stockholm.
Habermas, Jurgen (1984), *The Theory of Communicative Action 1: Reason and Rationalization of Society*, Boston, MA: Beacon Press.
Hanchey, J.R. (1975), *Public Involvement in the Corps of Engineers Planning Process*, report 75-R-4, Fort Belvoir, VA: US Army Corps of Engineers, Institute for Water Resources.
Kenworthy, T. (1996), *The Washington Post*, 27 March, A17.
Kettering Foundation (1991), 'Citizens and politics: a view from main street', a report by the Harwood Groups, June.
Lasswell, Harold (1958), *Politics: Who Gets What, When and How*, Cleveland, OH: Meridian.
Lewis, Martin W. (1994), 'Introduction', *Green Delusions: An Environmentalist Critique of Radical Environmentalism*, Durham, NC: Duke University Press.
Masters, Roger D. (1998), *Fortune is a River*, New York, NY: The Free Press.
Montville, J. and Jerome Delli Priscoli (1998), *Conflict Prevention in Central Europe*, PEW.
Peden, William (ed.) (1954), *Thomas Jefferson, Notes on the State of Virginia*, New York, NY: Norton Library, W.W. Norton & Co., Inc..
Pericles, 'Funeral oration' in Thucydides, *The Peloponnesian War*.
Reich, Robert (1996), 'Policy making in a democracy', in Robert Reich (ed.), *The Power of Public Ideas*, Cambridge, MA: Harvard University Press, p. 125.
Teclaff, Ludwig A. (1967), *The River Basin in History and Law*, The Hague: Martinus Nijhoff.
Vick, Stephen G. (2002), *Degrees of Belief: Subjective Probability and Engineering Judgment*, Reston, VA: ASCE Press.
Widditsch, A. (1972), *Public Involvement Workshops on the Puget Sound and Adjacent Waters Study: An Evaluation*, report 72-2, Fort Belvoir, VA: US Army Corps of Engineers, Institute for Water Resources.

Select USACE IWR Bibliography

Articles

Alternative Dispute Resolution (ADR) Procedures (1989).
Conflict Resolution in Water Resources: Two 404 General Permits (1987).
Citizen Participation: The Enduring Myths of Public Involvement (1982).
DOD Partnering – Quick Start Guide (1996).
Journal of Water Resources Planning and Management (1987), **114** (1).
Partnering Guide for Environmental Missions (1996).
Public Involvement and Teaming in Planning-Participants Workbook (1978).
'Public involvement and social impact analysis: union looking for marriage', (January 1978), IWR Working Paper 78-WP-2.
Public Involvement Techniques: A Reader of Ten Years Experience (September 1998), IWR Report 82-R-1.
'Public involvement, conflict management: means to EQ and social objectives', *Journal of Water Resources Planning and Management* (1989), **115** (1).
Public Involvement and Dispute Resolution (1998), IWR Report 98-R-5.
'Retraining the modern civil engineer', *The Environmentalist* (1983).
Social Assessment and Resources Policy: Lessons from Water Planning (1995).
'Twelve challenges for public participation practice', *Interact* (1995), **1** (1).
'What is public participation in water resources management and why is it important?', *IWRA Water International* (June 2004), **29** (2).
When Partnering Doesn't Work (Well): An Analysis of Less Successful Partnering Cases (1998).
'Why the federal and regional interest in public involvement in water resources development', (January 1978), IWR Working Paper 78-WP-1.

Case studies

89-ADR-CS-1 – Tenn Tom Constructors, Inc.
89-ADR-CS-2 – Granite Construction Company.
89-ADR-CS-3 – Olson Mechanical and Heavy Rigging, Inc.
89-ADR-CS-4 – Bechtel National, Inc.
89-ADR-CS-5 – Goodyear Tire and Rubber Company.
91-ADR-CS-6 – Corps of Engineers Uses Mediation to Settle Hydropower Dispute.
92-ADR-CS-7 – Brutoco Engineering and Construction, Inc.
92-ADR-CS-8 – Bassett Creek Water Management Commission.
92-ADR-CS-9 – General Roofing Company.
94-ADR-CS-10 – Small Projects Partnering: The Drayton Hall Stream-Bank Protection Project Charleston County, South Carolina.
94-ADR-CS-11 – The J6 Partnering Case Study – (J6 Large Rocket Test Facility).
94-ADR-CS-12 – Fort Drum Disputers Review Panel – A Case Study in the Alternative Dispute Resolution Series.
95-ADR-CS-13 – Use of Facilitated Task Force to Develop a General Permit in Colorado.
97-ADR-CS-14 – A Case Study in Dispute Resolution System Design: The Corps of Engineers Early Resolution Program (CEERP) for Allegations of Discrimination.

Pamphlets

89-ADR-P-1 – *The Mini-Trial.*
90-ADR-P-2 – *Non-Binding Arbitration.*
91-ADR-P-3 – *Mediation.*
91-ADR-P-4 – *Partnering.*
96-ADR-P-5 – *Overview of Alternative Dispute Resolution (ADR): A Handbook for Corps Managers.*
95-ADR-P-6 – *Deciding Whether or Not to Partner on Small Projects: A Guide for US Army Corps Engineers Managers.*
98-ADR-P-7 – *Partnering Guide for Civil Missions.*

Research reports

89-ADR-R-1 – *Using ASDR in the US Army Corps of Engineers: A Framework for Decision-Making.*

Working papers

90-ADR-WP-1 – 'ADR round table: US Army Corps of Engineers (South Atlantic Division)'.
90-ADR-WP-2 – 'Public involvement; conflict management, and dispute resolution in water resources and environmental decision making'.
90-ADR-WP-3 – 'Getting to the table'.
90-ADR-WP-4 – 'Environmental ends and engineering means: becoming environmental engineers for the nation and the world'.
94-ADR-WP-5 – 'Partnership councils: building successful labor management relationships'.
96-ADR-WP-6 – 'Conflict resolution, collaboration and management in international water resource issues'.
96-ADR-WP-7 – 'Public participation in designing our environmental future'.
96-ADR-WP-8 – 'Partnering, consensus building, and alternative dispute resolution: current uses and opportunities in the US Army Corps of Engineers'.
96-ADR-WP-9 – 'An organizational assessment of the US Army Corps of Engineers in regard to public involvement practices and challenges'.

APPENDIX 2.2 NEBRASKA NATURAL RESOURCE DISTRICTS

In 1939 there were 172 special-purpose organizations designed to deal with some aspect of Nebraska's waters (Fischer, 1981). As greater demands were placed on this resource, additional governmental units emerged to address special needs. By 1969 the population of such organizations had grown to about 500 narrowly focused organizations, with overlapping responsibilities, duplication of services and taxation and limited ability to cope with problems encompassing more than one jurisdiction. They included soil and water conservation districts, watershed conservancy districts, watershed districts, watershed planning boards, irrigation districts, reclamation districts, sanitary drainage districts, drainage districts and groundwater conservation districts.

To provide a better basis for solving the state's water problems, the legislature determined that a consolidation of districts would be appropriate and that a new set of regional water management districts should be devised to blanket the state. Thus, in 1969 the legislature established 24 Natural Resource Districts (NRDs). The legislature's intent was to create governmental units with sufficient powers to address a broad range of natural resources issues and to implement programs or projects to resolve them. Although only about 300 of the previous districts were merged or abolished in the process of setting up the NRDs, the new organizations had much greater capacity for managing water and other natural resources than their predecessors (ibid.). The original intent of the NRD movement was to bring about a total consolidation of existing entities. This was not politically feasible at the time and so a compromise was struck, with the remaining special-purpose districts encouraged to cooperate and if possible to merge with the NRDs. In addition, the legislature specified that no new districts of previous form could be established after the passage of the legislation.

Supervisory control of the NRDs is vested in the state's Natural Resources Commission. This semi-autonomous agency has broad powers and is charged with the task of coordinating the activities of the NRDs, other state agencies responsible for natural resources and other substate entities including counties, municipalities and those special-purpose districts not abolished or merged into the NRDs. The principal state agencies involved are the Department of Water Resources (responsible for administering the water rights of the state), the USDA and the Department of Environmental Control (the state's counterpart to the EPA). Nebraska's Natural Resources Commission also interfaces with federal agencies whose programs affect development and management of the state's waters.

The legislation gave the NRDs broad responsibilities. These included soil conservation and erosion control; flood and sedimentation control; water supply; development and management of ground and surface waters; solid waste disposal, sanitary drainage and pollution control; drainage and channel improvements; and responsibilities relative to fish and wildlife habitats, recreation, forestry and range management. The legislature also provided the NRDs with the authority needed to get their jobs done, including taxation; eminent domain; construction and maintenance of facilities; acquisition and disposal of water rights; financial assistance for projects; regulation of groundwater use; development, storage and distribution of water; regulation of land use in certain cases; rate setting for water furnished; development of facilities for solid waste disposal; provision of technical assistance; assignment of charges to beneficiaries for services; and initiation and conduct of studies. While the NRDs may obtain water rights, they have little control over water allocations, which are administered by the Department of Water Resources.

An advantage the NRDs hold over their predecessors is that of spatial dimension. On average, the NRDs cover areas about four times larger than the average Nebraska county. This scale gives them the financial capability to obtain qualified technical staffs and suggests that many localized problems can be resolved within the bounds of a single NRD (ibid.). The NRDs also have access to a state resource development fund that may be used to fund or partially fund meritorious state projects.

Reference

Fischer, L.K. (1981), 'A critique of Nebraska natural resource districts', Unpublished manuscript, University of Nebraska, Lincoln.

3. The theory and practice of benefit-cost analysis

John J. Boland, Nicholas Flores and Charles W. Howe

INTRODUCTION

Economic reasoning began to influence decisions about water resources development and management even before a recognized discipline of economics existed (eighteenth century) but since World War II economics has received increasing weight in the planning for and management of water resources. This has been stimulated by the increasing scarcity of water relative to the multiple demands imposed on it.

Economic analysis can inform water resources planning at several levels. Benefit-cost analysis discussed in this chapter is intended to promote the efficient use of resources at the project level by guiding the design of individual projects and their operating rules, by measuring the economic gains generated by alternative projects and then by allowing the comparison of competing projects in terms of their benefits to society. Economic analysis at a more macro or regional level can assess the broader impacts of changes in water availability on parties other than the direct water user, for example, on activities that service irrigated agriculture or the effects of water supply availability on regional economic growth. These higher levels of economic analysis use different tools or models than those used in benefit-cost analysis of individual projects and are not discussed in this volume.

To assist in the design and evaluation of water projects and related policies, it is necessary to identify all project effects, beneficial and adverse (benefits and costs), then to quantify those effects in physical terms and, wherever possible, to place monetary values on the physical measures. Examples would be changes in agricultural outputs resulting from increased or more reliable irrigation supplies or changes in urban supplies. Market prices usually exist for agricultural products, while urban rate structures allow us to place values on levels of urban water use. Cost savings from improved navigation can be calculated. More difficult to deal with would be the impacts of increased flood control, improved recreational opportunities or the long-term health effects of improved water quality, for which no obvious market prices exist. Some impacts such as endangered species preservation may elude credible monetization entirely (but should not be ignored).

Then measured benefits and costs of individual projects can be compared to see if, giving consideration to non-monetized impacts, each project alternative's benefits justify its costs and which, among competing projects, delivers the greatest benefits net of costs. While the logic of economic analysis is straightforward, this simplicity is easily lost in the many details of actual application. This chapter provides the reader with sufficient background to understand and begin to apply benefit-cost analysis.

What follows is a brief overview of the economic logic of benefit-cost analysis, which is referred to in economic jargon as 'welfare economics'. An understanding of this basic logic should be helpful in following later discussions of specific techniques. Following the overview, a section provides a historical perspective on the evolution of the current 'tool box' in response to changing social values and institutions. There it will be seen, for example, that, with the rise of environmental concerns, economists developed techniques to measure non-market environmental benefits and damages to ecosystems. This evolution of benefit-cost analysis was accompanied (sometimes with considerable time lags) by federal legislation directing federal agency programs and practices as described in Chapter 2. Next, we explain how benefits and costs can be measured directly through markets, indirectly through markets or by techniques that can substitute for market prices. That section provides the reader with the basic techniques and an appreciation of their broad applicability, but also of their limitations. Another section integrates the concepts and measurement techniques into a comprehensive framework for application. Finally, an overview and assessment of the state of benefit-cost analysis is presented, with suggested directions for future development.

THE LOGIC OF ECONOMIC ANALYSIS

The appropriate framework for the analysis of most water projects is the river basin since the effects can often be felt throughout the basin, both upstream and downstream of the project. For example, a dam to produce power and facilitate navigation will alter the hydrology of the basin. These changes will impact the flood plains along the river and the ability of users to divert water from the stream. New electric power supplies may change power prices. Changes in land use are likely, affecting land values and tax bases. Some recreational opportunities will be created (for example, reservoir boating) while others will be eliminated (for example, white water canoeing). Bird, fish and plant populations of riparian ecosystems will change. Taken together, these changes will make some people better off (winners) while making others worse off (losers).

Welfare economics in the form of benefit-cost analysis attempts to assess the impacts on the winners and the losers and to judge the net impact on society.[1] But how can the gains to winners be compared with the losses to losers? Even if all impacts can be monetized, a monetary value of $1000 may be insignificant to some parties and crucial to others. Thus in evaluating projects that involve interpersonal comparisons of values, the only way to conclude that a project is unambiguously desirable from society's point of view is if some people gain from the project while no one loses. Such an outcome is called a 'Pareto improvement'.[2]

Unfortunately, Pareto improvements are rare in the real world: gains to some are almost always associated with losses to others. This creates the need for a more practical test. A weaker criterion is to determine whether the winners have gained enough that they could monetarily compensate the losers – rendering them no worse off – while retaining sufficient gains to remain winners. This criterion is called the 'compensation principle' and a project meeting this criterion is said to pass the 'compensation test'. The adoption of this criterion does not, however, solve the problem of having a foolproof criterion since the monetary compensation required to make the losers as well off as they were before must be determined and this is not an easy task, especially if many parties are involved.

For each winner and loser we can, in principle, determine the amount of money subtracted from their income (for the winners) or added to it (for the losers) that would make that person just indifferent between having the project relative to not having the project. The technical term for this measure is 'compensating variation'.[3] For winners, we would need to take away money so the compensating variation is positive. For losers, we would need to give money so the compensating variation is negative. If we could sum up individual compensating variations for all people, we could determine whether the compensation test was satisfied, whether or not the compensation is actually paid. A positive sum would indicate that the compensation test was passed while a negative sum would indicate that the project failed the compensation test.

An alternative way of saying this is that the sum of project benefits outweighs the total costs, where both costs and benefits are measured in ways consistent with the notion of the relevant compensating variations. The ability to measure compensating variation for the many changes occasioned by water projects has grown over the past 50 years by extending the range of impacts that can be assessed in monetary terms.[4] Initially benefit-cost analysis took account of only those project impacts for which benefits and costs could be measured directly from markets, for example, changes in profits for producers and commodity prices for consumers. Service flows not traded directly in markets, such as public recreation and ecological preservation, were relegated to the category of intangibles.[5] The mid 1960s saw a burst of research activity aimed at incorporating monetary benefits and costs for non-marketed service flows into project analysis. As Russell and Sagoff note in Chapter 5 of this book, Krutilla's work (1967) marked a paradigm shift in the way economists view environmental/ecological services in project analysis. He argued (1) that benefits and costs related to the environment are naturally and logically part of neoclassical economics and (2) that adequately gauging the economic efficiency of large-scale water projects will increasingly depend on the ability of analysts to measure environmental benefits and costs.[6]

The changing needs and concerns of society pose continuing challenges to benefit-cost analysis. Eckstein (1958) and Krutilla (1967) represent successive generations of benefit-cost analysis as an evolutionary process of response to changing social values. Economic analysis has lagged behind new social concerns as economists attempt to develop new tools to address these new concerns. However, the increasing scarcity of water has made the case for an increasingly important role for economic analysis in project and policy assessments.

In order to understand economic analysis of water projects as it is carried out today, it is useful to understand the evolutionary interaction of societal concerns and economic techniques of analysis since this same evolutionary process is active today and will almost certainly continue.[7] To this end, we now turn to a historical overview of the evolution of economic analysis including that of water policy legislation.

EVOLUTION OF ECONOMIC ANALYSIS THROUGH A HISTORICAL LENS

Early Foundations

It is commonly thought that the application of economic analysis to the design and evaluation of water policies and projects was initiated by the US Flood Control Act of 1936. However, the use of basic economic concepts in the selection and evaluation of publicly funded water projects began early in US history.

In 1807 the US Senate directed Albert Gallatin, Secretary of the Treasury, to undertake a survey and analysis of the system of roads and canals in what was then the USA and to make recommendations for the expansion of that system. In his report Gallatin (1807) set forth economic guidelines that would still be considered appropriate in the light of contemporary welfare economics:

> It is sufficiently evident that whenever the annual expense of transportation on a certain route in its natural state exceeds the interest on the capital employed in improving the communication and the annual expense of transportation by the improved route (exclusive of the tolls), the difference is an annual additional income to the nation. . . . it also happens that (when construction proceeds slowly), the capital applied remains unproductive for a longer time . . . and the interest accruing during this period becomes, in fact, an injurious addition to the real expense of the undertaking. The general gain is not confined to the difference in expense of those articles which had formerly been conveyed by that route, but many which were brought to market by other channels will then find a new and more advantageous direction and those which, on account of their distance or weight could not be transported in any manner whatever will acquire a value and become a clear addition to the national wealth. . . . In countries possessed of a large capital, where property is sufficiently secure to induce individuals to lay out that capital on permanent undertakings and where a compact population creates an extensive commercial intercourse . . . those improvements may often . . . be left to individual exertion without a direct aid from Government.
>
> There are, however, some circumstances that check the application of private capital and enterprise to improvements on a large scale. . . . The great demand for capital in the U.S. and the extent of territory compared with the population are, it is believed, the true causes that prevent new undertakings. . . . The general government can alone remove these obstacles. . . . Good roads and canals will shorten distances, facilitate commercial and personal intercourse and unite . . . the most remote quarters of the U.S. (Gallatin, 1807, p. 724)

Current economics texts could hardly state these principles of project evaluation and economic development more clearly. Gallatin sets forth the annualized comparison of benefits and costs including interest during construction and interest return on the total investment. He calls for a systems analysis of the diversion and creation of traffic. He clearly states the issue of capital scarcity and the property right conditions needed to call forth private undertakings and adds that, when national interests require infrastructure investments not privately attractive due to dispersed populations and security problems, government should take on the tasks.

Outside the USA, engineers at the French Ecole National de Ponts et Chaussees (ENPC) in the eighteenth and first half of the nineteenth centuries addressed the problem of evaluating the benefits and costs of public services like bridges and roadways (Ekelund and Herbert, 1973).

The major early contributors were Henri Navier, Joseph Minard and Jules Dupuis.

Navier published an article in the *Annales des Ponts et Chaussees* in 1832 that presented a systematic discussion of extending a market spatially by reducing costs to the shipper. Joseph Minard established a course in public economics at ENPC in 1831, which emphasized factors influencing demand for transport services and demand-supply interaction to determine prices. His benefit measure was cost of the best alternative (still used today as a shortcut). He presented an explicit consideration of time in the benefit-cost assessments: the production period, the durability of capital goods and the use of compound interest.

Jules Dupuit (1844) formalized the concept of diminishing marginal utility and its relationship to the demand curve. He recognized the appropriate area under a demand curve as a measure of benefit. He argued the advantages of competitive equilibrium in markets and the removal of barriers to free trade. Thus, it is clear that sophisticated economic concepts had been formulated and applied to roads and canals during the first half of the nineteenth century.

By the early twentieth century, the English economist, A.C. Pigou, in the various editions of his famous *The Economics of Welfare* (first published in 1920), while not dealing explicitly with water, was extending economic analysis by identifying the problems of (negative and positive) externalities and the use of taxes and subsidies to correct market allocations of goods and services. He also recognized that objectives other than economic efficiency will be important in some situations and was concerned with the distribution of economic welfare and possible conflicts between economic efficiency and equity:

> The misery and squalor that surround us, the injurious luxury of some wealthy families, the terrible uncertainty overshadowing many families of the poor – these are evils too plain to be ignored . . . the question is raised in what circumstances it is possible for the absolute share of the dividend accruing to the poor to be increased without, at the same time, diminishing the volume of the dividend as a whole. . . (Pigou, 1932, p. vii)

United States Guidelines for Water Resources Evaluation[8]

Though the ideas antedated the law, federal guidelines for water resources project evaluation did spring from the Flood Control Act of 1936, wherein Congress directed that federal flood control projects be undertaken 'if the benefits to whomsoever they may accrue are in excess of the estimated costs and if the lives and social security of people are not otherwise adversely affected' (33 USC 701a). The application of this legislative provision has been far wider than just to flood control projects. Either by statute or by administrative order, this provision has been made broadly applicable to all water resources projects of US Army Corps of Engineers (USACE), US Bureau of Reclamation (USBR) and National Resource Conservation Service (NRCS).

The importance of this provision was to inject economic analysis into water planning. The opportunity afforded by Congress to apply this normative theory to the field of water and related land resource use and development was welcomed by economists and reflected in the work of those within the federal government, with outside support from academics. These efforts were interrupted by exigencies of World War II, but after 1945, the elaboration of benefit-cost analysis began in earnest.

The first product of this activity was popularly known as the 'Green Book' (it had a green cover), a report of the Subcommittee on Benefits and Costs of the Federal Interagency River Basin Committee, published in 1950 and bearing the title, *Proposed Practices for Economic Analysis of River Basin Projects* (USIACWR, 1950). This report embodied Pigouvian theory of public finance and an analysis of externalities and market failure. With minor additions and changes, a revised edition was published in 1958. The *Proposed Practices* set forth 'criteria and principles' of 'general economic welfare' for 'application by agencies within the framework of their particular programs and responsibilities'. Goals or objectives other than economic efficiency from a 'comprehensive public viewpoint' were recognized as relevant (paraphrased from Caulfield, 2000, p. 14).

The 'Green Book', moreover, called for identification of all beneficial or adverse effects of a project in both tangible (that is, monetary) and intangible terms. An intangible beneficial effect of a flood control project would be risk reduction and the saving of human life, effects Congress clearly had in mind when establishing flood control as a national, largely non-reimbursable, project purpose. However, because of the weight given by the US Bureau of the Budget (BOB, now the Office of Management and Budget (OMB)) and Congress to achieving a 1.0 or greater ratio of tangible benefits to tangible costs as the basic criterion for authorization and funding of water development projects, all other goals were (implicitly) secondary. For example, regional development was secondary to the goal of national economic efficiency.

The 'Green Book' was never adopted by the Federal Interagency River Basin Committee (FIARBC) or its successor committees, largely due to continuing interagency disagreements over inclusion of secondary benefits in project reports. The secondary benefits issue refers to the appropriateness of including the additional incomes generated in activities linked to the project as providers of inputs or users of project outputs. The controversy continues today. Budget Circular A-47, (BOB, 1952), embodied the basic philosophy and criteria and principles of the 'Green Book'. Its most fundamental standards and procedures were these:

- The relative economy of alternative means available for meeting national needs was to be set forth for consideration.
- Benefits and costs, in total and separately for each project purpose, were to be set forth. Where benefits and costs could not be estimated in monetary terms, their relative significance was to be stated in as precise and quantitative terms as possible.
- 'While it is recognized that a comparison of estimated benefits with estimated costs does not provide a precise measure of the absolute merits of any particular program or project, one essential criterion in justifying any program or projects will, except in unusual cases where adequate justification is presented, be that its estimated benefits to whomsoever they may accrue exceed its estimated costs' (Caulfield, 2000, p. 15).

The BOB attempted to apply A-47 to all projects presented to it for review in the 1950s. This effort led to great dissatisfaction with A-47 within Congress, beginning about 1956. Few, if any, in Congress called for abandonment of the benefit-cost analysis per se, but there was a widespread call for its liberalization. Democrats in Congress declared the Eisenhower Administration had a no new starts policy.

A panel of consultants to the BOB (M.M. Hufschmidt, J. Krutilla, J. Margolis and S.A. Marglin) produced an innovative report, titled *Standards and Criteria for Formulating and Evaluating Federal Water Resources Developments* (Hufschmidt et al., 1961). David Bell, Director of the BOB, commended the report for consideration by all agencies involved in water management and it exerted a strong influence on subsequent policies and standards. The report first addressed the objectives of water development and management: the efficiency objective, distributional objectives, preservation of aesthetic and cultural values and merit wants in general. Thus, as with the earlier reports, the need to recognize multiple objectives was emphasized.

The report also discussed discount rates extensively, emphasizing the existence of different private and social rates, as well as the appropriate discount rate in the light of national stabilization policy and budget constraints. A stable social discount rate for purposes of project design was recommended, along with a contemporary opportunity cost rate to assess the desirability of proceeding with the project.

The secondary benefits issue, which had led to controversy over the

'Green Book' and A-47, was covered as well. It was pointed out that federal agencies were wont to include so-called 'secondaries' to enhance the desirability of the project. The economics profession, then and now, has followed the full employment-competitive market model to conclude that secondary impacts should be ignored on the grounds that the resources used in a project would be drawn from equally productive activities elsewhere or that alternative projects precluded by the one under consideration would have equivalent secondary impacts. However, according to the report, secondary benefits could, under circumstances deviating from the full employment-competitive condition, constitute legitimate national benefits not captured in the willingness-to-pay (WTP) of direct beneficiaries. The report suggested situations in which secondary benefits would legitimately be included from an economic efficiency point of view.

Other topics covered in innovative ways included risk and uncertainty, the use of alternative cost, recreational values, the importance of repayment policy in motivating responsible project assessment and the need for integrated river basin planning.

Senate Document 97, *Policies, Standards and Procedures in the Formulation, Evaluation and Review of Plans for Use and Development of Water and Related Land Resources* (US Senate, 1962) replaced the BOB Circular A-47 on 15 May 1962. Consideration was to be given to three objectives with 'reasoned choices made between them when they conflict':

- Economic development (a new label for economic efficiency) – Water and related land resource development and management were taken to be essential to economic development and growth, including outdoor recreation, fish and wildlife enhancement.
- Preservation – Proper stewardship of the nation's natural bounty was taken to require preservation in particular instances of open space, green space, wild areas of rivers, lakes, beaches and mountains and areas of unique natural beauty, historical and scientific interest. Such preservation was required to support outdoor recreation and fish and wildlife enhancement.[9]
- Well-being of people – Hardship and basic needs of particular groups were to be of concern, as was the saving of human life.

In Senate Document 97 an initial economic efficiency baseline river basin plan was to be identified having the following characteristics: (a) tangible benefits must exceed project economic costs; (b) each separable unit or purpose must provide benefits at least equal to its costs; (c) the scope of the development must be such as to provide the maximum net benefits; (d) there must be no more economical means, evaluated on a comparable basis, of accomplishing the same purpose. Such optimum plans were to provide baselines from which alternative plans reflecting different objectives could be judged (for example, by determining the efficiency benefits forgone if preservation of a reach of a scenic river was considered important). Regional, state and local points of view or objectives were to be considered as well as national points of view. In contrast to A-47, there was no requirement that projects must exhibit a benefit-cost ratio greater than 1.0 but the BOB was not to be barred from adopting such a requirement. Before President Kennedy approved Senate Document 97, the Council of Economic Advisors established a group of distinguished academic economists led by Kenneth Arrow to review the agreement. Approval was given, subject to a committee to further study the discount rate.

The Water Resources Planning Act (WRPA) of 1965 created an active, well-staffed Water Resources Council (WRC).[10] Under Section 103 of the Act, the Council was required to promulgate its own principles, standards and procedures for application by all federal water and related land resource projects. The multi-objective approach was retained, represented by the two primary objectives of national economic development (NED) (economic efficiency) and environmental quality (EQ). In addition, the effects on regional development and social well-being were to be displayed. The discount rate formula was changed to reflect contemporary federal borrowing rates, calculated as the average nominal rate on Treasury bonds outstanding with maturities of 15 or more years. These new *Principles and Standards* (P&S) (WRC, 1973) superseded Senate Document 97. A simplified set of *Principles and Guidelines* (P&G) was issued by Presidential order in 1983 (WRC, 1983). But, shortly after that, the Reagan Administration abolished the active program of WRC, including the federal-state river basin commissions (RBCs) created under the WRPA.

Academic Contributions and Controversies

In the late 1950s and early 1960s path-breaking contributions to the economic analysis of water systems appeared from Harvard, Resources for the Future (RFF), RAND Corporation and elsewhere. Clawson (1959) and Clawson and Knetsch (1966) elaborated the travel cost method for assessing the value of water-based recreation.[11] Kneese (1964), Kneese and Bower (1968), Davis (1968) and others at RFF were developing the economics of water quality management. The concepts of option value, introduced by Weisbrod (1964) and existence value, introduced by Krutilla (1967), brought out new dimensions of resource management reflecting society's changing values. Techniques for measuring these new values became a major objective of large numbers of environmental economists, thus extending the reach of efficiency analysis, though not necessarily to the exclusion of other descriptive measures. More of the impacts earlier described under the EQ account of the P&S could now be brought under the economic efficiency umbrella. However, the reconciliation is still not complete. There is, for example, little agreement on measuring community and cultural values associated with water allocation and development. There also remain questions of how far the benefit quantification techniques like contingent valuation and hedonics can be credibly pushed: to assess existence values or to value endangered species? There remains a role for the multi-objective planning and evaluation process first acknowledged by Gallatin and the French engineers at ENPC. These developments are treated in following sections of this chapter.

Two major books were published in 1958: Otto Eckstein's *Water-Resource Development: The Economics of Project Evaluation* (Eckstein, 1958) and the Krutilla-Eckstein volume *Multiple Purpose River Development: Studies in Applied Economic Analysis* (Krutilla and Eckstein, 1958). Eckstein's book was a revision of his PhD dissertation at Harvard but it was destined to become one of those classics that remain relevant over the decades. The book critiques the procedures for measuring benefits and costs used by USBR and USACE, using welfare economics as the basis of critique and assuming that distributional, political and social objectives can be left to other public sector programs. The later chapters apply the principles to flood control, irrigation, navigation and electric power generation. The importance of cost-sharing in motivating socially responsible project selection is emphasized.

The Krutilla-Eckstein book concentrates on the river basin as the natural unit for planning and project analysis, emphasizing the interdependence of projects and purposes and situations of complementarity and substitutability between projects. These principles are then applied to several detailed case studies: the Hells Canyon case that compares the benefits and costs of a high dam to those of three low dams and a two dam plan. The analysis includes assessment of a natural river and flat-water recreation benefits, pointing to the unique values of the natural river and the existence of extensive flat-water opportunities already in the region. Much of the analysis was done in connection with the Federal Power Commission (FPC) hearings on license applications from the Idaho Power Company. Conclusions of the study included the sensitivity of plan selection to the discount rate and the importance of requiring licensees to take into account the effects of their stream regulation on downstream power potential.

Hirschleifer et al. (1960) produced *Water Supply: Economics, Technology and Policy* (1960) (sponsored by RAND and published by University of Chicago Press), to educate the public, especially that of California, on principles for evaluating the economic worth of water projects. This book was published at the time the large California State Water Project was being undertaken and one intent of the book was to demonstrate the economic superiority of conservation, reallocation of existing supplies and better irrigation technologies over further large-scale construction. The importance of water prices was emphasized while pointing out that raw water supplies were grossly underpriced by both the earlier Central Valley Project (USBR) and the new State Water Project. Recommendations of the study include (1) adopting marginal (rather than average) cost pricing of water; (2) clarifying property rights in water so that efficient trading would be encouraged; (3) establishing procedures to reduce negative externalities from water use and water development; and (4) providing the public with information on the alternatives available.

The Harvard Water Program began in 1955 as a program of engineering and economics innovation as well as training for many public agency personnel. The research purpose was to improve the methods for designing water resources systems taking advantage of emerging advances in probability theory, statistics, operations research and welfare economics. The resulting methodology involved (a) identifying the objectives of design, (b) translating these objectives into design criteria, (c) optimizing specific water systems and (d) evaluating the consequences of the developed plans. A major advance was to join engineering and economics in the analysis of complex river basin systems for which analytical production functions could not be specified. Uncertain hydrology was innovatively handled through the invention of synthetic hydrology that permitted the derivation of probability distributions of system outputs and extended the analysis beyond reliance on the historical hydrologic record. The analysis of water demand was also extended and its role in system design strengthened. A major product of the program's early years, *The Design of Water-Resource Systems: New Techniques for Relating Economic Objectives, Engineering Analysis and Governmental Planning* (Maass et al., 1962) is a classic in the water resources field.

Table 3.1 summarizes in chronological order the major contributions described previously and puts them in the context of the evolving federal guideline documents. In the light of the enormous quantity of work summarized in Table 3.1, it is instructive and somewhat amusing to note some of the reactions to the 1973 P&S by groups from the academic economics profession. Paraphrasing Bromley (2000, pp. 7–8):

> The academic community, or that exceedingly minor fraction of it that paid any attention to Federal water policy, was choosing sides. It is not unduly melodramatic to refer to these as *the water wars*. In one camp we found the *Axis Powers* emanating from Washington, D.C. (Knetsch, Haveman, Krutilla, Brewer, Howe . . .) that saw water policy as pork barrel politics that could be stopped only

Table 3.1 Historical contributions to the economic analysis of water resources

Contributor		New Insights
1807	Albert Gallatin	Economic efficiency in terms of annual benefits and costs: • transport savings • interest during construction • interest on total invested capital Necessary role for government Systems analysis of induced traffic
1831–44	(French) ENPC	Economic efficiency: • transport savings • alternative cost measure of benefits • compound interest and discounting • diminishing marginal utility • derivation of the demand curve • area under the demand curve as the benefit measure Supply-demand price determination Importance of competition and free trade
1920	A.C. Pigou	Externalities and use of taxes and subsidies: • importance of distribution of benefits and costs • efficiency-equity trade-offs
1936	Flood Control Act	The benefit-cost test of all flood control projects Public safety and well-being objective
1950	The 'Green Book' (Federal Interagency Committee)	Economic efficiency in monetized present values Intangible benefits, including saving of life Regional benefit and cost calculation Applicability of secondary benefits and costs
1952	Budget Circular A-47 (US Bureau of the Budget)	Comparative benefit-cost assessment of alternatives The benefit-cost assessment in total and by project purpose

Table 3.1 (continued)

Contributor		New Insights
		Other purposes stated in quantitative terms (with lesser weight)
1958	Otto Eckstein, *Water Resource Development: The Economics of Project Evaluation*	Welfare economic foundations of the benefit-cost analysis Only economic efficiency (other programs take care of equity and so on) Applications of the benefit-cost on a uniform basis to flood control, irrigation, navigation and power
1958	Krutilla-Eckstein, *Multiple Purpose River Development: Studies in Applied Economic Analysis*	The river basin as the natural and necessary unit of analysis Importance of the choice of discount rate Natural river and flat-water recreational values differentiated
1960	Hirschleifer, Dehaven and Milliman, *Water Supply: Economic Technology and Policy*	River basin as the natural unit of analysis Alternatives to new supplies: reallocation, conservation, irrigation improvements, water marketing Marginal cost pricing Importance of property rights in water Public education on water issues
1960s		Development of methods for non-market valuation: travel cost, hedonics, early contingent valuation
1961	Hufschmidt, Krutilla, Margolis and Marglin, *Standards and Criteria for Formulating and Evaluating Federal Water Resources Developments*	Economic efficiency objective Need for integrated river basin planning Distributional objectives Aesthetic and cultural values to be taken into account General merit wants Private versus social discount rates Secondary benefits and costs applicable under less than full employment conditions Risk and uncertainty to be considered Importance of reimbursement policies

Table 3.1 (continued)

Contributor		New Insights
1961	Senate Document 97, *Policies, Standards and Procedures in the Formulation, Evaluation and Review of Plans for Use and Development of Water and Related Land Resources*	Three objectives: • economic development (efficiency) • preservation of environment and resources • well-being of people (hardship, basic needs, saving of life) Economic efficiency baseline river basin plans from which to measure the implied costs of other objectives No requirement for the benefit-cost > 1.0
1962	Harvard Water Program, *The Design of Water-Resource Systems* (Maass, Hufschmidt, Dorfman, Thomas, Marglin and Fair 1962)	Methods for design of water systems Objectives; economic design criteria; economic evaluation Use of stochastic methods of analysis, including synthetic hydrology and optimization Study of water demand functions
1973	*Principles, Standards and Procedures* (P&S) (WRC)	Multi-objective approach: • NED (economic efficiency) • environmental quality • regional development • social well-being Discount rate = federal opportunity cost of funds
1983	*Principles and Guidelines* (P&G) (Presidential order)	Single objective: NED

with hard-edged economic analysis. This was a time when unnecessary dams and bizarre inland seaports like Lewiston, Idaho and Tulsa, Oklahoma were being proposed and constructed. The *Axis Powers* saw the P&S as soft analysis that would continue to justify such projects. A pamphlet on the indispensability of efficiency *über alles* (*Federal Natural Resource Development: Basic Issues in Benefit and Cost Measurement*) was published in May (Knetsch et al., 1969).

The Allied Powers (Kalter, Lord, Allee, Castle, Kelso, Smith, Ciriacy-Wantrup, Weisbrod, Bromley . . .) produced a countervailing 1969 pamphlet *Criteria for Federal Evaluation of Resource Investments* and declared the war to be over. In essence, the struggle was over the nature and scope of *welfare economics* and its ability to identify the *public interest* in selecting public investments. The *Axis Powers* placed more credence in this weapon, based on the first half of the Flood Control Act's 'if the benefits . . . are in excess of the estimated costs . . .' to justify a holy war against waste – if not corruption. The Allied Powers understood that water policy was a complex mix of regional development, agricultural issues, transportation policies and other issues and concluded that welfare economics alone was simply unable to identify the public interest in selecting public projects. While the benefit-cost analysis (based on welfare economics) was indispensable in organizing the many impacts of a public investment, it was neither necessary nor sufficient to link a proposed project with its impact on social welfare (Kalter et al., 1969).

MEASURING PROJECT BENEFITS AND COSTS

We now turn to more specific descriptions of how we measure compensating variation for different changes associated with water projects. Following up on the historical perspective provided in the previous section, the section begins with benefits and costs directly measurable through markets and then addresses benefits and costs for environmental/ecological flows and services not directly traded in markets.

Measuring Benefits and Costs in Markets

Price changes and consumers

We begin by considering the impacts of a commodity price change, first on consumers and then on producers. Absent other changes, a price increase for consumers resulting from a project is a bad thing and so compensating variation is negative, meaning consumers would need to be compensated in order to make them indifferent to the change.[12] For a price decrease, compensating variation is positive, meaning consumers are winners and money would have to be taken away to make them indifferent.

Compensating variation for a price change is approximated using the demand curve for the commodity. A commodity demand curve has two interpretations. The first is that it registers the quantity demanded of a good given that good's price and the prices of other goods consumed. In a functional form, demand for good *i*, depends on the good's own price, p_i, a vector of other commodity prices, $P_{\{-i\}}$, and the consumer's income, y:

$$x = x_i(p_i, P_{\{-i\}}, y) \tag{3.1}$$

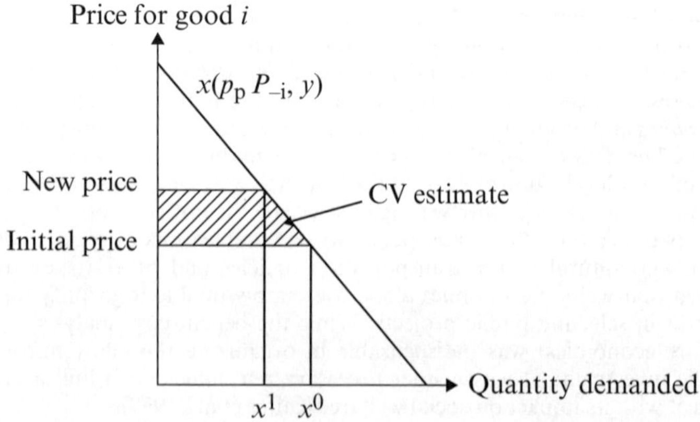

Figure 3.1 Compensating variation estimate for a price increase

The second interpretation of the demand curve, important for measuring the benefits and costs of price changes, is as a marginal valuation curve or function. The logic behind this is simple. In a free-choice, market situation a consumer gets to choose how much of their income to spend on a good. If the consumer is trying to achieve as much satisfaction/utility as possible through commodity choice, consumption will occur up to the point where the marginal benefit of consuming the good exactly equals its price. Thus, we know that at the current price, a utility-maximizing consumer has a marginal value for the good equal to its price. If this were not the case, the consumer could do better by adjusting consumption down when the marginal benefit is below the marginal cost or up when the marginal benefit is greater than the marginal cost. Hence, movement along the demand curve reflects quantity demanded at the market price and the marginal value of consumption of the selected quantity. Integrating the demand curve over the price change produces a monetary measure of the benefit of a price decrease or the cost of a price increase. Figure 3.1 depicts the integral for a price increase as the hatched area between prices to the left of the demand curve.[13]

For a price decrease, the figure looks similar, with the exception that the initial price would lie above the new price. In the case of a price decrease, the monetary measure would have to be taken away from the consumer to make them indifferent; for a price increase, the monetary measure would be given as compensation.

Compensating variation requires that the consumer be made indifferent to the price change, which in economic terms requires that the consumer's satisfaction/utility level remains as before the price change. Movement in prices along the demand curve, however, results in a utility decrease for a price increase and a utility increase for a price decrease. Hicks (1943) developed the conceptual relationship between demand and compensating variation. As it turns out, for goods where demand goes up with income, this integral/area will underestimate the magnitude of compensating variation for a price increase and overestimate the magnitude for a price decrease. As pointed out by Willig (1976), the degree of error is small in most cases.[14]

When multiple commodity price changes occur, the analysis should be conducted as a sequence of price changes. The analysis would proceed as: (1) calculate compensating variation for the first commodity price change;[15] (2) adjust income accordingly; (3) calculate compensating variation for the second price change, but at the adjusted income; (4) add together the compensating variation for the first price change to the compensating variation obtained from step three; and then (5) repeat for all remaining price changes.

Changes that affect producers and workers

On the production side of the economy, project analysis mainly focuses on changes in outputs and the associated changes in commodity supply. For consumers, significant supply impacts will be felt through price changes, which are valued as described previously. For producers, supply impacts may result in changes in profits, which are revenues minus costs. In project analysis, changes in producer profits are the producer-side equivalent to compensating variation. Thus, when a project affects a firms' productive capacity, the effect of price changes should be considered on the consumer side along with changes in producers' profits.

Positive or negative changes in employment resulting from project impacts on firms are counted only to the extent workers' incomes change (assuming full-time employment levels). For example, a project resulting in a firm's closure and the layoff of workers typically does not reduce income by the total of the laid off workers' wages. In a properly functioning labor market these workers would typically find other jobs. For these workers, losses are only the reduction in income, if the new wage is less than the old, not the total income loss from their previous job. Changes in wages and employment hours are slightly more complicated. A wage increase may result in an increase in labor supplied while a wage decrease may result in a decrease in labor supplied. In the case of a wage increase, the change in income overstates the benefit to the worker because some leisure was given up in order to work more. For the wage decrease, the change in income overstates the loss because the worker made the decision to work fewer hours and gained some leisure. The degree that changes in income overstate benefits or losses of wage change will depend on the responsiveness of labor supply to the wage.

Land use changes

Projects often result in a variety of land use changes. For example, some land may be inundated by a large water project, rendering the land useless. At the same time, other land may become lake front property. For economic analysis, the proper measure of accounting is the change in affected land's market value. It is important to recognize that through the marketplace for land, land is treated as a replaceable commodity by businesses and residents. In response to land use changes, residents and profitable firms, even farmers and ranchers, can usually relocate. Firms and residents adequately compensated for their replaceable land, including relocation expenses, are not any worse off than before the project. Some care needs to be exercised when full compensation does not take place. A firm not fully compensated for loss of the use of its land may be forced out of business, thus costing it profits and potentially resulting in income changes for workers. When this is the case, changes in profits and workers' income should be included in the analysis.

Hydroelectric benefits

Many large water planning projects involve changes in hydroelectric power production. In unfettered electricity markets the market benefits and costs of changing hydroelectric production are measured as described previously.[16] Changes in production affect supply, which affects prices for consumers and thus consumer costs or benefits are reflected in compensating variation for those price changes. On the producer side, benefits and costs are reflected in changes in profits.

In many regions, however, electricity prices are regulated. Utilities are required to meet electricity demand while utilities' cost structure determines allowable prices. In regulated electricity markets in the USA prices are regulated to allow for the recovery of capital and operating costs of meeting demand, including a rate of return on invested capital. Electricity consumers face a price that reflects these allowances regardless of temporal demand. When prices are regulated in this fashion, the economic benefits and costs of changes in hydroelectric production are measured through the change in capital and operating costs relative to the most likely replacement for the electricity produced through the project.[17]

Further insights from demand curves: changes in output

Much relevant information can be gleaned from a simple estimated demand curve for a project-produced commodity: What change in price

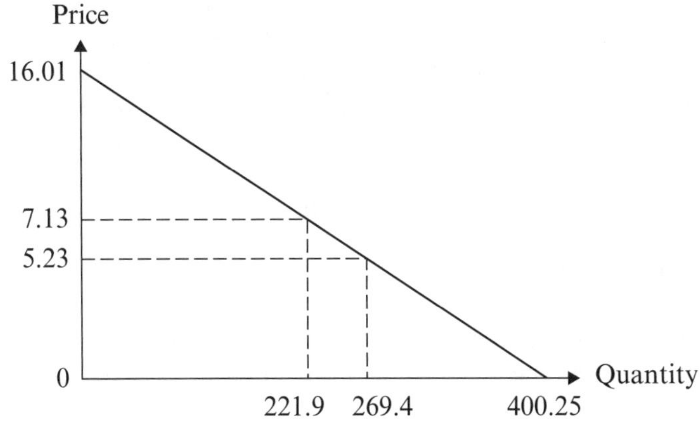

Figure 3.2 Estimated demand curve for Idaho potatoes

is likely to result? What gain in consumers' surplus will result? If the new output will be produced by new producers entering the market, what revenues will they receive? For the producers previously in the market, how much revenue will they lose as a result of the price change? Estimates of these values can be determined from the demand curve.

An example is seen in Figure 3.2. In the 1960s the USBR undertook a large irrigation project in Idaho for the production of potatoes. Data derived from earlier expansions of output and the current price-output point resulted in the estimated demand curve for Idaho potatoes (Howe, 1971):

$$P = 16.01 - 0.04\,Q \tag{3.2}$$

where:
P = price of potatoes ($ per hundredweight)
Q = potato harvest (millions of hundredweight)

The average experience over the previous several years was an output of 221.9 million hundredweight and a price of $7.13. The new project was estimated to add 47.5 million hundredweight annually. The demand curve then enables us to approximate the new market-clearing price of $5.23, a substantial reduction. Planners must know this change to determine whether or not the new farmers will make a profit and how much revenue the old farmers will lose. In spite of the price fall, the added output has a substantial value to society, namely $293.5 million per year under the demand curve between the old output (221.9) and the new output (269.4).

Of this, \$248.4 million will be paid to the producers and \$45.1 is consumer's surplus from the new production. The customers purchasing the former output will gain \$421.6 million per year in consumer surplus, which equals the loss of revenue to the producers of the prior output. While the consumer surplus measures are not identical to the theoretical measure of compensating variation described earlier, they serve to inform us who gains and who loses from the proposed project.

Non-Market Benefits and Costs

Often projects affect goods and services not directly traded in markets. For example, a project may change the availability of different types of recreational activities not priced in the marketplace. Similarly, a project may affect the management area's ecology. A number of techniques specifically address these issues. We begin with a discussion of measuring benefits and costs associated with recreation benefits.

Recreation benefits

Conceptually, recreation can be viewed as any other good. People participate in recreation to the extent that the benefit to them outweighs their costs. For ordinary marketed goods, the cost of consumption is readily observable through posted prices. Data on prices and quantities demanded facilitates estimation of demand curves that can then be used to measure the economic benefits and costs (compensating variation) of price changes or quantity restrictions, as just illustrated. For recreation experiences, costs are not directly observable, other than occasional entrance fees, which are not the full cost. The first non-market technique we consider, the travel cost method,[18] provides a way of inferring consumer costs that then facilitate recreation demand estimation. These demands can be used to value changes in recreation as well as changes in environmental quality at recreation sites.

Travel cost method The key breakthrough of the travel cost method was the recognition that much of the cost of recreation can be attributed to time spent traveling to the recreation site. Price variation for recreationists in a single time period can be observed since people travel from different home locations to a given recreational site. Home location, used to infer travel costs, combined with the number of trips suggests an avenue for statistically estimating the relation between trips demanded and price. The economic value of a trip is linked to the notion of consumer's surplus, as graphically depicted in Figure 3.3. This figure depicts the relationship between trips demanded and price. For consumers, who face trip

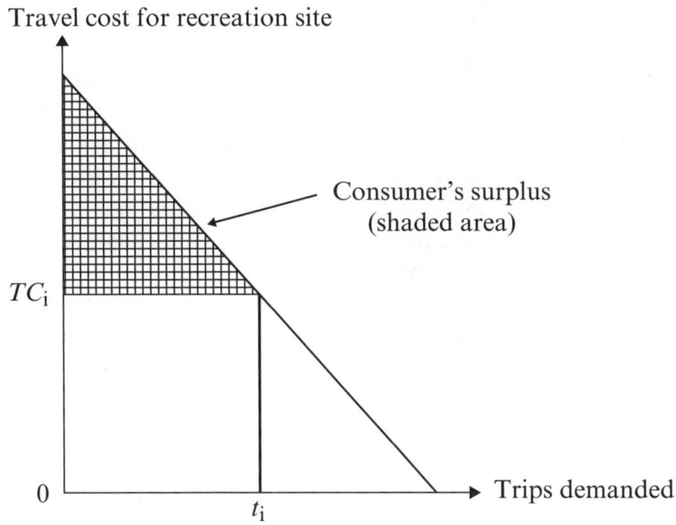

Figure 3.3 Recreation demand and travel cost (a)

cost, TC_i, the number of trips demanded is t_i. As mentioned earlier, in addition to providing the relationship between quantity demanded and price, a demand curve also shows the marginal value of units chosen at different levels of consumption. In Figure 3.3 the value of another trip to the (arbitrarily identified) marginal consumer at the current level of trips demanded, t_i, is exactly equal to the cost of the trip, TC_i. Consumer surplus is the shaded area above the price line and under the demand curve (the difference between the gross value of consumption and its cost).

For market goods where all consumers face the same price, like the example of potato harvest previously, it makes sense to aggregate demand across consumers by horizontally summing individual demand into market demand. For the travel cost method, demand can be aggregated, but consumers face different prices and so we do not get the simple graphical representation that is available for market goods with a single market price. Calculating aggregate consumer surplus requires us to calculate each consumer's surplus individually and then sum across individuals. For this reason, we focus our analysis at the individual level.

If we were to price individual *i* out of the market for recreation at the site, the change in that consumer's surplus would simply equal the individual's entire surplus. Thus, if we eliminated this recreation site, the lost surplus would be equal to the entire area under the demand curve. (This, of course, simplifies by ignoring the existence of substitute sites, a matter discussed in future sections.) Working in the opposite direction, where a site is opened, the consumer surplus represents *i*'s economic benefit from the new site. Given the travel demand concept, economic analysis of closing a recreation site is accomplished by determining the increase from current travel cost to the travel cost that completely chokes off demand. A site opening is analysed as the surplus generated by a price change from the choke price to the actual travel cost faced by the individual. Discussions of the value of adding or taking away recreational opportunities are usually cast in terms of average consumer surplus per trip.[19]

The primary methodological contribution of travel cost is the fact that by virtue of different home locations for recreationists we observe price (travel cost) variation for a target site in a single time period/season.[20] It was once believed this variation facilitated appropriate statistical estimation of the relationship between trips demanded and travel cost, accomplished by fitting a regression line of trip demand on travel cost. Unfortunately, while there is price variability across recreationists for the target site, there is also price variability for all other substitute recreation sites people might visit. Ignoring price variability across recreationists for other substitute sites will result in biased demand estimates for the target site. This is true because for each recreationist, trip demand for the target site is a function of the target site's travel costs as well as the travel costs to other sites. If we change the travel cost associated with one of the substitute sites a recreationist visits, their individual demand curve for the target site will shift. Similarly, since other recreationists face different travel costs for both the target site and substitute sites, their observed demand for the target site falls along different, shifted individual demand curves. The only way to remedy this problem is to estimate demands for the target site along with substitute sites, which is considerably more data intensive. Ignoring the problem often results in significantly biased estimates of consumer's surplus, in most cases overstating the economic benefit of recreation.

Valuing changes in environmental quality through travel cost A further important application of travel cost is to value changes in environmental quality at a target recreation site. Conceptually, demand for recreational activities, such as hiking and fishing, will be positively related to environmental quality.[21] In these cases improvements in the environmental quality will result in a shift in demand for site recreation and thus changes in recreation benefits. Figure 3.4 depicts this shift in demand from D_0 to D_1. The shaded area shows the change in consumer's surplus associated with the demand shift.

Given weak complementarity, a concept introduced by Mäler (1974), the change in consumer's surplus associated with the change in quality

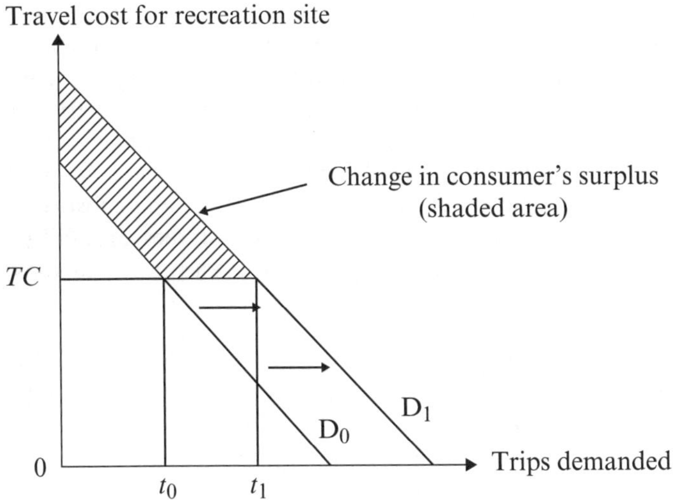

Figure 3.4 Recreation demand and travel cost (b)

at the site in question will closely approximate compensating variation for environmental quality. Weak complementarity is the condition that environmental quality improvements are of zero value when the demand for the complementary good, here recreation at the given site, is zero. This condition implies that recreationists only care about environmental quality when they use a site. In many cases weak complementarity is not satisfied. For example, hikers may still care about environmental quality of an area, even if denied access. In cases where weak complementarity is not satisfied, the change in consumer surplus measured on the recreation demand curve will underestimate both the economic benefits of environmental improvement and the economic costs of environmental degradation.

Correctly estimating the benefits of changes in environmental quality through travel cost requires estimating the demand functions for the target site and substitute sites as a function of their prices and environmental qualities. Ordinary demand estimation requires data containing variation in trips demanded, variation in travel costs for each site and variation in environmental quality at each site. Though variation in trips demanded and travel costs is generally satisfied, the last requirement of variation in environmental quality for each site is rarely satisfied. In order to circumvent this problem, Morey (1981) adapted a different approach called random utility modeling, which takes the probability of demand for each site to be a function of differences in travel costs and differences in environmental quality across the sites. In this framework variation in environmental quality is only required across sites as opposed to the ordinary demand system approach that requires variation in environmental quality for each site. Conceptually the change in consumer's surplus is still used as an approximation for compensating variation.[22] The random utility approach represents the current state-of-the-art in recreation demand modeling. In particular, random utility modeling is the most effective way of modeling demand for a target site and substitute sites in relation to environmental quality. Travel cost studies that fail to model substitutes should be viewed as suspect for the reasons raised above.

Survey approaches to estimating recreation benefits Survey research is usually needed to collect basic trip demand data. One natural extension is to ask questions about maximum WTP per trip to recreate under hypothetical scenarios of quality. This maximum WTP has been interpreted as representing average total consumer's surplus or compensating variation, for on-site recreation. Questioning of this kind was the first application of what is now referred to as the contingent valuation/method. Davis (1963) introduced this approach and was soon followed by Cicchetti and Smith (1973), Brown and Hammack (1973), Brown and Hammack (1974) and later by many others. The advantage to a survey approach is that recreation demand curves need not be estimated if the goal of the analysis is to determine compensating variation. The questions attempt to directly measure compensating variation as opposed to estimating recreation demand curves and then deriving consumer's surplus (and thus compensating variation) changes from the estimated demand curves.[23]

Another survey approach to estimating recreation benefits is to ask recreationists about how their demand would change under varying environmental quality scenarios across sites. These stated choices can then be used to estimate demand for the relevant sites, facilitating benefit estimation for a variety of environmental quality scenarios, including site closure. Standard demand analysis or an attribute-based, random utility approach can be used to estimate demand. As in the case with actual recreation data, careful attention must be paid to substitute sites when estimating demand to avoid biased demand and hence biased benefit estimates.

Amenity benefits and costs

Many people value the amenities provided by natural environments. Because water projects may affect these amenities, the economic benefits and costs of these changes should be considered in economic analysis. People are exposed to these amenities in several ways. One way is through recreation, the recreation techniques described above are often used to estimate amenity benefits and costs. If amenities can be quantitatively measured, then these amenities are a form of environmental quality that can be considered in a random utility framework. In the case of unique resources, such as the Grand Canyon, amenities are not easily quantified, particularly in relation to substitute sites. In instances of unique resources, survey methods are the primary avenue for measuring amenity benefits and costs associated with recreation.

Hedonic techniques Another way people are exposed to amenities is through their residential location choices. If residential sites have different relative amenities and people value these amenities, then the price of houses should vary with amenities, after all other sources of variation are 'removed'. Obvious candidates include proximity to the beach or lake and canyon views. A large water project might positively affect property by creating more lake front lots and lake views, while, at the same time, perhaps eliminating canyon views for some lots. Given that the prices of houses and lots vary with amenities, an indirect market for amenities in the housing market exists.

Rosen (1974) developed the hedonic method around the idea, originally suggested by Lancaster (1966), that goods, such as houses, can be viewed as bundles of valuable attributes. In the case of housing, these attributes include structural characteristics, such as size, number of bedrooms, number of bathrooms; neighborhood characteristics, such as school quality and safety services; and site characteristics such as amenities and lot topography.[24] In the housing market the differentiation of housing by these characteristics is the basis of price variation. The relative supply and demand of these characteristics determines price characteristics. Home purchasers buy these characteristics up to the point where the marginal benefit equals the marginal cost, the attribute's market price. Thus the market price of the attribute reflects its marginal value.

Statistical estimation of attribute prices is fairly straightforward. Multivariate regression is used to model housing prices. The standard approach is to regress the natural logarithm of individual house prices on the houses' structural, neighborhood and amenity characteristics. The estimated regression coefficients can then be used to infer the marginal values of characteristics. This technique provides an estimate of the marginal benefit of amenities, but care must be exercised when inferring benefits or costs for non-marginal changes. For example, multiplying the amount of amenity improvement by the marginal value of the amenity will tend to overestimate benefits because, as the amenity before the change is increased, the marginal benefit typically goes down. The reverse is true for declining quality. It is important to recognize that this approach assumes that changes in environmental quality are localized to the extent that they do not affect the overall price equilibrium. Bartik (1987) pointed out that large environmental quality changes imply an overall shift in supply of environmental quality and that the price equilibrium will shift. Large supply shifts create a fundamental problem for identifying, and even bounding, the benefits or costs from an estimated hedonic price function.

Non-use benefits

The approach to recreation and amenity benefits discussed in the previous section revolves around use of a target recreation or residential site that will be affected by a project. Krutilla (1967) raised the prospect of benefits from the natural environment even for people who do not currently use the resource. In particular Krutilla noted that people such as the spiritual descendants of John Muir may value natural areas or scenic wonders for their mere existence. The Arctic National Wildlife Refuge in Alaska is a good example, with many non-users valuing preservation, as Congress has discovered when considering allowing oil and natural gas development in the refuge. Many constituents who have never visited nor intend to visit the refuge have protested the prospect of such development to their Congressional representatives by letter, fax, email and telephone. Measuring this class of benefits has, however, proven to be both difficult and controversial. Non-use benefits are difficult to measure because non-users, unlike consumers of a product, recreationists and so on, leave no behavioral trail to link them to the resource. Even the identification of non-users is difficult since those who value preserving a natural area are likely to be geographically and demographically dispersed. Some progress on this challenge has, however, been made by application of so-called 'contingent valuation' techniques. Because contingent valuation (CV), as it is commonly known, has also been applied much more widely than just in search of non-use values, the following subsections discuss it and one of its important cousins in that broader context.

Contingent valuation Survey techniques, especially the CV method,[25] have been applied extensively to measure environmental benefits and costs, including non-use benefits and costs. The idea behind these surveys is to create a hypothetical market from which individuals' values can be inferred. Survey respondents are contacted using random sampling techniques. These surveys can be administered in person, by mail, by telephone, by Internet, as well as combinations of these modes (for example, telephone and mail). A properly designed valuation survey carefully explains how a particular project or program will affect a resource. Then a hypothetical payment proposal is made to the survey participant. When CV was first applied, payment proposals simply asked open-ended questions such as: what is the most you would be willing to pay for this program? Open-ended questions are easily manipulated. For example, people who really want the project may express very high amounts for their maximum WTP, even though they may not be willing to pay the stated amount. To reduce manipulation, payment proposals took a discrete form such as: would you favor the program if it cost your household $10 for a one-time tax assessment? If the respondent says yes, then the analyst infers the most this person is willing to pay, their compensating variation, is more than $10. A no response is interpreted as implying that this person's compensating variation is less than $10. In order to estimate the distribution of individual compensating variations, the cost amount is randomly varied across participants. Typically, analyses focus on estimating the mean of the distribution of individual compensating variation. The estimated mean can be used to calculate total benefits by multiplying the estimated mean and the number of households in the affected population.

The CV method has been applied extensively to value the environment and other public goods. In a recent bibliography Carson (2004) notes over 5500 CV studies. While CV applications are plentiful and growing more so, the method has its critics.[26] An obvious issue is that survey respondents state their preferences and their choices are non-binding.[27] Another potential problem is that many survey respondents may lack familiarity with the affected area and yet they still respond. Finally, unlike marketing research where stated preference estimation can be checked against actual market choices, external validation for CV-based benefit estimates is often quite difficult because of the difficulty of matching the changes being valued in different studies using different methods. In cases of benefits involving use, such as recreation and housing amenities, there have been comparisons of values obtained from CV and those obtained using methods such as travel cost and hedonic analysis. Carson et al., (1996) gathered 83 studies that provide 616 comparisons, in which the CV estimates averaged slightly lower than the estimates obtained from the other methods.

Much of the liveliest CV controversy arose because of its applications to natural resource damage assessment cases, where real money would be changing hands. In the court case *Ohio* vs *US Department of Interior* (USDOI), the US Federal Court of Appeals ruled that Congress intended for non-use values to be included in natural resource damage assessments conducted under the Comprehensive Environmental Response, Compensation and Liability Act (CERCLA), the same law that established the Superfund. The Court further ruled that CV was the only method capable of measuring non-use values. Probably the most prominent application example is the CV application that valued protecting Alaska's Prince William Sound from future oil spills like the one created by the grounding of the Exxon Valdez in 1989 (Carson et al., 1992). Estimates of the non-use economic damages from that study were in the order of $2.8 billion. Potential liability from natural resource injuries to non-users of this magnitude created considerable concern among potentially responsible parties from industry. By the late 1980s, the CV method was so embroiled in controversy that the National Oceanic and Atmospheric Agency (NOAA), the federal trustee for natural damage assessments in navigable waters of the USA, convened a panel of prominent economists, including two Nobel laureates, to assess the validity of CV in damage assessment cases. In their report, published in the *Federal Register*, Arrow et al. (1993) concluded 'contingent valuation studies can produce estimates reliable enough to be the starting point for a judicial or administrative determination of natural resource damages – including lost passive-use value' (p. 4610).

Choice-based conjoint While the NOAA panel supported the use of CV, it is being replaced in natural resource damage assessment by a related, but distinct technique referred to as choice-based conjoint (Adamowicz et al., 1999). Choice-based conjoint is useful when projects can be represented according to the quantitative levels of the major attributes provided by the project. Like CV, choice-based conjoint is a survey-based technique and survey respondents state their choices. The primary difference is that choice-based conjoint provides hypothetical choices between alternative projects that differ by the levels of these attributes, including cost. Typically a single survey respondent makes multiple choices between different 'designs' at each choice occasion. In contrast, CV survey participants typically face one choice: between the proposed project (or policy) with some form of payment and the option of doing nothing at no cost, that is, the status quo. Similar to the hedonic method, in choice-based conjoint analysis the marginal values for the attributes are inferred from the data, only here the data reflects stated rather than market choices.

Federal statutes require that money recovered in natural resource damage litigation be directed exclusively toward restoration of injured resources and the restoration of other resources as a form of compensation. Choice-based conjoint has gained popularity in natural resource damage assessment because it facilitates measuring damages in both monetary and compensatory resource terms.[28] In most cases of water planning project analyses, however, only monetary measures are required. Nonetheless, there are those situations in which projects are most clearly described in terms of attribute levels. For these cases, choice-based conjoint can provide an avenue for easily considering projects of different make-up and scale, particularly when compensatory restoration will be used to offset ecological losses.

Overall, the stated choice methods of benefit and damage estimation have a major advantage, flexibility, over the older methods that rely on revealed preference data from markets and complex reasoning and econometrics to tease out estimates. That is, stated choice surveys can be designed to ask exactly what is at issue, and the value of preserving something or of building something or of putting in place a particular policy. It is often difficult to design revealed preference studies that can address what is actually of interest and the analyst may be forced to measure a highly imperfect proxy. It is also true, as noted in passing previously, that CV or conjoint studies can reveal non-use values, but in general only as parts of the aggregate benefit or damage estimates and not as separate numbers.

Inferring Non-Market Benefits Using Benefits Transfer

Many planning exercises have insufficient financial resources or insufficient time to conduct original studies to estimate non-market benefits and costs. Lacking resources, the method of benefits transfer can sometimes be used to analyse projects, particularly in preliminary stages of planning. As the name suggests, benefits transfer applies results from existing economic analyses to infer costs and benefits for the project at hand. While the way benefits are transferred can vary considerably, some basic guidelines exist for evaluating a benefits transfer.[29]

First, the benefits transfer should carefully lay out the benefit and cost data requirements necessary to adequately evaluate the project, regardless of the availability of existing studies. This process includes laying out the likely impacts of the project and then identifying the population likely to be affected. Second, the benefits transfer should identify as many relevant studies as possible for the task at hand, even studies not ultimately used to infer benefits. The burden is then on the analyst to convincingly explain the logic behind the choice of studies to include in the benefits transfer and studies to exclude. Two primary screens for selecting projects are overall analytical quality and correspondence of conditions. The quality of a benefits transfer relies on the quality of the existing studies used to generate the benefits. Studies using outdated techniques or substandard research methods, while worthy of mention for potential relevance, should not be considered in a benefits transfer, no matter how convenient. There also needs to be reasonable correspondence between the character of the project being analysed and conditions reflected in the studies included in the data set. The resources involved for the target project should be similar to the resources involved in existing studies. For example, when considering changes in recreation benefits for a Rocky Mountain trout fishery, the analyst should favor existing studies that estimate benefits for similar fisheries, as opposed to fisheries with flat water and different fish species. The demographic composition of the population affected by the target project should also be similar to the demographic composition of the population in the chosen studies. Lacking correspondence on all dimensions, the analyst should explain what, if any, problems are likely implied by this lack of correspondence.

The first major type of benefits transfer is often called 'unit value transfer'. A common example is the estimation of the average consumer's surplus estimate for a day's recreation of a particular kind. Returning to the Rocky Mountain trout fishery, average per trip consumer's surplus estimates from several studies of other Rocky Mountain trout fisheries may exist and the average of those unit values could be transferred from the existing studies to the new problem setting. Non-use benefits can, in principle, also be transferred. For example, suppose a project would eliminate natural habitat. There may exist CV studies that value natural habitat preservation in other similar areas. These will usually reflect both use and non-use values and separating the two may or may not be possible. But the unit value of compensating variation per household could be transferred from these existing studies so that some unknown amount of non-use value will be reflected in the analysis.

A second type of transfer is that of activity data. Returning to recreation, we may need the change in recreational demand resulting from the project in addition to a unit value. Studies estimating demand shifts for similar areas can be used to infer demand shifts for the target area.

The final type of value transfer we mention is 'value function' transfer. This method uses the estimated demand or preference functions from existing studies and then predicts using data for the existing study. For example, an existing study may correspond closely except with regard to the income distribution. If the estimated demand or preference function from the existing study depends on income, the benefit estimates can be adjusted through the estimated function.

In an environment of declining budgets, benefits transfer is likely to play an increasing role in project analysis. Though traditionally touted as a preliminary screening device, benefits transfer is quickly becoming an inexpensive substitute for original analysis, even for large projects. Credibility of original analysis requires adhering to best practice research standards. High quality benefits transfer requires form (studies used must meet best practice standards) but also requires art, where this is the process of justifying the use of particular existing studies and explaining their relevance to the task at hand.

Benefit-cost inference and incomplete economic analysis

In some cases time or resource constraints may result in an analysis lacking benefit or cost estimates for some categories, most often in areas involving non-market benefits and costs. Fortunately, in many instances, an incomplete analysis is still sufficient for judging the economic merits of the project. Suppose, for example, a project will result in environmental losses affecting recreational fishing and white water boating. Further suppose the losses are only measured for recreational fishing, but that these are larger than the benefits of the project. No loss estimates are required for white water boating, although the analysis should mention the prospect of these losses because, even without the recreational boating losses, the project fails to generate positive net economic benefits. Similarly, a project may provide several categories of benefits, with some of these going unmeasured, while all expected costs are satisfactorily measured. Again, if the estimated categories provide a total larger than estimated costs, an incomplete analysis is sufficient for the benefit-cost test.

At other times, a determination cannot be made because of missing benefits or cost estimates. In these cases good practice dictates a consideration of the magnitude of missing benefits or costs that would result in a project failing or passing the benefit-cost test. Suppose a project will provide water supply benefits valued at \$4.2 million per year at a construction and maintenance cost of \$3 million per year. The only unmeasured costs are lost white water recreation opportunities. From area visitation surveys, analysts infer there were 5000 white water recreation days in the last year. The relevant question is whether the economic losses from reduced white water recreation exceed \$1.2 million. Given the potential for substitution to other recreation sites, 5000 lost white water recreation days represents an upper bound to the reduction in demand for white water recreation. Using this upper bound, we can construct the required per trip value that would equate benefits to costs (that is, divide \$1.2 million by 5000 which equals \$240 per trip). A survey of the recreational demand literature suggests that \$240 per trip is well outside the range of existing WTP estimates for a day of white water recreation. The large requisite per trip value and the conservative estimate of trip loss allows for credible inference that the project passes the benefit-cost test.

Economic Analysis at the Margin

As the preceding discussion suggests, economic analysis relies on the notion that people have preferences for those things provided, or perhaps destroyed, by competing projects and that knowledge of these preferences is potentially useful in helping decision makers weigh the merits of competing alternatives. Some scholars[30] fundamentally reject both the notion and role of individual preferences in public decision making. We believe most economists, ourselves included, accept the notion and usefulness of preferences without apology. Regardless of whether the reader accepts or rejects the notion and usefulness of preferences, the central conceptual foundation underlying economic project analysis is likely to continue to be preference based for the foreseeable future.

As pointed out by Russell and Sagoff in Chapter 5, economists view choices as a window on preferences. Assuming people weigh competing alternatives, economists reason that their choices will generally provide insight into what they want (that is, their preferences). It is important to recognize, however, that in order to draw meaningful inferences regarding preferences the analyst must identify the margin on which people operate, which is not always obvious. Following in this same tradition, economists also tend to view projects in terms of their marginal contributions, a world view Russell and Sagoff contrast with that of ecologists, for whom the total environment is always at risk. We readily admit that analysts, when inferring preferences, can misidentify the margin on which people operate. Similarly, public policies may not be designed to lead to the appropriate margin. However, there is a flip side to this coin and that is that if the proper margins are identified, then the calculus of choice may indeed positively serve society.

SPECIAL ISSUES IN THE ESTIMATION OF COSTS

Many costs take the form of foregone benefits; so many of the techniques described previously apply directly to estimating that part of the cost side. However, some issues are unique to the cost side. For example, questions on the appropriateness of market prices of inputs are important. These prices can be distorted by monopoly suppliers, by deviations between traditional wages and real opportunity costs, by price support programs like those applied to agricultural products, by manipulated exchange rates and so on. But not all costs are communicated through market prices. As water volumes, quality and flow patterns change negative externalities prevail. Damage to riparian ecosystems frequently occurs, while changes in groundwater levels (beneficial or damaging) can result from reservoir storage.

Much discussed in the literature is the question of how to allocate the total cost for a multi-purpose project to its various purposes. Such allocations are desirable for appropriate pricing of the several outputs and in meeting various financial requirements, such as cost repayment and no profit conditions for public utilities. The problem arises from the existence of joint project components that are parts of the project that lie behind the successful fulfillment of more than one purpose. The obvious example is a dam, the existence of which allows for flood control, navigation improvement, electric power generation and perhaps irrigation. Technical personnel may identify the primary purpose of the project and then other purposes that may warrant inclusion. Design is carried out along with cost estimation. Separable costs are easily assigned (for example, water distribution system costs for irrigation, power plant costs for electric generation, locks and associated facilities for navigation). However, the joint costs (for example, the costs of the reservoir) pose a problem. Any procedure for dividing those costs is arbitrary (Young, 1985). Procedures have been developed (the separable costs-remaining benefits method) that do the job in a reasonable way in the sense of public perception, but distortion of output prices may still result.

INTEGRATING BENEFITS AND COSTS

The foregoing discussion of benefits and costs neglects a critical dimension of project evaluation: that of time. The fact that all benefits and all costs do not occur at the same instant creates a number of concerns not yet treated here. For one thing, monetary values change over time (price inflation). For another, neither individuals nor society are indifferent as to when benefits or costs occur (time preference). Also, the passage of time reduces the certainty with which effects can be measured (risk and uncertainty). Finally, because of the long lives and long-term impacts of many water resources projects, questions arise about the desire of society to transfer benefits or costs to future generations (intergenerational equity).

Temporal Issues in Project Analysis

Water resources projects, like other investments, incur most of the costs early in the life of the project, while most benefits accrue later. This, in itself, creates an evaluation problem, since costs at one time cannot be directly compared to benefits at another. Moreover, neither costs nor benefits occur at a single time; they are continuously varying streams of expenditures or benefits that extend throughout the life of a project and sometimes beyond. Even a simple question such as: what is the cost of this project? requires attention to the temporal dimension of cost. The answer to this question is found by calculating the present value of project costs – a single sum at a specified time that is, given certain assumptions, equivalent to the stream of costs over the life of the project. A comparison of benefits to costs, then, requires calculation of the present value of benefits and the present value of costs. These two single sums can be compared and conclusions drawn regarding the worth of the project.

Price inflation

Since project effects are forecasted over time and then monetized, it is important to note that the value of money changes over time. In most cases the value of money falls from year to year. This fact is communicated to consumers by rising market prices for goods and services. Wages, pension payments and other amounts also increase as the value of money decreases, often through the use of Cost of Living Adjustments (COLAs) or other escalator clauses. Changes in the value of money are described as price inflation and measured by one of a number of indices. Different indices are appropriate in different circumstances, but most discussions center on a version of the Consumer Price Index (CPI), the Producer Price Index (PPI) or the Gross Domestic Product Implicit Price Deflator series. The CPI for all urban consumers (CPI-U) is the most frequently quoted measure of price inflation, while the CPI for urban wage earners and clerical workers (CPI-W) is commonly used to escalate wages and pension payments.

Monetizing project effects requires knowledge of prices, wages and other values related to prices and wages. Generally, these values are known at the present time. However, since project evaluation deals entirely with hypothesized future events, some assumption must be made about future prices and wages. Two approaches are possible: (1) make some assumption about the rate of price inflation from now until the time of the valuation (the time when the cost or benefit is projected to occur); or (2) value all future costs and benefits in terms of present-day prices and values. The first approach produces an estimate of nominal costs and benefits, an estimate that depends on the assumed rate of price inflation. The second approach produces an estimate of real costs and benefits. Conventional practice in public sector benefit-cost analysis is to employ real estimates of benefits and costs, often referred to as measuring values in today's dollars. As will be seen below, both methods produce the same present value provided appropriate discount rates are used.

The convention of using real values does not entirely dispose of the issue of price changes. In certain circumstances, prices of specific goods or services change over time for reasons other than general price inflation. For example, consider a period when prices in general are escalating at an annual rate of 3.0 per cent. But suppose that prices for gasoline and other petroleum products increase at an average annual rate of 7.0 per cent. This rate of increase is partly due to general price inflation, but also reflects some other factor or factors. Perhaps the world demand for petroleum products is growing, causing the price to be bid up. Or perhaps the increase is due to the exercise of market power by oil-exporting countries. Whatever the reason, it is clear that prices of petroleum products are rising faster than prices in general. The difference is expressed by the following equation:

$$\frac{1.07}{1.03} = 1.0388 \tag{3.3}$$

Based on this calculation, the price of petroleum products is increasing 3.88 percentage points faster than prices in general. This is the annual rate of differential inflation.

Even when project impacts are expressed in real terms (that is, in today's prices), it is still necessary to identify goods or services that may be subject to differential inflation. These items must still be escalated: not at the projected rate of price increase, but at the differential rate. Note that negative differential price changes (deflation) may also occur; for example, in the case of electronic equipment. This is handled in the same way, except that the rate of differential inflation is negative.

Principle of present value

If an individual is promised a sum of money, they will probably prefer to receive it now rather than receive the same sum at some future time. Similarly, if a debt must be paid, most people prefer to make the payment later, as compared to paying the same sum now. These preferences reflect the factors noted previously (time preference, price inflation, risk). Since these same factors affect governments and society as a whole, similar concerns are expected at all levels of aggregation.

In order to compare sums received or paid at different times, it is necessary to develop some notion of equivalence. This is done by observing that there must be some sum of money, received or paid at the present time, which would be regarded as equivalent to the future sum. In the case of a sum to be received in the future, a smaller amount received now may be equivalent. This equivalent amount is the present value of the future sum. If a debt must be paid in the future, the equivalent present value is also smaller than the actual amount to be paid. In both cases the test of equivalence is that the individual is indifferent between the actual future sum and its present value.

Applying this notion to water resources development, projects have future costs and future benefits and each cost and benefit has an equivalent present value. Once all future costs have been restated as their equivalent present values, they can be added to give the present value of project cost. This is a consistent measure of total cost, taking into account not only the amounts that must be expended in the future, but the time at which those expenditures occur. The same logic applies to benefits: if all future benefits are restated as their equivalent present values, they can be summed to yield the present value project benefit. Since both costs and benefits are stated at present value as of some base year, they can be compared to each other or to the costs and benefits of other projects stated as present values for the same base year.

The calculation of present values is accomplished through the use of a discount rate, defined as the rate with which the present value of a sum changes from period to period. The present value as of time = *0* of a single benefit received or cost incurred in time t is found as follows:

$$P.V.(S_t) = \frac{1}{(1+i)^t} S_t \tag{3.4}$$

Where:
S_t = benefit or cost occurring at time t
i = discount rate

The present value of a stream of benefits or costs occurring over the life of a project, T, is found by adding individual present values:

$$P.V.(\overline{S}) = \sum_{t=1}^{T} \left[\frac{1}{(1+i)^t} S_t \right] \tag{3.5}$$

Where:
$\overline{S}$ = vector of future benefits or costs
T = project life

In both cases the present value is calculated as of time = *0*.

Choice of appropriate discount rate

In the case of market transactions involving future payments, the associated market interest rate performs the function of the discount rate. For public sector decision making, market interest rates are either not available or of dubious applicability, so an appropriate discount rate must be determined. This subject has been the focus of considerable controversy over the years and remains unsettled to some degree. The specific areas of disagreement can be identified by considering the following decomposition of a discount rate:[31]

$$(1+i) = (1+r)(1+p)(1+a) \tag{3.6}$$

Where:
i = discount rate
r = simple rate of time preference (also called consumption discount rate)
p = risk premium
a = inflation allowance

The first set of controversies applies to the rate of time preference. Some argue that this should reflect the time preference characterizing market transactions. For example, the rate of time preference reflected in US Treasury Notes and Bonds (assuming that risk is zero and after removing the effect of price inflation) has typically fluctuated in the range of 1.0 to 4.0 per cent per year. For the 2007–10 period, the OMB forecasts this rate at 2.5 per cent (OMB, 2007). Another school of thought says that since society consists of both present and future generations, there should be no time preference; that is, the rate of time preference should be zero. Yet another view is that in the face of future environmental events that may reduce the welfare of society compared to present levels (resource exhaustion, global warming), considering a negative rate of time preference is appropriate (Mäler, 1997).

All market interest rates incorporate some allowance for risk. Indeed the wide range of risk associated with various financial instruments is the major source of variation in observed interest rates (consider, for example, interest rates for home mortgages as compared to those for unsecured credit card debt). Some would argue that public sector discount rates should reflect either (1) the risk associated with the specific project, (2) portfolio risk for a class of projects, or (3) government-wide investment risk. In the latter case most would agree that government investments as a whole are so many and diverse as to render the overall risk premium negligible.

The inclusion of an inflation allowance in the discount rate reflects whatever inflation rate was incorporated in the estimates of the future benefits and costs that are to be discounted. If all future amounts have been escalated at a constant 4.0 per cent annual rate, the inflation allowance should be 4.0 per cent. Similarly, if the usual convention of the benefit-cost analysis is applied so that all future amounts are measured in real terms (escalation rate = 0), the inflation allowance should also be zero. Both methods result in the same present value. This can be seen by examining the following equality:

$$\sum_{t=1}^{T}\left[\frac{(1+a)^t}{[(1+r)(1+p)(1+a)]^t}S_t\right] = \sum_{t=1}^{T}\left[\frac{1}{[(1+r)(1+p)(1+0)]^t}S_t\right] \tag{3.7}$$

The convention, therefore, is to utilize real (inflation-free) valuations of future benefits and costs and to discount them with a real (inflation-free) discount rate. The real discount rate has two components: time preference and risk premium. Alternatively, full consideration of inflation gives the same value. In both cases the discount rate and the valuations must reflect the same assumption.

In Circular A-94 (of 1992) the OMB proposed that government investments and regulations be evaluated using a real discount rate of 7.0 per cent. This rate is meant to reflect the real pre-tax time preference observed in the private sector, together with the marginal risk premium characterizing private sector investments (OMB, 1992). The calculation is ultimately derived from the work of Stockfisch (1969), who concluded that private sector investments produce an average real return between 7.0 and 10.0 per cent. The rationale for using private sector pre-tax preferences and risk premiums is complex, but the basic idea is that funds spent in the public sector can be viewed as having been diverted from the private sector; therefore, it is reasonable to expect similar economic performance.

The OMB rate of 7.0 per cent does not apply to water resources projects, however. The Water Resources Development Act (WRDA) of 1974 requires that these projects be evaluated using a discount rate based on the average yield of US Treasury Securities with remaining terms of 15 or more years. This rate is calculated annually. For example, it was set at 5.625 per cent for fiscal year 2004 (USDOI, 2004). Although quantitatively similar, the water resources rate differs conceptually from the OMB rate. First of all, since it is an average of market interest rates, it incorporates assumptions regarding future inflation; in other words, it is a nominal, not a real rate. Second, since the reference market is US Government Securities, the resulting discount rate incorporates a low risk premium, perhaps approaching zero. Finally, the rate reflects the time preferences of those private sector investors active in the market for US Government Securities: it is not a social or a resource-constrained time preference. However, Federal Law requires the application of the nominal water resources interest rate, even though benefits and costs are measured in real terms. The calculation, therefore, is conceptually inconsistent.

Another approach to the discount rate debate would be to combine the following assumptions: (1) social rate of time preference of zero or near zero, (2) risk premium of zero, reflecting diversified investment by the government, and (3) inflation allowance of zero reflecting measurements of future benefits and costs in real terms. This would produce a discount rate near zero. Since benefits tend to appear late in project lives, while costs are incurred early, lower discount rates make projects appear more worthy. The OMB rate of 7.0 per cent would result in approving the fewest projects, the zero rate would favor the most projects and the water resources rate of 5.625 would fall between these extremes. While some advocates of public investment favor a very low rate, this could also result in substantial distortion of investment policies (marginal returns on investment would be much higher in the private sector than in the public sector). The result could be less, rather than more, public investment.

Intergenerational equity

Because of their long lives, water resources projects have the potential to reallocate benefits and costs between generations. Development projects, such as dams and waterways, create costs for the present generation while providing economic benefits to future generations. The same projects, however, may create environmental costs in the future. Ecosystem restoration projects, in effect, pose the opposite problem because the failure to implement ecosystem restoration may impose the environmental costs of present economic activities on future generations. All of these examples raise ethical issues concerning the present generation's rights and responsibilities as the steward of the environment.

Many critics of water resources policy pointed to discounting as a problem for intergenerational equity. For example, some projects may be evaluated at a particular discount rate and judged infeasible, even though they would be feasible at a lower discount rate. Future generations have, thereby, been denied access to the benefits of these projects because of the present generation's myopic time preference. But to manipulate the discount rate in order to achieve some distributional goal destroys the information needed to allocate capital efficiently in the present, possibly to the detriment of future generations. Attempts to employ discounting as a tool of intergenerational equity, or to blame discounting for failures to achieve intergenerational equity, rest on faulty logic. More important, they conceal the real ethical issues and trade-offs. A better approach is to identify the kinds of redistributions that are unacceptable and should be avoided and to plan water resources development within these constraints.

The decision criterion

The purpose of identifying and measuring the effects of a water resources project and of monetizing the measurements wherever possible is to help find answers to a number of basic questions about the project. Is the project worth doing? Would the project be more desirable if it was larger, smaller or otherwise reformulated? Should the project be implemented now or would it be better to wait? What priority should be assigned to the project, given a finite budget and the existence of competing projects?

The original goal of benefit-cost analysis was to develop a single decision criterion, a metric that could be used to provide answers to these questions.[32]

The first step in developing a decision criterion is to convert all monetized effects to present values. Then, at least three metrics can be considered:

- Net present worth – the excess of the present value of benefits over the present value of costs, given the selected discount rate.
- The benefit-cost ratio – the ratio of the present value of benefits to the present value of costs, given the selected discount rate.
- Internal rate of return – the discount rate at which the net present worth is zero.

Although common in the private sector, internal rate of return is not used much in the public sector. In the case of real discount rates, it offers few advantages over other decision criteria.

Both the net present worth (also known as net present value) and the benefit-cost ratio answer the question of whether a particular project is worth doing. A positive net present worth and a benefit-cost ratio greater than unity convey the same information: the project is economically feasible. If the question is which of two (or more) projects, all aimed at essentially the same outcomes, is the better (or best) the two criteria are again, for practical purposes, identical. But, if the decision to be made involves choosing from among a large number of substantially different, discrete projects, a subset that makes the best use of a fixed investment budget, neither criterion leads to optimality.[33] This is a problem of the 'knapsack' variety and requires, in effect, complete enumeration of all feasible combinations, though the integer programming technique can be used to cut down on the need for brute force. Nevertheless, both the P&G (WRC, 1983) and OMB's Circular A-94 (OMB, 1992) advocate formulating projects to maximize net present worth, as well as ranking projects by the same criterion.

Uncertainty in Benefit-Cost Analysis

The procedure for identifying the beneficial and adverse consequences of a project is to project future conditions without the project, then to project all conditions again with the project. Any differences between the with- and without-project projections are considered to be the effects of the project. A major characteristic of this approach is the high level of uncertainty surrounding many estimates of project effects. Forecasts of all kinds are inherently uncertain, due to imprecision of underlying data and model assumptions and to the influence of unknown but possible exogenous events. That uncertainty rises as the forecast periods lengthen. Differences between forecasts may be more or less uncertain than the forecasts themselves, depending on the models used.

Most benefit-cost analyses are conducted by developing single estimates of all effects and values, then treating those estimates as if they were deterministic. This method omits important information about the project. For example, in comparing alternative projects, those with relatively higher levels of uncertainty may be less desirable than projects with lower but more certain benefit-cost ratios. Financial markets account for uncertainty by building a risk premium into the interest rate. As noted in the discussion of discount rates, the same approach can be taken in the pubic sector. But this is a relatively crude approach and, furthermore, it is precluded by legislation that fixes the discount rate on federal water resources projects.

A preferable method is to deal with uncertainty explicitly, identifying the principal sources of uncertainty and quantifying the impact on project decision criteria where possible.

Scenario methods

Where the major sources of uncertainty are believed to be assumptions about major drivers of the phenomena being forecast (for example, population, household income, unemployment and so on), it may be helpful to define a number of scenarios, each characterized by a set of specific assumptions about those drivers. The probability of any one scenario actually occurring is not generally known. However, they should collectively represent a reasonable range of plausible outcomes. The project is then evaluated under each scenario and the range of outcomes examined. Projects that prove feasible for most or all scenarios are considered robust and good candidates for implementation. Those feasible under one or a few scenarios, but not under others, may require further study.

Sensitivity analysis

Another approach to examining the impact of uncertainty on project evaluation is sensitivity analysis. Major assumptions are varied systematically and the project evaluation is recomputed for each value. Where the project evaluation proves sensitive to a particular assumption, the assumption is subjected to further analysis to improve accuracy. It is also possible to vary more than one assumption at a time, but this quickly becomes complex.

Simulation techniques

Ideally, the analyst would have available probability distributions for all key elements of the benefit-cost analysis, leading ultimately to a probability distribution for the decision criterion (for example, benefit-cost ratio). However, this kind of information is rarely found. Instead, where something is known of the parameters of uncertainty for some assumptions and outcomes, it is possible to simulate a range of values, approximating a probability distribution. If the simulation model is extended to include the entire project and all benefits and costs, then methods such as Monte Carlo simulation can be used to obtain a probability distribution for the decision criterion (Vaughan et al., 2000).

The Importance of Financial Analysis and Financial Policies

The preceding sections describe how benefit-cost analysis brings together in present value terms benefits and costs to reflect the positive and negative impacts of projects (or policies or programs) on human welfare. These impacts may or may not take the form of cash flows or observable market transactions (for example, the non-monetary items previously discussed). Also, benefit-cost pays no attention to the incidence of these benefits and costs (for example, how project beneficiaries will share in paying project costs). These issues are among the concerns of financial planning and the results of financial policies.

In a broad sense, financial planning is concerned with a project's inflows and outflows of cash: who will pay for project outputs and who will cover project costs, both the initial capital cost and continuing operations, maintenance and repair costs. Construction costs must be paid out of accumulated funds, by current appropriations of public funds or by the issuance of bonds. How and what parts of these construction costs must be repaid by beneficiaries or others (for example, real estate tax payers) represents part of the financial policy of the relevant agency or governmental unit. The payment of ongoing operations, maintenance and repair costs and often repayment of construction costs depend heavily on the pricing of project services. Clearly, careful financial analysis and planning is needed to permit the project to meet its financial and contractual obligations.

The realities of the cash flows and financial arrangements for a project are likely to differ substantially from the flows of benefits and costs used to evaluate a project from an economic point of view. This can motivate decisions by private and public actors and at least some of these are likely to be economically inefficient. For example, it is obvious that policies reducing cost repayment for beneficiaries will affect the beneficiaries' private assessment of the project. It is then likely political pressures will be used to promote projects regardless of the economic benefit-cost assessment.

In a prominent article, Krutilla (1966) emphasized the importance of repayment policies, hopefully policies that would motivate political and professional decision makers to mimic correct benefit-cost assessments of projects. As an example, the early navigation work of the USACE was all publicly funded. Following the Flood Control Act of 1936, the USACE continued to fund the reservoir storage components of flood plans, while requiring cost sharing by local entities for levees. Local areas bore any costs associated with zoning and other non-structural measures. This motivated local entities to advocate reservoir storage even in situations where storage was not the most effective strategy.

The Water Resources Development Act of 1986 required cost sharing for the USACE and NRCS projects. At present, there is a range of required cost sharing (see Table 2.7 in Chapter 2 for details). Thus, large elements of subsidy remain and these separate the economics from the financing of projects and are likely to continue to stimulate inefficient project promotion and design.

The history of the Reclamation Program that started in 1902 exhibits a pattern of increasing subsidies to irrigated agriculture through decreasing repayment requirements. The initial Reclamation Fund of $10 million was to be loaned to irrigation sponsor organizations for project construction and to be repaid in ten years. The repayment of capital costs was never accomplished within the specified period and Congress repeatedly extended the repayment period, finally to 50 or more years. Repayment contracts with the USBR require no payment of interest on the unpaid balances, nor are any allowances made for inflation, repayment being in nominal (inflated) dollars. Three other financial arrangements serve to further reduce the real values of repayment: (1) the acceptability of balloon payments wherein much of the nominal repayment was allowed to be made in the last few years of the repayment period; (2) the specification of non-reimbursable project purposes, such as flood control, recreation, Native American uses, fish and wildlife enhancement; and (3) the ability-to-pay limit on beneficiary repayment. Since cost allocation among purposes is usually quite arbitrary, the existence of non-reimbursable purposes motivates allocation of costs toward non-reimbursable purposes. The introduction of the ability-to-pay limit (Reclamation Project Act of 1939) means that beneficiaries of poor projects are relieved of a large part of any repayment obligation. Under the Reclamation Program overall only 10.5 per cent of costs allocated to irrigation are repaid in real terms by beneficiaries (GAO, 1996).

This recital of financial arrangements makes quite clear that the financial attractiveness of projects can differ greatly from the economic efficiency measure used in the benefit-cost analysis. This is particularly true from the point of view of the beneficiaries who are often relieved of a large part of project costs by virtue of special interest-oriented financial arrangements. This is not to deny the need for careful financial analysis so that project financial obligations and contract requirements are met. However, these financial arrangements have historically been subject to manipulation and serious distortion from an economic efficiency point of view.

OVERVIEW AND ASSESSMENT

The idea that water resources development should be subject to some kind of economic calculus is older than the economics profession itself. Some of the earliest manifestations of applied economic reasoning dealing with the benefits and costs of public investment appear at the beginning of the nineteenth century. Water resources projects figure prominently in these writings. In the USA the Flood Control Act of 1936 set into motion an intensive study of water resources project evaluation, culminating in the development of the first detailed procedures for a benefit-cost analysis. These procedures, first published in 1950, underwent continuous and extensive revision and augmentation over the years.

In reviewing the history of economic analysis of water resources projects, two things are evident: (1) the conceptual simplicity of benefit-cost analysis, despite the complexity of implementation and (2) the close linkage between the state-of-the-art and changing social goals and values.

Benefit-cost analysis is a simple idea. The effects of a project are identified, measured and monetized where possible; beneficial effects are compared to adverse effects. Projects demonstrating a favorable comparison (benefits exceed costs) are declared feasible. Those with the most favorable comparisons are placed at the top of priority lists. But in applying these simple ideas, numerous complications arise. We need to know: how to identify project effects, how to place monetary values on effects, what to do with effects that cannot be monetized, how to find equivalent present values for future values, how to evaluate and rank competing projects and so on. These and many other questions occupied the profession for almost 60 years and much progress has been made.

But it is instructive to note the areas in which the major breakthroughs occurred. As the broader environmental and social implications of water resources development attracted notice in the 1950s and 1960s, benefit-cost analysis incorporated the notions of non-monetized effects and multi-objectives. At the same time, major strides were made toward making analysis more transparent and reducing opportunities for misallocating public funds. As concern for impacts on the environment grew in the

1970s and 1980s, pioneering work was done on the economic valuation of non-market goods, such as recreation and environmental quality. The techniques developed during this period proved useful in other applications, including the determination of natural resource damages due to release of hazardous wastes. At the end of the twentieth century, prior developments continued to evolve and mature while additional progress was made in rendering project planning more accountable to local needs. The principal lesson to be learned from this history is the extent to which economic theory and economic analysis kept pace with changing social goals and values. This relationship is evident today and will doubtless continue in the future.

The result has been a highly evolved technique for economic analysis of water resources projects, one that has largely kept pace with the concerns and demands of society. Benefit-cost analysis today is a disciplined process for identifying and measuring the impacts of a project on society. But some developments are not complete; some problems are not yet solved.

Published Standards for Benefit-Cost Analysis

A specialized set of principles, standards and procedures, known most recently as the P&G, governs the benefit-cost analysis for water resources projects (WRC, 1983). From 1965 to 1983, the predecessors to the P&G were published and periodically revised by the WRC. That body passed out of existence with the issuance of the last revision in 1983. Since then, the IWR has maintained the P&G informally for the USACE. This ad hoc arrangement is unlikely to be adequate to the demands of the future, which may require substantial revision and broader dissemination of the P&G.

The Role of Willingness-to-Accept

The advent of stated preference methods for valuing environmental goods (such as the CV method) gave researchers the opportunity to explore willingness-to-accept (WTA) valuations as well as the customary WTP. Whereas a WTP valuation measures the amount a respondent would pay for something of value (or for removal of some undesirable condition), WTA measures the amount that would be accepted as compensation for tolerating an undesirable condition (or foregoing something of value). In the terminology adopted in this chapter, WTP to gain something of value is a measure of compensating variation, whereas WTA the absence of that same thing is a measure of equivalent variation.

It is possible to think of many environmental goods from either perspective and CV surveys have inquired about both measures. For example, respondents may be asked their WTP for a recreation opportunity or they may be asked their WTA in the absence of that same opportunity. One might assume that the results would be similar, as is the case for many market goods, but early attempts at measurement often found wide variances between WTP and WTA. For a variety of reasons, including WTP's intrinsic similarity to familiar market transactions, most practitioners concluded that the WTP was the most appropriate measure of value for non-market environmental goods. Many thought that the unfamiliarity of the WTA choice scenario produced arbitrary and unreliable responses, thus explaining the large divergences between WTP and WTA. The NOAA panel concurred with this view (Arrow et al., 1993) and the WTA measures were generally abandoned after that time.

But several decades of work in experimental and behavioral economics have demonstrated clear reasons why the WTP measures differ from the WTA measures of the same choice. In fact, the disparities are pervasive and predictable (Kahneman et al., 1990). In particular, when a WTP measure is used to measure a negative environmental impact (the WTP to avoid), the true value of that impact may be significantly understated (Knetsch, 2004).

This work has been largely ignored in the benefit-cost community, which continues to rely on the WTP measures for all applications of stated preference methods. But there are definable situations where this measure will understate or overstate value. Improved guidance is needed to identify the correct value measure in each type of situation.

The Appropriate Discount Rate

Much scholarly and what might be called political attention has been paid to the question of the appropriate discount rate for evaluating public sector investments such as water resources projects. The conceptual bases and implications of the various theories regarding discount rates are now widely understood and the possibility of reaching a consensus on this matter appears closer. Yet water resources project analysis remains mired in the largely discredited notion of using the cost of federal borrowing as an estimator of the discount rate. This practice was imposed by Congress in the WRDA of 1974, despite the obvious inconsistency of applying a nominal discount rate to real data. Over the years, no real effort has been invested to either (1) build support for a change in the law or (2) modify benefit-cost procedures to be consistent with the existing law.

Treatment of Uncertainty

Despite much discussion of the importance of full consideration of uncertainty, few examples in the water resources benefit-cost literature of serious engagement with this problem exist. A number of techniques have been proposed, but little is known of their practicality or usefulness in actual project planning. If project selection is to reflect both expected net benefits and relative uncertainty, much work needs to be done.

Non-Monetized and Non-Quantified Effects

Perhaps the most impressive achievement of the past several decades is the development of sound, practical methods for placing monetary values on certain kinds of non-market goods. This work, which proceeded apace with public demands for more attention to the environmental consequences of public investment, dramatically improved the reach of benefit-cost analysis. Previously, non-monetized and non-quantified effects could be identified and described, but they were often given little weight in the final evaluation. Some kinds of non-market goods can now be included with more conventional market-oriented project effects. This work must go on and should be extended to new classes of non-market goods wherever possible. But many project effects will never be monetized and some seem unlikely to be even quantified. Benefit-cost analysis must evolve to incorporate and to give appropriate weight to all project effects.

Intergenerational Equity

Large, long-lived water resources projects are often criticized for their possible impact on the distribution of benefits and costs among successive generations. Some commentators fear that the present generation will underinvest in benefits for future generations and many suggest that changes in discounting practices will correct this perceived problem. Actually, such changes may promote inefficient investment and may create more problems than they cure. There is a need for a better understanding of this problem and a clearer idea of possible strategies.

Ecosystem Restoration

At the beginning of the twenty-first century, some of the largest water resources projects under consideration are not development projects but rather ecosystem restoration projects. The benefits from these projects may be in part the restoration of lost economic values, but they are more likely to be the avoidance of future environmental costs, achieved by arresting further ecosystem deterioration. Also, most such avoided costs are non-monetized and some are non-quantified. While conventional approaches to identifying and measuring benefits and costs have been applied to some of these projects, it is not clear that they are fully appropriate. In particular, where individual projects are to work in concert with other past and future projects to benefit a large interconnected ecosystem and where the benefits of such individual projects consist mostly of future system-level improvements, conventional benefit-cost analysis provides little assistance. This area merits substantial attention to improving both economic theory and economic analysis.

NOTES

1. The origins of modern welfare economics can be traced to Pigou (1932), Kaldor (1939) and Hicks (1943).
2. This concept was developed by the nineteenth century Italian economist Vilfredo Pareto.
3. Another, perhaps more familiar, term is 'consumer surplus'. In most cases consumer surplus is a useful approximation to compensating variation (Willig, 1976).
4. These advances have only partially solved the practical (and moral) problem of determining true compensating variation for winners (that is, their 'willingness-to-pay') and for losers (their 'willingness-to-accept').
5. For evidence of this practice, see Eckstein (1958) which at the time of its publication represented the state-of-the-art in the economic analysis of water projects.
6. While Krutilla's ideas are not now viewed as controversial, there were at the time criticisms of his reasoning, for example, Cummings and Norton (1974).
7. The discussion in Chapter 5 of this book, on the difficulties of reconciling concerns of economists and ecologists, affirms the persistence of this problem.
8. This section is quoted and paraphrased from Caulfield (2000). Henry P. Caulfield, Jr was a Professor of Political Sciences, Colorado State University, after a distinguished public service career, having served as Assistant Director and Director of the Resources Program Staff, Office of the Secretary, Department of the Interior (1961–65) and as the first Executive Director of the Water Resources Council (WRC) (1966–69).
9. Wild areas of rivers had already been officially proposed in the interdepartmental comprehensive study of the Arkansas, Red, White River Basin Study at the urging of Irving Fox representing the Department of the Interior.
10. This replaced the President's WRC created by Executive Order several years earlier.
11. A similar method had been suggested earlier by Harold Hotelling, but Clawson's approach was developed independently (personal communication, Jack L. Knetsch to Charles W. Howe, 15 September 2004).
12. Recall that compensating variation is the amount subtracted from or added to income that makes a person indifferent to the project.
13. This area is also known as the change in consumer's surplus where consumer's surplus is the area under the demand curve above the market price.
14. Hausman (1981) provides one way to reconcile the difference between compensating variation for price changes and the approximation discussed here.
15. The order of price changes considered matters due to the fact that this method approximates compensating variation. The best rule of thumb for price increases is to order

by relative size of independent compensating variation (considering each price as the only change), from largest to smallest independent compensating variation. For price decreases, the ordering is reversed. This rule of thumb will result in the closest approximation for multiple price changes.

16. Here market benefits and costs refer to those benefits and costs that can be measured directly in markets. There are often non-market benefits and costs associated with changes in hydroelectric production. Non-market benefits are taken up in future sections.
17. Black et al. (1998) provide a comprehensive analysis and explanation of this issue.
18. The concept of recreational demand modeling through travel cost is typically traced back to an unpublished letter from Harold Hotelling to the Director of the National Park Service (NPS) in 1947. But current practice is derived from the later and apparently independent work of Clawson (1959).
19. Morey (1984).
20. Normally demand estimation requires data from multiple periods in order to observe variation in price and quantity demanded. Across individuals in a single period we have price variation (through differences in home location) and individual trip demand variation.
21. In particular, changes in water quality often affect site demand for fishing. For this reason the travel cost method is used to identify and measure benefits for water quality improvement or degradation. The CV method, which is discussed in a future section, has also been used to measure the benefits of water quality improvements both for recreationists and non-recreationists. A frequently cited CV study is Carson and Mitchell (1993) who estimate the public's willingness-to-pay for boatable, fishable and swimmable water quality as mandated by the Clean Water Act (CWA).
22. In the random utility framework the change in consumer's surplus is expressed in probabilistic expectation. Though derivation of the expected change in consumer's surplus is different from the derivation of estimated consumer's surplus from ordinary demand system estimation, the basic concepts and their relation to welfare economics are the same.
23. Later paragraphs discuss perceived problems with survey approaches to measuring benefits.
24. Amenities can include many things such as proximity to good things (beach, lake and so on), proximity to bad things (hazardous waste site, landfill), views (beach, mountains, power plant) and air quality.
25. While the recreation application of Davis (1963) discussed above is the earliest application of CV, a later landmark is the highly influential book by Mitchell and Carson (1989).
26. The *Journal of Economic Perspectives* published three articles on the reliability of CV. The first article is an introduction to the controversy (Portney, 1994), the second article is a defense of the technique (Hanemann, 1994) and the last article (Diamond and Hausman, 1994) is a criticism of the technique.
27. This is the basis of Bohm's criticism of the method. For example, see Bohm (1994).
28. Using a goods-for-goods approach in natural resource damage assessment is sometimes referred to as habitat equivalency. Flores and Thacher (2002) provide discussion and analysis of the ability to use and measure compensatory resources in natural resource damage assessment.
29. Here we touch on some of the basic issues faced in benefits transfer. For a comprehensive discussion offering multiple points of view, see the collection of papers in *Water Resources Research*, **28** (3), 1992.
30. See, for example, Sagoff (2003a), Sagoff (2003b) and Sagoff (1994).
31. Note that financial institutions conventionally decompose market interest rates in the same way, except that they typically neglect cross-products so that $I = r + p + a$. This is a close approximation provided that all components are small.
32. Although the single decision criterion remains at the heart of benefit-cost analysis,

there has long been recognition that significant non-monetized benefits and costs exist, requiring the use of multiple criteria decision methods and other approaches.

33. If the projects are infinitely divisible into tiny pieces, and therefore can be arrayed along a continuum as though they constituted one large project, the benefit-cost ratio can be used as the choice criterion.

REFERENCES

Adamowicz, W.L., P.C. Boxall, J.J. Louviere, J. Swait and M. Williams (1999), 'Stated-preference methods for valuing environmental amenities', in I.J. Bateman and K.G. Willis (eds), *Valuing Environmental Preferences: Theory and Practice of the Contingent Valuation Method in the U.S., EU and Developing Countries*, Oxford: Oxford University Press.

Arrow, K.J., R. Solow, P.R. Portney, E.E. Leamer, R. Radner and H. Schuman (1993), 'Report of the National Oceanic and Atmospheric Administration panel on contingent valuation', *Federal Register*, **58** (10), 4601–14.

Bartik, T. (1987), 'The estimation of demand parameters in hedonic price models', *Journal of Political Economy*, **95** (1), 81–8.

Black, R., N.E. Flores, B. McKenney and R. Unsworth (1998), 'Economic analysis for hydropower project relicensing: guidance and alternative methods', paper prepared for Division of Economics, US Fish and Wildlife Service, US Department of the Interior, Cambridge, MA, and Industrial Economics, Inc., University of Colorado, Boulder, CO.

Bohm, P. (1994), 'CVM spells responses to hypothetical questions', *Natural Resources Journal*, **34** (Winter), 37–50.

Bromley, D. (2000), 'Program evaluation and the purpose of rivers', *Water Resources Update*, **116**, 7–10.

Brown, Jr, G.M. and J. Hammack (1973), 'Dynamic economic management of migratory waterfowl', *Review of Economics and Statistics*, **55** (1), 73–82.

Brown, Jr, G.M. and J. Hammack (1974), *Waterfowl and Wetlands: Toward Bioeconomic Analysis*, Baltimore, MD: Johns Hopkins University Press, p. 95.

Carson, R.T. (2004), *Contingent Valuation: A Comprehensive Bibliography and History*, Cheltenham, UK and Northampton, MA, USA: Edward Elgar.

Carson, R.T. and R.C. Mitchell (1993), 'The value of clean water: the public's willingness to pay for boatable, fishable and swimmable quality water', *Water Resources Research*, **29**, 2445–54.

Carson, R.T., R.C. Mitchell, W.M. Hanemann, R.J. Kopp, S. Presser and P.A. Ruud (1992), *A Contingent Valuation Study of Lost Passive Use Values Resulting from the Exxon Valdez Oil Spill*, La Jolla, CA: Natural Resources Damage Assessment, Inc.

Carson, R.T., N.E. Flores, K.M. Martin and J.L. Wright (1996), 'Contingent valuation and revealed preference methodologies: comparing the estimates for quasi-public goods', *Land Economics*, **72** (1), 80–99.

Caulfield, Jr, H.P. (2000), 'Early Federal guidelines for water resource evaluation', *Water Resources Update*, **116**, 14–17.

Cicchetti, C.J. and V.K. Smith (1973), 'Congestion, quality deterioration and optimal use: wilderness recreation in the Spanish peaks primitive area', *Social Science Research*, **2** (1), 15–30.

Clawson, M. (1959), *Methods of Measuring the Demand for a Value of Outdoor Recreation*, reprint no. 10, Washington, DC: Resources for the Future.
Clawson, M. and J.L. Knetsch (1966), *Economics of Outdoor Recreation*, Baltimore, MD: Johns Hopkins University Press.
Cummings, R. and V. Norton (1974), 'The economics of environmental preservation', *American Economic Review*, **64** (6), 1021–4.
Davis, R.K. (1963), *The Value of Outdoor Recreation: An Economic Study of the Maine Woods*, Cambridge, MA: Department of Economics, Harvard University.
Davis, R.K. (1968), *The Range of Choice in Water Management: A Study of Dissolved Oxygen in the Potomac Estuary*, Baltimore, MD: Johns Hopkins Press.
Diamond, P.A. and J.A. Hausman (1994), 'Contingent valuation: is some number better than no number?', *Journal of Economic Perspectives*, **8** (4), 45–64.
Dupuit, J. (1844), 'On the measurement of utility of public works', translated by R.H. Barback (1952) for *International Economic Papers*, no. 2, London: Macmillan, pp. 83–110.
Eckstein, O. (1958), *Water-Resource Development: The Economics of Project Evaluation*, Cambridge, MA: Harvard University Press.
Ekelund, Jr, R.B. and R.F. Herbert (1973), 'Public economics at the Ecole des Ponts et Chaussees: 1830–1850', *Journal of Public Economics*, **2**, 241–56.
Flores, N.E. and J. Thacher (2002), 'Money, who needs it? Natural resource damage assessment', *Contemporary Economic Policy*, **20** (2), 171–8.
Gallatin, A. (2 March 1807), *Report of the Secretary of the Treasury on the Subject of Public Roads and Canals Made in Pursuance of a Resolution of Senate*, Washington, DC: R.C. Weightman.
Hanemann, W.M. (1994), 'Valuing the environment through contingent valuation', *Journal of Economic Perspectives*, **8** (4), 19–43.
Hausman, J.A. (1981), 'Exact consumer's surplus and deadweight loss', *American Economic Review*, **71** (4), 662–76.
Hicks, J.R. (1943), 'The four consumer's surpluses', *Review of Economic Studies*, **XI**, 31–41.
Hirshleifer, J., J.C. DeHaven and J.W. Milliman (1960), *Water Supply: Economics, Technology and Policy*, Chicago, IL: University of Chicago Press.
Howe, C.W. (1971), *Benefit-Cost Analysis for Water System Planning*, Washington, DC: American Geophysical Union.
Hufschmidt, M.M., J.V. Krutilla, J. Margolis and S. Marglin (1961), *Standards and Criteria for Formulating and Evaluating Federal Water Resources Developments*, Washington, DC: US Bureau of the Budget.
Kahneman, D., J.L. Knetsch and R.H. Thaler (1990), 'Experimental tests of the endowment effect and the Coase Theorem', *Journal of Political Economy*, **98**, 1325–48.
Kaldor, N. (1939), 'Welfare propositions of economics and interpersonal comparisons of utility', *The Economic Journal*, **49** (195), 549–52.
Kalter, R.J., W.B. Lord, D.J. Allee, E.N. Castle, M.M. Kelso, D.W. Bromley, S.C. Smith, S.V. Ciriayy-Wantrup and B.A. Weisbrod (1969), 'Criteria for federal evaluation of resource investments', Water Resources and Marine Sciences Center, Cornell University, Ithaca, NY.
Kneese, A.V. (1964), *The Economics of Regional Water Quality Management*, Baltimore, MD: Johns Hopkins Press.

Kneese, A.V. and B.T. Bower (1968), *Managing Water Quality: Economics, Technology, Institutions*, Baltimore, MD: Johns Hopkins Press.
Knetsch, J.L. (2004), 'Gains, losses and the U.S. EPA economic analyses guidelines: a hazardous product?', *Environmental and Resource Economics*, **32** (1), 91–112.
Knetsch, J.L., R.H. Haveman, C.W. Howe, J.V. Krutilla and M.F. Brewer (1969), *Federal Natural Resources Development: Basic Issues in Benefit-Cost Analysis*, Natural Resource Policy Center, Washington, DC: George Washington University.
Krutilla, J.V. (January 1966), 'Is public intervention in water resources development conducive to economic efficiency?', *Natural Resources Journal*, **6**, 60–75.
Krutilla, J.V. (1967), 'Conservation reconsidered', *American Economic Review*, **57**, 777–86.
Krutilla, J.V. and O. Eckstein (1958), *Multiple Purpose River Development: Studies in Applied Economic Analysis*, Baltimore, MD: Johns Hopkins Press.
Lancaster, K.J. (April 1966), 'A new approach to consumer theory', *Journal of Political Economy*, **74**, 132–57.
Maass, A., M.M. Hufschmidt, R. Dorfman, H.A. Thomas, Jr, S.A. Marglin and G.M. Fair (1962), *The Design of Water-Resource Systems: New Techniques for Relating Economic Objectives, Engineering Analysis and Governmental Planning*, Cambridge, MA: Harvard University Press.
Mäler, K.G. (1974), *Environmental Economics: A Theoretical Inquiry*, Baltimore, MD: Johns Hopkins Press.
Mäler, K.G. (1997), 'Social discount rates, environmental resources and global warming', lecture given to the International Institute for Applied Systems Analysis, 11 June, Laxenburg, Austria.
Mitchell, R.C. and R.T. Carson (1989), *Using Surveys to Value Public Goods: The Contingent Valuation Method*, Washington, DC: Resources for the Future.
Morey, E.R. (December 1981), 'The demand for site-specific recreational activities: a characteristics approach', *Journal of Environmental Economics and Management*, **8** (4), 345–71.
Morey, E.R. (1984), 'Confuser surplus', *American Economic Review*, **74** (1), 163–73.
Office of Management and Budget (OMB) (29 October 1992), *Circular Number A-94, Revised*, Washington, DC: US Government Printing Office.
Office of Management and Budget (OMB) (January 2007), *Appendix C, Circular Number A-94, Revised*, Washington, DC: US Government Printing Office.
Pigou, A.C. (1932), *The Economics of Welfare*, 4th edn, London: Macmillan and Company.
Portney, P.R. (1994), 'The contingent valuation debate: why economists should care', *Journal of Economic Perspectives*, **8** (4), 3–18.
Rosen, S. (1974), 'Hedonic markets and implicit markets: product differentiation in perfect competition', *Journal of Political Economy*, **82** (1), 34–55.
Sagoff, M. (1994), 'Should preferences count?', *Land Economics*, **70** (2), 127–44.
Sagoff, M. (2003a), 'On the relation between preference and choice', *Journal of Socio-Economics*, **31** (6), 587–98.
Sagoff, M. (2003b), 'Cows are better than condos, or how economists help solve problems', *Environmental Values*, **12** (4), 449–70.
Stockfisch, J.A. (1969), 'Measuring the opportunity cost of government investment', Institute for Defense Analysis research paper, no. 490, p. 29.

US Bureau of the Budget (BOB) (1952), *Budget Circular A-47*, Washington, DC: US Government Printing Office.

US Department of Interior (USDOI) (26 April 2004), 'Change in the discount rate for water resources planning', *Federal Register*, **69** (80), 22556.

US Government Accountability Office (GAO) (1996), *U.S. Bureau of Reclamation: Information on Allocation and Repayment of Costs of Constructing Water Projects*, US Governmental Accountability Office/RCED-96-109, Washington, DC: US Government Printing Office.

US Interagency Committee on Water Resources (USIACWR) (1950), *Proposed Practices for Economic Analysis of River Basin Projects*, The Green Book, revised 1958, Washington, DC: US Government Printing Office.

US Senate (1962), *Policies, Standards and Procedures in the Formulation, Evaluation and Review of Plans for Use and Development of Water and Related Land Resources*, Senate Document 97, 87th Congress, 2nd Session, Washington, DC: US Government Printing Office.

US Water Resources Council (WRC) (1973), 'Establishment of principles and standards for planning water and land resources', *Federal Register*, **38** (174), 24778.

US Water Resources Council (WRC) (1983), *Economic and Environmental Principles and Guidelines for Water and Related Land Resources Implementation Studies*, Washington, DC: US Government Printing Office.

Vaughan, W.J., C. Russell, D. Rodriguez and A.C. Darling (2000), 'Cost-benefit analysis based on referendum CV: dealing with uncertainty', *Journal of Water Resources Planning and Management*, (November/December), 351–7.

Weisbrod, B.A. (1964), 'Collective-consumption services of individual-consumption goods', *Quarterly Journal of Economics*, **78** (3), 471–7.

Willig, R.D. (1976), 'Consumer's surplus without apology', *American Economic Review*, **66** (4), 589–97.

Young, H.P. (1985), 'Methods and principles of cost allocation', in H.P. Young (ed.), *Cost Allocation: Methods, Principles, Applications*, New York: North-Holland.

4. Environmental issues and options in water resources planning and decision making

David H. Moreau and Daniel P. Loucks

INTRODUCTION

When asked, Americans usually express environmental concerns about a variety of water-related issues, including: drinking water quality; ambient water quality in streams and lakes as this relates to water-contact recreation; health of aquatic ecosystems and the abundance of game fish; preservation of streams and related habitat, including lands of natural, scenic and historical interest; and water supply in ample amount and sufficient quality for industry and agriculture. These concerns are outward expressions of values increasingly woven into the fabric of US culture, especially since 1970. That is not to say that all citizens share the same priorities, but there is evidence that most share the same broad goals and concerns.

Related advances in science, policy formulation, and project planning, evaluation and implementation, have been substantial, especially over the past four decades, yet major uncertainties and issues remain. Examining the emergence of policy and planning techniques addressing water resources issues, will help us identify the matters yet to be resolved.

ENVIRONMENTAL VALUES

Environmental concerns expressed by Americans arise from several basic values. Kempton et al. (1995) relied on several studies as well as their own anthropological research to conclude:

> Americans' environmental values derive from three sources: (1) religion, whether traditional Judeo-Christian religious teaching or a more abstract feeling of spirituality; (2) anthropocentric (human-centered) values, which are largely utilitarian and are concerned with only those environmental changes that affect human welfare; and (3) biocentric (living-thing-centered) values,

which grant nature itself intrinsic rights, particularly the rights of species to continue to exist. (p. 87)

Whatever their ultimate source or sources, environmental values are manifested in at least four themes of public policies: (1) preservation of areas of natural beauty and natural features; (2) protection of individual species from extinction, either from overharvesting or destruction of habitats; (3) protection of public health; and (4) protection of complex ecosystems. In examining two periods, pre- and post-1965, we shall find specific policies emerging from those themes and be in a position to assess how well the evolution of planning techniques, especially environmental effect prediction modeling, has served the needs of those formulating and implementing these policies.

PRE-1965 ENVIRONMENTAL POLICIES

Preservation of Natural Areas

Early attitudes about environmental values associated with water resources cannot be divorced from attitudes about riparian land resources. Over half of the 220 million acres of wetlands existing in the coterminous USA at the time of the Revolutionary War have been lost (Dahl, 1990). As the country developed and as the population grew and moved westward into the Lower Mississippi River Valley in the first half of the nineteenth century, vast wetlands of that region were drained and transformed into productive agricultural lands. Swamps and overflowed lands with their rich and productive soils were seen as opportunities for economic gain.

For more than 20 years states and landowners in the Lower Mississippi Valley petitioned Congress to transfer those lands to the private sector. Congress eventually responded by passing the Swamp Lands Acts of 1849 and 1850. These acts eventually led to the transfer of 64.9 million acres to states, approximately 4 per cent of all the 1840 million acres of public domain lands in the USA (US Bureau of Land Management (USBLM), 2003). If those lands were all wetlands, as currently defined, they would have accounted for nearly 30 per cent of wetlands existing during the colonial period. Four states, Louisiana, Arkansas, Missouri and Mississippi, got 24 million acres. Robert Harrison referred to those acts as the ‘first important Federal legislation relating to land reclamation’. Transfers of lands to states under these acts were made on the condition that they were to be sold. Proceeds from sales were allocated to build levees and drainage works for the purpose of economic development (Harrison, 1961, p. 68).

The Swamplands Acts were an early part of the great land rush of the late 1800s that gave scant attention to environmental values. From 1875 to 1900, the federal government either gave away or sold at minimal prices over 1 billion acres of land, more than three-fourths of all lands acquired by the USA from 1781 up to the time Alaska was purchased in 1867. Mineral and forest rights were largely sold or given with rights to the land.

Some seeds of change had been sown in the 1850s. A number of writers and artists, including Thoreau, began calling attention to the need for preserving some lands for recreation and inspiration. Their calls did not go entirely unheeded. Numerous individuals urged President Lincoln to take steps to preserve lands around Yosemite Valley in California. Most notable among them was Galen Clark, a miner from New England, who moved to the area to establish a homestead. Lincoln acceded to these requests by signing a bill in 1864 granting California lands to be held for public use and recreation, lands now part of Yosemite National Park. The conservationist John Muir first visited the area in 1868 and began writing of the need to preserve it as early as 1869. Muir and Robert Underwood Johnson, the influential editor of *Century Magazine,* convinced Congress in 1890 to establish the area around Yosemite Valley as a national park. A decade later, Muir, with the help of railroad magnate Edward Harriman and President Theodore Roosevelt, managed to get California to cede Yosemite Valley back to the federal government as part of the new park.

Yellowstone National Park had been the first of the national parks, created in 1872 when President Ulysses Grant signed the originating legislation. That action followed several explorations of the area that documented its unique natural features (Dombeck et al., 2003).

The conservation movement that flourished under the administration of President Theodore Roosevelt had its roots in the last quarter of the nineteenth century, but its guiding philosophy was wise use of resources, not preservation. In 1878 Major John Wesley Powell, prominent explorer of the West, delivered his famous *Report on the Lands of the Arid Region of the West*. In that report Powell argued for reform of land policy so as to better coordinate the use of land and water resources. Soon after that report was delivered, Congress created the US Geological Survey (USGS) and Powell was appointed its director in 1881. He attracted a number of bright and energetic people to the USGS, people who would take prominent roles in the Roosevelt Administration and promote the philosophy of rational development of the nation's water resources. Among them were Frederick Newell, the second director of the USGS and W.J. McGee, who has been described as the chief theorist of the conservation movement (Hays, 1959).

A parallel development was taking place in forestry under the influence of Gifford Pinchot, a Yale graduate and European trained forester and a pioneer in scientific management of forest resources in the USA. Pinchot began his career managing the Biltmore forests near Asheville, North Carolina in 1892. He quickly built a national reputation and, after serving on the National Forestry Commission, he took a position with the Division of Forestry in the Department of the Interior (USDOI) in 1897. He later became Chief of the Division and a prominent advisor to Presidents McKinley and Roosevelt.

McGee, Pinchot and Newell had many occasions during these administrations to advocate their views. One of their proposals was establishment of the Inland Waterways Commission (IWC). After acting on their recommendation in 1907, the President then appointed the three of them, as well as several leaders of Congress, to the IWC. The Commission's preliminary report issued in 1908 articulated several fundamental principles for efficient use of water resources, including treatment of an entire river basin as a single hydrologic system, development of multi-purpose facilities and comprehensive planning.

Reconciliation of conflicts between those promoting wise use and those seeking to preserve resources in their natural state was not always possible then as it is not always possible today. Among the most heated controversies was the debate over use of the Hetch-Hetchy watershed in Yosemite Valley as a water supply for San Francisco. Hayes (1959) recounts the long and bitter conflict over this issue that began in 1901 and placed Roosevelt between his friend John Muir and the wise use advocates Pinchot, Newell and other influential officials of the administration. The fight to prevent construction of the reservoir continued until it was approved in 1914, and continues to this day, now fought by those advocating removal of the dam.

Protection of Individual Species

Destruction of habitat and depletion of populations of fish and wildlife accompanied the massive program of land grants. As the population grew at a rapid rate, large areas of land were converted to animal and row-crop agriculture. Perhaps the best known symbol of wildlife depletion was the elimination of large herds of bison from their original rangelands, but the number of species that have become extinct, not just depleted, since the colonial period is estimated to be in excess of 500. Fragmentation of habitat is commonly cited as the reason for the extinction of over 90 species, subspecies and varieties of plants in the continental USA and over 270 in Hawaii (Czech and Krausman, 2001).

Advocates for the protection of wildlife came from both preservationists and sport hunting groups. Establishment of Yellowstone National Park in 1872 was in part a response to these interests and in 1894 Yellowstone was established as a de facto national wildlife preserve when Congress passed the Yellowstone Park Protection Act (ibid.).

President Theodore Roosevelt established the first of the official wildlife reserves. At the turn of the century Pelican Island, Florida was the last breeding ground for brown pelicans along the east coast of Florida. At the urging of a number of prominent people, Roosevelt elevated the importance of wildlife protection to a level of national concern when, by executive action, he established the Pelican Island Wildlife Refuge in March 1903 (US Fish and Wildlife Service (USFWS), 2007a). Unlike later actions taken by hunters to preserve migratory game, this step marked one of the first times the public acted to preserve a species for its intrinsic rather than its utilitarian value. During Roosevelt's Administrations, a total of 53 wildlife reserves were established.

Attitudes toward wetlands remained largely unchanged until game hunters became alarmed at the declining population of migratory birds, particularly along the flyway of the Mississippi River during the late 1920s and the Dustbowl era of the 1930s. The Migratory Bird Conservation Act, passed in 1929, authorized the USDOI to purchase or rent water and water-related lands to establish waterfowl refuges. Money to support that activity was limited until passage of the Migratory Bird Hunting and Conservation Stamp Act of 1934. This Act established what has become known as duck stamps, a fee charged on hunting licenses. Funds derived largely from that source have been used to acquire over 4 million acres of migratory bird habitat, most of which are wetlands (US Government Accountability Office (GAO), 1991; USFWS, 2007b).

With the acceleration of large dam construction in the 1920s, concerns grew over the effects they might have on fish and wildlife. Public Law 121, now referred to as the Fish and Wildlife Coordination Act of 1934, took the first step toward integrating water resources developments with fish and wildlife concerns. Although it did not give any explicit authority to the fish and wildlife agencies to alter primary uses of projects, the Act did require that the Bureau of Fisheries be given an opportunity to use all federal impoundments for fish culture stations and resting places for migratory birds. The Act also required the construction agencies to consult with the Bureau of Fisheries before any new federal dam was built. Any necessary and feasible means to mitigate blockage of migratory patterns was required to be incorporated in the project. Amendments to the Coordination Act in 1946 extended the required consultation with

USFWS to include consultation, for the purpose of preventing loss of or damage to wildlife resources, with state agencies on all projects that would impound, divert, control or otherwise modify streams. Stronger language was added in 1958 requiring equal consideration and coordination of wildlife conservation with other water resources development purposes (USFWS, 1980).

Protection of Public Health and Aquatic Life

Even though the geographic center of the American population steadily moved westward after 1850, American cities in the East were also growing rapidly. In 1840 only five cities claimed a population of 50 000 or more. That number increased dramatically as shown in Figure 4.1, especially after 1840, tripling by 1860 and doubling again by 1880. As shown in Figure 4.2, about 6 million people or about 20 per cent of the population lived in urban places in 1860. That population exploded to over 30 million by 1900 when 40 per cent of the total population lived in urban places. Urban services could not keep pace with growth. Sanitation in many of those cities was deplorable, especially for the poor.

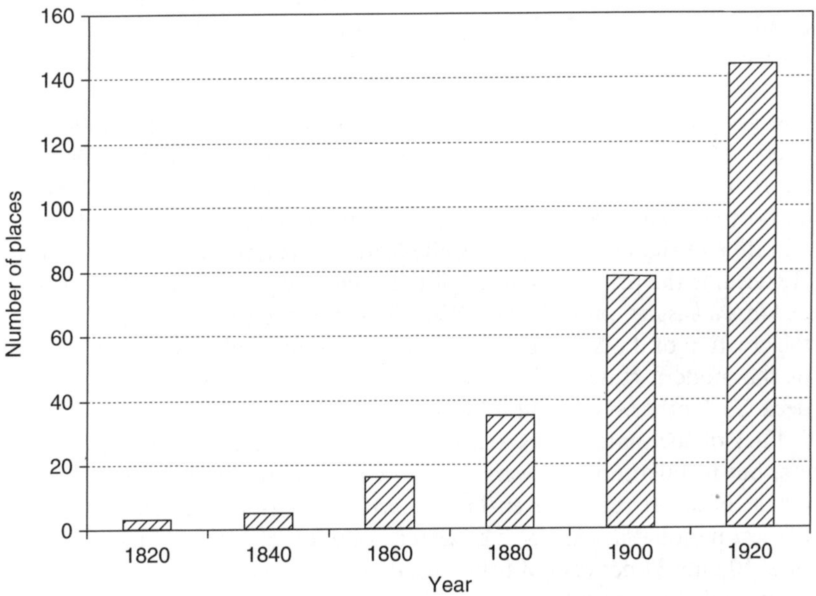

Figure 4.1 Number of urban places in the USA with population over 50 000

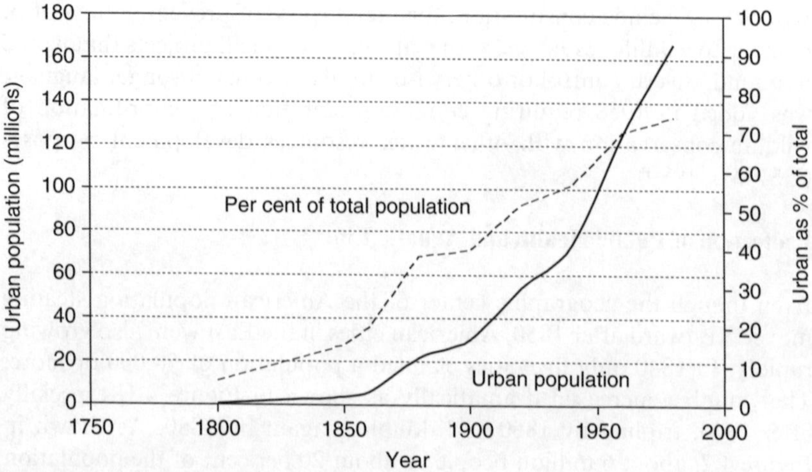

Figure 4.2 Urban population of the USA

In 1838 Edwin Chadwick, the principal author of the 1842 *Report of the Poor Law Commissioners Concerning the Labouring Population of Great Britain*, had launched a movement toward the cleanup of England's cities. Chadwick's continued advocacy for reform was a key motivation for the 1848 Public Health Act. While the Act was a timid first step, it did establish the General Board of Health and required the mapping of districts for sewage systems, an unprecedented requirement for cities (Platt, 1996).

US cities, taking a lead from England, awakened to the need for improvements in sanitation in the 1850s. Lemuel Shattuck of Boston, author, merchant, member of the common council of Boston and representative in the legislature, took the lead in pushing for sanitary reform. He became the principal author of the *Report of the Sanitary Commission of Massachusetts*, published in 1850. That report led eventually, in 1869, to the creation of the Massachusetts State Board of Health, as 'the prototype of the modern state health authority' (Hynning, 1939, p. 72). Within a decade, 17 other states had followed suit.

Lack of adequate sewers was a matter of high priority for urban reformers, but installation of sewers was slow in coming. National data on the extent of sewer service even in the early 1900s is sparse, but one of the earliest national assessments of water pollution control estimated that as of 1910 only 37 per cent of urban residents were served by sanitary sewers (National Resources Committee, 1939). Trends given in that report are shown in Figure 4.3. By 1938, only 56 per cent of urban residents were served by sewers.

Figure 4.3 *Urban population served by sewers and sewage treatment 1910 to 1938*

Sewage treatment lagged further behind. In 1910 only 9 per cent of urban residents were connected to sewer systems for which any treatment was provided. That percentage had risen by 1938 to 54 per cent, but that figure is likely to be somewhat misleading. No information in the report indicated how effective that treatment was, though it was referred to as 'secondary'. There is little doubt, however, that it was substantially less effective than what qualifies as secondary treatment today. If these numbers are reasonably accurate, they indicate that in excess of 90 per cent of municipal wastewater was discharged as raw sewage in 1910. When direct discharge of industrial waste is added, it is not difficult to imagine the conditions that must have existed in the streams receiving these wastes. Although it is difficult to find data on ambient water quality for the period, the adverse impacts on both human health and aquatic life of streams must have been appallingly large.

Effects of pollution on public water supplies were the initial concerns that brought the issue to lawmakers' agendas. Massachusetts was the first state to take legislative action to address deterioration of water quality with passage of 'An Act to Protect the Purity of Inland Waters' in 1886. It authorized funding of a full-time engineering staff in the state board of health (Fair, 1950). Even though at least 40 states had some law on their books regarding water pollution by 1905, many were vague and subsumed under broad powers to protect public health. Only eight states had explicit enforcement authority (Tarr et al., 1980). But by 1938 almost every state had vested authority to control water pollution in its board of health, though explicit enforcement authority still existed in only 20 states (National Resources Committee, 1939).

Federal action on water quality began in 1912 and then only with a research program. In that year the US Public Health Service gained approval to extend its research to include sanitation and pollution. The resulting research program in Cincinnati, Ohio attracted some of the nation's most distinguished sanitary engineers and scientists, including Harold Streeter and Earle Phelps, who conducted extensive research on water pollution in the Ohio River. Twenty-five years later, in 1937, bills were introduced in Congress to provide financial assistance for pollution control to the states. Separate versions of the bill passed in the House and Senate, but a conference committee could not resolve their differences before World War II intervened.

A Congressional bill, similar to the one proposed in 1937, passed shortly after World War II and was known as the Water Pollution Control Act of 1948 (WPCA). It authorized the Public Health Service to develop and adopt comprehensive programs in cooperation with states, local governments and industries; authorized federal grants to states and interstate agencies to support studies; authorized grants for plans and engineering of treatment plants; encouraged adoption of uniform state laws; and established an enforcement policy to be implemented with consent of states after all state efforts were exhausted (Davies, 1970).

The permanent Federal Water Pollution Control Act (FWPCA) passed in 1956 as Public Law 84-660, but its effect was primarily limited to interstate water bodies. States were required to establish a system of stream classifications and related water quality standards for those streams. Classifications were to reflect the highest and best use for each stream segment. Many states had already established classifications and standards; the 1956 Act required that for all states but only for interstate streams. The Act also authorized grants to states and interstate agencies to support comprehensive pollution control programs and included authorization for construction grants.

A 1962 state-by-state survey by McKee and Wolf (1963) identified about 20 states with reasonably comprehensive pollution control programs but also revealed that nearly half of the states had no water quality standards or only minimal guidelines.

Progress toward cleaning up wastewater discharges continued to be slow. The Federal Water Pollution Control Administration (FWPCA), one of the predecessors of the US Environmental Protection Agency

(EPA), estimated that in 1960 the sewered population of the country was about 110 million. Only 56 per cent of that population was served by secondary treatment (FWPCA, 1969). Even though the data are limited, estimates of sewered population and wastewater treatment and the status of state institutions for water pollution control indicate that by the 1960s there remained much to be done in protecting water quality. Those factors set the stage for bold federal initiatives beginning in 1965.

Environmental Values In Water Resources Planning Programs

Planning for the rational use of the nation's water resources was an important part of President Franklin Roosevelt's New Deal programs. The National Planning Board (NPB) was established in 1933, the President's Committee on Water Flow and the National Resources Board (NRB) in 1934 and the National Resources Planning Board (NRPB) in 1939. Negative Congressional reaction to the proliferation of new agencies led to their demise, but in 1943, the Departments of War, Interior and Agriculture and the Federal Power Commission (FPC) voluntarily created the Federal Interagency River Basin Committee (FIARBC). In 1946 that committee established a Subcommittee on Benefits and Cost and its report, *Proposed Practices for Economic Analysis of River Basin Projects*, published in 1950, is commonly referred to as the 'Green Book' (USIACWR, 1950).[1]

In the 'Green Book', distinctions were drawn between tangible and intangible effects. Intangibles were defined as those benefits impractical to express in monetary terms. Examples included scenic values, improvements to health and prevention of loss of life. Authors of the 'Green Book' argued that intangibles should be described and not ignored in project evaluation, but there was no guidance on what intangible effects should be included or how they were to be described.

A more balanced, multi-objective view was introduced by Senate Document 97 (US Senate, 1962), which defined the basic objective as 'to provide the best use, or combination of uses, of water and related land resources . . . (and that) full consideration shall be given to each of the following objectives and reasoned choices made between them when they conflict'. The three objectives were National Economic Development (NED), preservation and well-being of people. In this context, the preservation objective is particularly noteworthy. It included:

- Protection and rehabilitation of resources to insure their availability in time of need.
- Maintenance and use of open space, green space and wild areas of streams and mountains for recreational use.

- Preservation of areas of unique natural beauty, historical and scientific interest.

Standards in Senate Document 97 directed federal agencies to use the plan that maximized net benefits as the baseline against which to consider effects of intangibles. Agencies were directed to estimate the extent to which they departed from the maximum net benefit plan when they took intangibles into account.

Even while addressing a number of issues related to environmental quality, Senate Document 97 used the word environment only once and then only to refer to the general setting for planning based on the expectation of an expanding national economy, growing population and higher incomes. The term was not used to refer to the quantity and quality of natural resources.

ENVIRONMENTAL POLICIES AFTER 1965

It is clear from the above that environmental values were increasingly brought into consideration in water resources policy and planning guidance prior to 1965. The extent to which water resources development reflected those policies and planning directives is debatable, but both state and federal policies in the post-World War II era reflect a very different attitude about environmental values than had been the norm in the nineteenth and early twentieth centuries.

Kempton et al. (1995) demonstrate, using national survey data, that environmental values were increasingly shared by the American population after 1960. They argue further that the change goes beyond shifts in attitudes and opinions to core values and fundamental beliefs. Hays (1987) used a variety of indicators, including Congressional and state legislative voting patterns, growth in environmental organizations, presidential responses and responses of advocacy organizations and management agencies to reach similar conclusions. One illustration of the growth of interest is membership in the Sierra Club from its beginning in 1892 with 182 members to a 1982 membership of 325 000 with over 90 per cent of that increase after 1960 as shown in Figure 4.4 (Sierra Club, 2003).

Between 1965 and 1980, a flurry of roughly a dozen major federal laws were passed reflecting the public's shift in environmental values broadly and those related to water resources specifically. These legislative actions (see Tables 2.4 and 2.5) built on basic themes that had emerged prior to 1965 and on a fundamentally new theme – protection of complex ecosystems to minimize destruction of basic life-support processes.

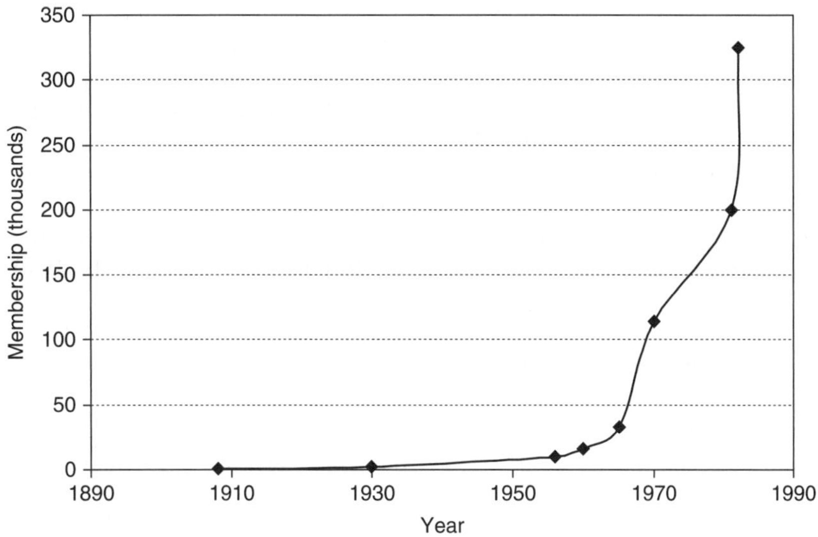

Figure 4.4 Growth in membership of Sierra Club 1908 to 1980

Preservation of Natural Areas

The preservation movement that had led to the establishment of the national parks was extended after 1965 to preservation of selected streams in their natural or near-natural state. The great dam-building era, begun in the 1920s, reached its peak in the 1960s. The loss of free-flowing streams and of riparian habitat associated with those impoundments made dam construction a primary target of preservationists. Congress responded in 1968 by passing the Wild and Scenic Rivers Act (Public Law 90-542). Section 5(d) of the Act directed the Secretary of Interior to identify wild and scenic river areas. It also directed federal agencies involved in development of water and related land resources to take into consideration and evaluate the effects of plans and projects on those areas. In response to that directive, the National Park Service (NPS) developed and continues to maintain the Nationwide Rivers Inventory (NRI) of potentially eligible stream segments. A river segment may be listed in the NRI if it meets several criteria. It must be free-flowing and it must have one or more outstanding remarkable values, among them exceptional scenery, fishing or boating, unusual geological formations, rare plant and animal life and cultural or historical artifacts judged to be of more than local or regional significance (www.nps.gov/ncrc/programs/rtca/nri/hist.html#pwsra). More than 3400 segments had been listed by 2003.

Preservation of the nation's wetlands was not explicitly mentioned in the Clean Water Act (CWA), but a lawsuit by the Natural Resources Defense Council over interpretation of what was included in 'waters of the United States' led to them being brought under jurisdiction of Section 404 dredge and fill permits. That decision had a pronounced effect on wetland preservation. During the period 1950–70 the rate of loss was approximately 460 000 acres per year, but under provisions of the CWA, as amended in 1972 and President George H.W. Bush's 'no net-loss' proclamation, losses were reduced to about 60 000 acres a year in the 1990s (Dahl, 2000).

Preservation of Individual Species

In addition to launching program expansions to preserve natural areas, the post-1965 proliferation of environmental legislation expanded protection of individual species. Following publication of Rachael Carson's *Silent Spring* in 1962 and the overwhelming public response, the Bureau of Sports Fisheries and Wildlife compiled and published a list of 63 endangered species. Congress passed a relatively weak Endangered Species Preservation Act in 1966 to protect endangered vertebrates to the extent practicable. A version to protect invertebrates passed in 1969. As the environmental movement strengthened, Congress responded by passing the Endangered Species Act (ESA) of 1973, a far-reaching step with a significant effect on water resources management (Czech and Krausman, 2001).

Section 7 of the ESA requires that all federal agencies, in consultation with the USDOI, conserve officially listed endangered and threatened species and must insure that all their actions are 'not likely to jeopardize the continued existence of any endangered species or threatened species or result in the destruction or adverse modification of habitat of such species', unless an agency has been granted an exemption by the cabinet-level Endangered Species Committee. That Committee can grant an exemption if it can be demonstrated by the petitioner that:

- There are no reasonable and prudent alternatives.
- The benefits of such action clearly outweigh the benefits of alternatives.
- The action is of regional or national significance.
- No irreversible or irretrievable commitment of resources has been made.
- Provisions are made for reasonable mitigation and enhancement measures.

Table 4.1 *Number of endangered and threatened species in the USA listed pursuant to the Endangered Species Act as of February 2007*

	Endangered	Threatened	Total
Animals	933	199	1132
Plants	599	148	747
Total	1532	347	1879

Source: http://endangered.fws.gov.

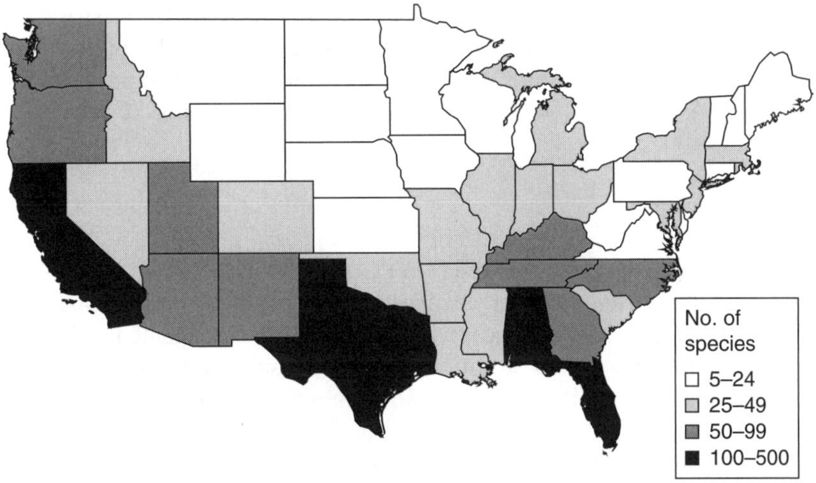

Figure 4.5 *Distribution of threatened and endangered species by states*

As of early 2007, almost 2000 species of plants and animals had been listed as endangered or threatened in the USA, as summarized in Table 4.1. See Figure 4.5 for the distribution of federally-listed species.

Water resources actions are not the only cause of endangerment of species, but they are important. Czech and Kraussman (2001) identified 18 categories of causes since passage of the ESA. They note several limitations of their analysis, including the facts that species are rarely endangered by a single cause and that it is often difficult to determine which of several causes may be the dominant one. Nonetheless, they rank reservoirs and running water diversions as the third leading cause in the continental USA; aquifer depletion and wetland draining and filling is ranked as the fifteenth leading cause. Pollution of air, water or soil is listed as the fifth leading cause, but their analysis does not differentiate among types of pollution.

Protection of Public Health and Aquatic Life

Action on water quality became fast and furious by the mid 1960s. The 1965 Water Quality Act (Public Law 89-234) required states to classify all streams and establish related water-quality standards, consistent with federal criteria, for each class of stream. Another provision moved the program out of the Public Health Service to a newly created Federal Water Quality Administration. Protection of groundwater also got a start in 1965 with passage of the Solid Waste Disposal Act that eliminated open dumps and directed the EPA to set standards for sanitary landfills. One year later, Congress passed the Clean Water Restoration Act, the main feature of which was an authorization of $3.9 billion over five years for construction grants. It also moved the program to the USDOI. A very significant reorganization occurred in 1970 when the EPA was created.

Clean Water Act

The 1972 amendments to the FWPCA, now known as the CWA, brought about fundamental changes to water quality management in the USA. It also had significant implications for management of water resources in general. In addition to the classification and standards requirements of the 1965 Act, its more important provisions included:

- States were required to develop basin-wide plans for achieving applicable water quality standards (Section 303(e)).
- All publicly-owned treatment works (POTW) were required to achieve at least secondary treatment (defined by the EPA as achieving 85 per cent removal of biochemical oxygen demand).
- All industries that discharged directly to streams were required to have best practicable treatment as defined by the EPA in effluent guidelines.
- If minimum treatment requirements for either municipalities or industries were not sufficient to satisfy water quality standards in a particular stream, more advanced treatment would be required (such streams are referred to as being water quality-limited).
- Grants to aid in construction of POTW authorized at a 3-year level of $18 billion.
- No discharge of wastewater to the waters of the USA was allowed without a permit (Section 402).

- Enforcement was based on compliance with effluent limits included in discharge permits where compliance was determined by self-monitoring and reporting.
- Without specific exemption, permits were required for any activity that dredged material from or placed fill material in the nation's waters (Section 404).
- Before a dredge or fill permit could be issued, the state would have to certify that the proposed action would not lead to a violation of water quality standards (Section 401).

Two major sources of pollution, non-point sources and urban storm water run-off, were not addressed by operative sections of the CWA until the amendments of 1987. This was in part because the extent and magnitude of the problems were not adequately known at the time. Nor was there a consensus on how they could or should be controlled. Finally, the political power of the farm lobby, particularly in the Senate, cannot be ignored. Some would argue that all this is still true today, but, nonetheless, Congress directed the EPA, in 1987, to take steps toward the management of these sources.

Section 319 of the CWA amendments of 1987 and subsequent EPA regulations for non-point sources required the states to identify:

- Streams in which water quality standards were violated because of non-point sources.
- Categories of non-point sources causing problems and the best management practices for each of them.
- State programs that address non-point sources, how those programs will be implemented over the short and long runs and annual milestones for tracking programs.
- Sources of funding for programs.

In response to the 1987 directive from Congress on urban storm water management, the EPA formulated a two-phase program: Phase I regulations, adopted in 1990, covered incorporated places and counties with populations over 100 000 and Phase II regulations, adopted in 1999, covered all urban areas with municipal separate storm sewer systems (MS4s) owned by public entities. The directive established a requirement for a discharge permit for facilities and activities that discharge storm water into surface waters from a pipe or channel. Under Phase I, the EPA required permit coverage for large urban storm water dischargers and 11 categories of industrial activity, including construction activity that disturbs five or more acres of land. Phase II requires permits for small MS4s and construction activities disturbing between 1 and 5 acres.

Another significant provision of the CWA was the anti-degradation policy (CFR, Title 40, Part 131.12). It required that the quality necessary to support existing in-stream uses be maintained and protected, with special attention to high quality waters (HQW) where existing stream conditions are substantially better than that required for protection of fish and recreation. The quality of the HQW must be maintained and protected except for special circumstances. Existing quality must be maintained and protected without exception in those HQWs that constitute outstanding national resources, such as national and state parks, wildlife refuges and waters of exceptional recreational or ecological significance.

A number of provisions of the CWA have implications for broader aspects of water resources management. First, because allowable loads on water quality-limited streams are directly proportional to stream flow, any modification to low flow regimes in those streams could result in changes to treatment requirements for dischargers. Second, any change in use of a stream segment that might be proposed as part of a water resources project would require a reclassification of the stream segment and impose a different set of water quality standards. For example, to develop a portion of a stream for public water supply that is currently classified for protection of aquatic life would require a formal reclassification process and imposition of a more stringent set of quality standards. Such a change could affect upstream as well as downstream dischargers because the hydrology of the receiving stream would be altered. Third, the anti-degradation policy could represent substantial barriers to development projects and other uses of protected streams.

Court challenges and subsequent modifications to regulations governing dredge and fill permits under Section 404 significantly affected all projects impacting wetlands. Sequencing requirements and compensatory mitigation altered planning processes and costs of projects requiring those permits. Section 404(b) (1) of the CWA requires an applicant for a permit to demonstrate no feasible alternative to filling of a wetland. The applicant must show compliance with a sequence of steps to avoid or minimize any adverse impacts to wetlands.

Implementation of the Clean Water Act

Compliance with some of the mandates of the CWA came about within reasonably short times. Thus, industrial sources were largely in compliance with technology-based treatment requirements within a decade. Progress toward achieving secondary treatment for publicly owned treatment was slower, but, as shown in Figure 4.6, virtually all publicly owned

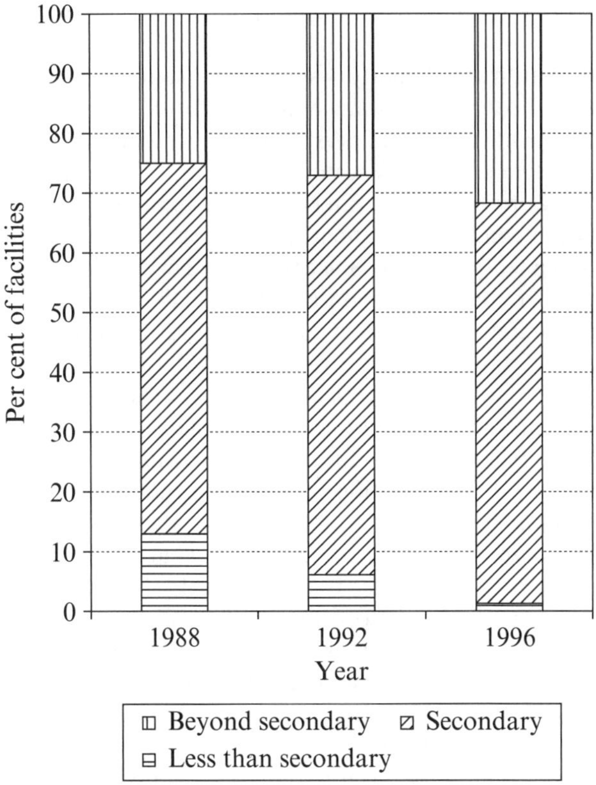

Source: USEPA, (2000).

Figure 4.6 Progress toward secondary treatment

facilities were at the secondary level or beyond by 1996 (EPA, 2000). More than 30 per cent are currently rated as being greater than secondary and those facilities serve about 44 per cent of the sewered population of the country.

With the exception of a few places like the Chesapeake Bay, tracking changes in water quality in the nation's streams has proved to be difficult. Section 305(b) of the CWA requires the EPA to prepare biennial reports on water quality conditions in the country. The EPA compiles those reports from data provided by each of the states. Several factors limit the value of the state data, however, including variation in the procedures by which states make assessments and changes in the guidance provided by the EPA over time. It is also worth noting that no attempt is made in the submissions to estimate what the conditions would be without the CWA programs.

The National Water Quality Assessment Program, conducted by the USGS, established in 1991, is much more scientific in its approach. It was designed to provide a national perspective on water quality though not to track the effectiveness of CWA implementation. The data are generated in studies of 42 river basins, watersheds and aquifer systems distributed throughout the country. The intent is to assess conditions in each study area on about a ten-year cycle. Since the second cycle of studies began only recently, quite limited time series data are available from that effort.

The need for reforming water quality monitoring programs has been noted by an assistant administrator of the EPA (Mehan, 2004). He cited the concluding comment in the *Draft Report on the Environment 2003* that there was insufficient information to assess the condition of the nation's water and watersheds with confidence and scientific credibility. He also cited a survey by the Association of State and Interstate Water Pollution Control Administrators that concluded that states are operating their monitoring programs at about 50 per cent of what is needed.

In addition to programs to assess physical, chemical and biological conditions of water bodies, efforts have been made to assess the economic benefits and costs associated with the CWA programs. The Regulatory Right-to-Know Act of 2001 now requires an annual estimate of benefits and costs of major federal programs by the Office of Management and Budget (OMB). In its 2003 report to Congress the OMB estimated that programs administered by the EPA Office of Water, of which the CWA programs are a dominant portion, had benefits in the range $0.89 to $8.08 billion, while costs ranged between $2.42 to $2.93 billion. Net benefits could range from a negative $2 billion to a positive $5 billion (OMB, 2003). Among all the difficulties and uncertainties associated with these estimates, two are especially important. First is the problem of estimating what conditions would be in the absence of federal programs, the baseline for comparing actual conditions. It cannot be assumed that no action would have been taken without the federal programs, but guessing what the actions would have been and what they would have accomplished clearly involves considerable uncertainty. Second, benefits of pollution control are measured by the public's willingness-to-pay (WTP) for protection of health, aesthetic qualities of the environment, recreation, protection of fish and wildlife, protection of ecosystems and other attributes of water quality. Most of these services are not marketed, so estimates of benefits must rely either on inferences based on what people actually spend in market situations where there is arguably a relation between water quality and marketed goods or services or on what people say they are willing to pay in hypothetical markets. The latter method has remained controversial, even after substantial developments over the past 20 years and after having been blessed for use in official natural resource damage assessments by a blue ribbon panel of Nobel laureates. (See Chapter 3 for a fuller discussion of techniques for damage and benefit estimation.)

Two other questions of interest concern the affordability of pollution control programs and how affordability may have changed from 1972 to 1997. To provide at least a rough answer, estimated expenditures by local governments (including federal grants) are divided by the number of housing units connected to public sewers to get expenditures per housing unit. That cost is then divided by median family income to get an estimate of expenditure for sewer service as a per cent of family income (PFI). Costs and incomes have been adjusted to 2001 dollars using the CPI for all urban consumers CPI-U-X1 price deflator (see *Mini Historical Statistics*, Table HS-25, Statistical Abstract of the United States). The results of this calculation, graphed in Figure 4.7, show that over the 25-year period, the real cost of sewer service per household rose from about \$226 to \$315 per year. That represents an increase in PFI from 0.55 per cent in 1972 to 0.64 per cent in 1997. For families at the median income level (about \$50 000 in 1997), the cost clearly has been and remains affordable.

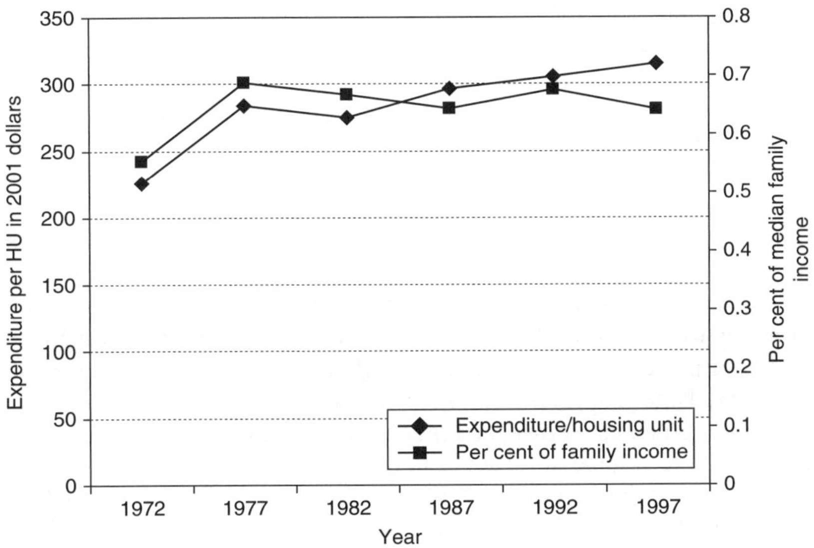

Source: United States Bureau of the Census.

Figure 4.7 Local government expenditures for sewage services

Safe Drinking Water Act

The Safe Drinking Water Act (SDWA) of 1973 directed the EPA to establish National Drinking Water Standards (NDWS). From the time it was enacted to 1986, the EPA established regulations on about two dozen substances, including inorganic chemicals, microbiological indicators, organic compounds and radionuclides. Dissatisfied with the pace at which the EPA was bringing those substances under the NDWS, Congress amended the Act in 1986. It directed the EPA to consider nearly 100 contaminants over a period of several years. Current standards apply to:

- Seven microbiological indicators – some specific to particular organisms, other indicators of possible pathogens.
- Four disinfection byproducts.
- Three disinfectants.
- Sixteen inorganic chemicals.
- Fifty-three organic chemicals.
- Four radionuclides.

Failure to satisfy these standards in a lake or stream does not necessarily disqualify use of that resource for public drinking water. Although withdrawing public drinking water from uncontaminated sources is preferable, a source may be acceptable after treatment. The SDWA Amendments of 1986 included the requirement that filtration be used as a treatment technique unless a water supplier can demonstrate that the source water is of sufficiently high quality that filtration is not necessary.

Compliance data for the NDWS, as shown in Figure 4.8, tend to reveal steady improvement in drinking water quality for community water supplies, with both the number of systems experiencing violations of maximum contaminant levels and the number of people affected by those violations generally declining from 1995 through 2000. Compliance with drinking water standards is not, however, the most direct measure of increased protection. Incidence of waterborne disease would be a better indicator. Data from the Center for Disease Control on the number of reported outbreaks, shown in Figure 4.9, indicates an overall decline.[2] However, the number of people affected by these outbreaks is highly sporadic. Over the past decade the single outbreak in Milwaukee in 1993 affected more than 400 000 people. Since then, reported outbreaks have affected about 1000 annually, but that data may not tell the whole story. It is very likely that many water-related outbreaks of disease affecting relatively small numbers of people go unreported. For some outbreaks of disease, the cause cannot be determined. A further limitation is that

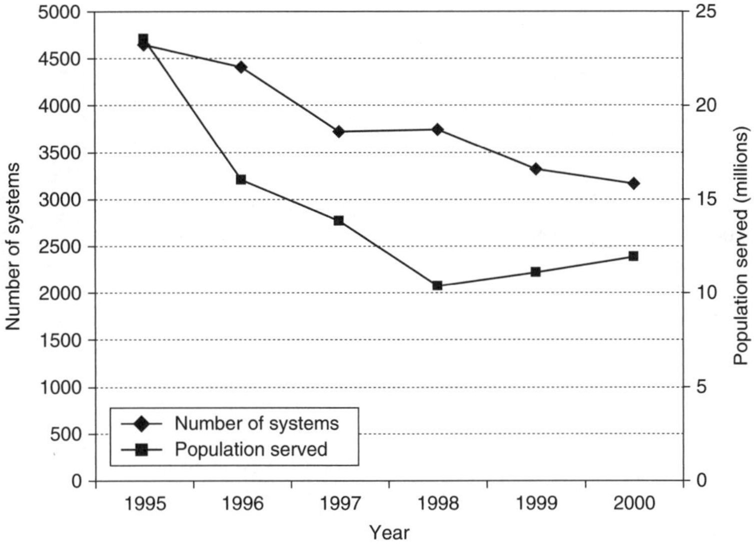

Source: US EPA Annual Compliance Reports.

Figure 4.8 Violations of maximum contaminant levels in national drinking water standards

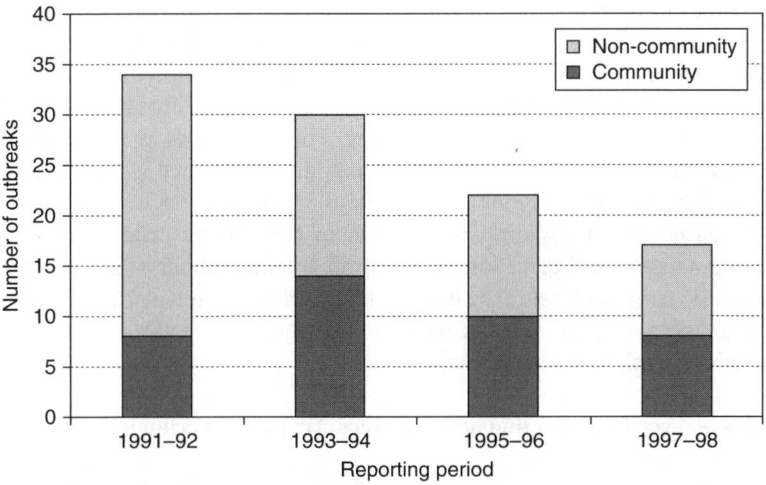

Source: CDC Survelliance Reports.

Figure 4.9 Outbreaks of waterborne disease in the USA

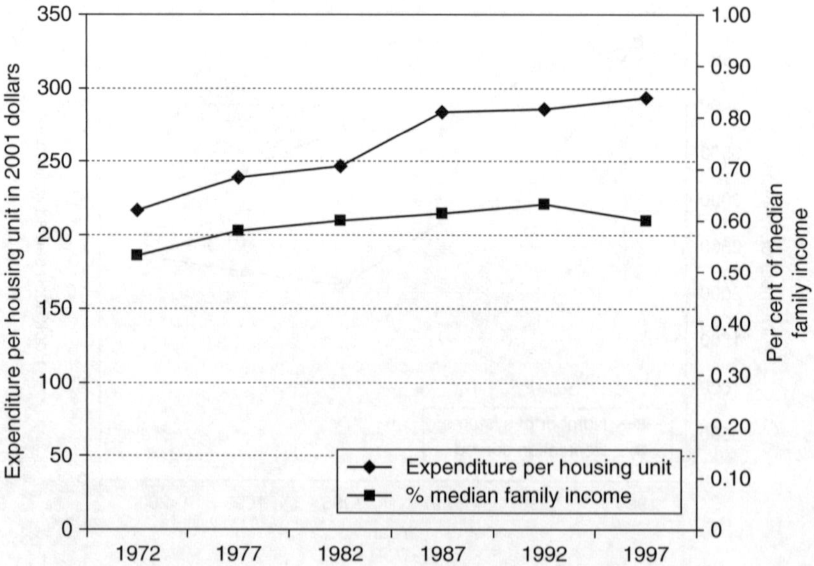

Figure 4.10 Local government expenditures for water supply

diseases resulting from long-term exposure to low levels of chemicals in water are not reported as outbreaks.

Increased protection of health due to enhanced drinking water standards comes at some increase in cost, but the service remains affordable to most Americans. As shown in Figure 4.10, local government expenditures per household on publicly owned water supplies rose from $217 in 1972 to $294 in 1997 in constant 2001 dollars. This represents an increase of 35 per cent, but in terms of per cent of median family income, the increase in the per cent of family income is from 0.53 to 0.60. Per household costs were estimated by dividing the Bureau of the Census estimates of local government expenditures for water supply by the number of housing units on public supplies (including both publicly and privately owned supplies). It was assumed that 85 per cent of housing units on public supplies are served by publicly owned systems.

The Resource Conservation and Recovery Act and Superfund

The CWA is directed toward chemical substances and biological organisms that are routinely discharged to streams. It does not directly address episodic releases of hazardous chemicals from industrial operations or leakage from active or abandoned waste disposal sites, the number of which is staggering. To address actual and potential environmental damage from those events, Congress passed the Resource Conservation and Recovery Act (RCRA) of 1976 and the Comprehensive Environmental Response, Compensation and Liability Act of 1980 (CERCLA) or Superfund.

The RCRA with its cradle-to-grave manifest system for hazardous substances was designed as a prevention strategy. Among its other provisions, Superfund was designed as a cleanup program for hazardous wastes with liabilities assigned for those sites where responsible parties are known and the use of trust funds for those sites where no responsible party could be identified. Under the Superfund law, the EPA is authorized to take two actions: (1) emergency, short-term action to prevent or remove substantial and imminent threats to human health or the environment and (2) long-term remediation to permanently remove the risk. Long-term remediation can occur only at sites formally added to the National Priorities List (NPL). Since passage of the Superfund program in 1980, the EPA and the states have made final assessment decisions on nearly 40 000 sites. A large number of those required no further action. From the time the NPL was created in 1983 to January 2007, about 1557 sites have been added to the list and 317 have been removed, leaving 1240 active sites (EPA, 2007).

Protection of Ecosystems

A fundamentally new theme, that of preserving complex ecosystems as basic life-support processes, was introduced by the Anti-degradation Policy of the CWA, the National Environmental Policy Act (NEPA), the ESA and later legislative actions. A White House panel to evaluate the effectiveness of NEPA referred to it as 'the foundation of modern American environmental protection' and as 'the first law to focus environmental concerns within a comprehensive national policy' (Council on Environmental Quality (CEQ), 1997). Congress declared it the continuing policy of the federal government, in cooperation with state and local governments and the private sector, to use all practical means and measures to protect and enhance environmental conditions. Many of the changes brought about by NEPA were procedural, but those changes broadened the scope of environmental concerns addressed by water resources agencies. By requiring federal agencies to address all significant environmental effects of developmental and regulatory actions, and by opening up the review process to third party intervention, NEPA expanded the scope of environmental assessments. An agency proposing to take an action must not only address specific issues mandated by other statutes, but must consider more general effects on ecosystems.

The NEPA and similar statues passed by a number of states greatly increased the extent to which environmental concerns are considered before actions requiring government approval can be undertaken. But the process is reactive in the sense that it is activated only when proposed actions would significantly affect the environment. It was not designed to initiate proactive measures to protect or enhance environmental resources.

More specific environmental responsibility was given to the US Army Corps of Engineers (USACE) in 1990. Section 306 of the 1990 Water Resources Development Act (WRDA) directed USACE to include environmental protection as one of its primary missions. It authorized USACE to undertake projects for the protection, restoration and creation of aquatic and ecologically related habitats in conjunction with navigation projects. Among the first and best known project undertaken with that authority is the Kissimmee River Restoration Project. The river was channelized by USACE in the 1960s, but soon after its completion, advocates began a movement to restore the river to its pre-channeled condition. In 1990 the state adopted a restoration plan prepared by the South Florida Water Management District (SFWMD) and Congress authorized a cost-shared project through the WRDA of 1992.

The ecological restoration authority of USACE was further broadened by Section 206 of the 1996 WRDA, under which USACE was authorized to engage generally in restoration of aquatic ecosystems, not simply to mitigate effects of its own projects or to restore areas it had previously degraded, but also to fix problems created by others. The plan to restore the Greater Everglades region in South Florida is one such effort.

Congress first authorized the Central and South Florida (C&SF) Project in 1948. The project resulted in a vast network of canals, levees and pump stations for controlling the flow of water through the Everglades to prevent flooding, provide water supply to agriculture and cities in South Florida, control salt water intrusion and protect fish and wildlife. Vast changes to regional ecological and hydrological systems, enormous growth of the population and conversion of land to urban uses and widespread embrace of environmental values brought demands for change. Responses came in both the WRDA 1992 and WRDA 1996 when USACE was authorized and directed to restudy the C&SF Project and develop a comprehensive restoration plan. Congress approved the Comprehensive Everglades Restoration Plan (CERP) in 2000 with an estimated price tag of \$7.8 billion for 60 projects to be built over 30 years.

Restoration projects by USACE are subject to cost sharing rules. On the one hand, modifications to cost sharing formulas in the 1986 WRDA (as discussed in Chapter 2) placed additional hurdles in the path of development projects that would have adverse environmental effects, but, on the other hand, those same obstacles stand in the path of environmental restoration.

Incorporation of Environmental Values in Water Resources Project Planning

Several of the environmental statutes directed administrative agencies to develop and adopt formal criteria and processes for environmental analysis to be incorporated into project formulation and evaluation. Provisions of the NEPA, the Water Resources Planning Act (WRPA) and the CWA are particularly noteworthy.

Among the more important provisions of the NEPA is the requirement that all federal agencies prepare detailed statements for every contemplated major action significantly affecting the quality of the human environment. The scoping process of the CEQ included in the regulations implementing the NEPA required an early identification of relevant environmental issues that should be addressed during the planning process.

Indeed, the NEPA, which was passed as the WRC was developing the *Principles and Standards* (P&S), heavily influenced their content. The multi-objective planning/evaluation model that the Water Resources Council (WRC) had under development and published in final form in 1973 (WRC, 1973) readily accommodated the new requirement, at least in principle, by requiring federal water resources agencies to formulate and evaluate plans with respect to beneficial and adverse effects on four accounts, namely NED, regional economic effects (REE), environmental quality (EQ) and other social effects (OSE). The NED and EQ effects were to be equally weighted in selecting a preferred project from among alternatives. How 'equal weights' were to be applied to objectives expressed in different metrics was not determined, at least not by formal criteria.

Beneficial and adverse effects of alternatives on the EQ objective were to address the separate resource elements listed in Table 4.2. Evaluation of effects on Classes A and B required assessments of the sizes and various measures of the quantities of resources, descriptions of the project's effects on those resources with and without a proposed plan, the extent of improvements and actions to protect and preserve these resources. For each Class C effect, evaluation of beneficial and adverse impacts was required for the full range of parameters relevant to applicable environmental standards.

When the *Principles and Guidelines* P&G replaced the P&S in 1983 (USACE, 2000), the EQ objective was eliminated. Instead, the federal objective was to contribute to the NED objective consistent with protecting

Table 4.2 Classes of environmental effects in Principles and Standards *(P&S)*

Class A	Class B	Class C
Open and green space	Archeological resources	Water quality
Wild and scenic rivers	Historical resources	Air quality
Lakes	Biological resources	Land quality
Beaches and shores	Geological resources	
Mountains and wilderness areas	Ecological systems	
Estuaries		
Other areas of natural beauty		

the nation's environment, pursuant to national environmental statues, applicable executive orders and other federal planning requirements.

Furthermore, the guidelines placed greater emphasis on a general evaluation framework and process and less emphasis on specific components of the EQ account and measurement of beneficial and adverse effects. How much change in plans was brought about by the change in objectives from the P&S to the P&G would be difficult to assess. Although the P&S required equal weighting of the NED and EQ objectives, no unambiguous measure existed for judging if equal weighting had been achieved. Although the P&G only requires the preparation of the NED plan that satisfies the stated objective, it also states: 'Other alternative plans should be formulated to adequately explore opportunities to address other Federal, state, local and international concerns not fully addressed by the NED plan.'

When the CWA passed, it authorized a separate multi-tiered framework for planning. Basin-wide plans were required in Section 303(e) as the basis for State Implementation Plans; area-wide plans were required in Section 208 for all complex urban-industrial areas where NPS and urban run-off could be significant sources and facility plans were required under Section 201 as a prerequisite to receipt of construction grants. Congress provided generous funding for these planning activities in the 1970s. Section 209 authorized completion of the comprehensive basin-wide and regional water resources plans as envisioned under WRPA, but no funds were ever provided under the CWA.

Although Congress never explicitly provided a directive or funding for watershed planning after about 1980, the EPA initiated its watershed protection approach in the early 1990s (EPA, 1991a, 1991b). Through that initiative, the EPA encouraged states to take a watershed approach to planning and regulatory activities. Despite its use of terms such as 'integrated' and 'holistic', the program was largely limited to problems of water quality and related land management. The framework document (EPA, 1991b) laid out a rather informal planning process.

The two examples that follow illustrate general observations about some strengths and weaknesses of watershed planning as practiced today. Some watershed planning activities have been started in response to the EPA regulations or other incentives; individual states, local governments or non-profit organizations have initiated other activities. One of the examples cited by the EPA early in its watershed approach was North Carolina's basin-wide water quality planning program, initiated by the Division of Water Quality of the Department of Environment and Natural Resources (DENR) in 1991. This program was developed to provide a rational basis for simultaneous issuance of all five-year National Pollution Discharge Elimination System (NPDES) permits within a basin. Since then it has been expanded to include a NPS program as required by Section 319 of the CWA.

North Carolina's basin-wide plans represented a major step forward. By providing a more complete picture of water quality conditions, sources of pollution and recommendations for improvements in each basin than had been available, they constitute a stronger basis for issuing permits and establishing priorities for developing policy and allocating available funds to reduce non-point source pollution. The highest priority in the first round generally was given to point source discharges and their effects on surface water quality. The Neuse and Tar-Pamlico River Basin plans did include the first set of basin-wide estimates for nitrogen and phosphorous loads. Supplemental studies for those two basins were necessary to establish basin-wide regulatory policies for nutrient load reductions and nutrient trading programs.

Although these efforts represent a substantial advance over previous planning activities, they are not comprehensive. Designated uses as specified in the existing stream classification system are taken as a given, but no consideration is given to future needs that could lead to changes in use. Perhaps the most significant omission is the absence of any analysis of evolving demands for, and supplies of, surface and groundwater withdrawals. Operating policies for reservoirs are not included as options for enhanced management. (See the discussion in Chapter 2 of the Washington, DC water supply study of the 1970s, in which altering operating rules was key to large cost savings.) Flood damage reduction is considered only incidentally to the protection of riparian areas for water quality improvements. Those omissions could have important consequences. In many instances balancing supply and demand for public water supplies, industrial supplies, agricultural uses and cooling water for thermoelectric power plants can have significant consequences on water quality and aquatic ecosystems. In North Carolina planning for water supply is primarily a local government responsibility. The state water supply plan, prepared by another division of the DENR, is largely a compilation of local plans with some state oversight.

Another example of watershed planning is Pennsylvania's Unified Watershed Assessment begun in 1998 to address non-point sources as required by the CWA. In that program major river basins in Pennsylvania were divided into sub-basins and within sub-basins watersheds were delineated by 8-digit Hydrologic Unit Codes. Watershed Restoration Action Strategies (WRAS) were then developed for each of the watersheds having the highest potential for pollution (www.dep.state.pa.us). As with North Carolina's basin-wide planning, the WRAS plans are primarily limited to existing water quality problems. They do not address demand for, and supply of, water and other potential uses of the resource. Indeed, one of the significant losses that has come from the demise of WRC is the lack of any integrated assessment of both quantitative and qualitative aspects of the nation's water resources.

Sustainability

The concept of sustainability or sustainable development has attracted widespread attention over the past two decades. For example, a keyword search of a major university library catalog using 'sustainable' turned up a list of 3200 references, not including articles in journals. That list covered a wide range of topics, including building materials, architecture, transportation, land use, work environments, natural environments, higher education, terrorism, communities, neighborhoods, enterprises, energy, natural resources, economics and diplomacy.

Kirby et al. (1995) trace the history of the concept to a report by the International Union for Conservation and Natural Resources (IUCN) entitled *World Conservation Strategy: Living Resource Conservation for Sustainable Development* (IUCN, 1980). They cite literature that reported the existence of 70 definitions of sustainable development, the most widely quoted being that of the report of the World Commission on Environment and Development (WCED), commonly referred to as the Brundtland Report (WCED, 1987). In brief, that source defined sustainable development as that which meets the needs of the present without compromising the needs of future generations.

Some have sought to add greater specificity to the concept as it may be applied to the management of water resources. A joint working group of the American Society of Civil Engineers (ASCE) and the United Nations Educational, Scientific and Cultural Organization (UNESCO) defined sustainable water resources systems as those that fully serve social objectives while maintaining ecological, environmental and hydrological integrity (ASCE and UNESCO, 1998). That report included a large number of recommended criteria for incorporating concepts of sustainability in designs for water resources systems.

Martin and Stakhiv (1999) examined a large body of literature on sustainability in search of concepts and goals that could be relevant to water resources programs of the civil works programs of the USACE. A particular focus of their review was the report of the President's Council on Sustainable Development (PCSD, 1996). In its view of sustainable development, the PCSD emphasized three goals – economic prosperity, environmental health and social well-being and equity. Although sustainable development, sustainable use and sustainability do not appear in any federal water resources statutes or regulations, Martin and Stakhiv point to a strong parallel between the PCSD's three goals and the four evaluation accounts in the WRC's P&S and P&G as discussed earlier. Recommendations of the PCSD never became directives to federal water resources planning agencies.

A major barrier to making operational multiple-objective or multiple-goal concepts of sustainability is the problem of weighting. While it is possible to use documents related to actual water resources decisions, determining if and how multiple goals were considered in the planning process, no common metric for comparing competing goals has yet been devised.

TECHNIQUES FOR PREDICTING ENVIRONMENTAL EFFECTS

Demand for Techniques

Inclusion of environmental analyses and values in water resources project planning and program and policy formulation, as required by provisions of water resources and environmental statutes, especially those of the last three decades of the twentieth century, has created a demand for analytical techniques to predict beneficial and detrimental environmental consequences of such projects and programs. This sort of evaluation requires predicting the states of the environment with and without the contemplated actions. In many, if not most, project and program evaluations, it is not sufficient to simply predict that some good things and some bad things will happen. It is most often the case that decision makers need to know how much good and how much bad will happen, where, when and to whom.

The need for predictive models is especially compelling when a policy dictates that one or more specific technologies be designed to achieve specific ambient environmental standards. Equally compelling is the case where policies require mitigation to offset adverse impacts of proposed projects. In those cases statutes require establishment of quantitative relationships between a proposed action and the consequences to the ambient environment. Despite the difficulties of establishing those relationships and of the substantial uncertainty often associated with them, agencies have had to develop or adapt techniques that could at least be judged as providing objective assessments of environmental consequences of proposed actions.[3]

Predictions of future states of the environment have been based on simulations of environmental systems, using either physical or mathematical models or both. Regardless of the type of model used, the strategy is to make adjustments to the model until it is reasonably representative of existing conditions, then it can be manipulated to predict how the system will respond to proposed projects or programs. Each of the two approaches, physical and mathematical, has its advantages and disadvantages. A principal limitation of physical models of ecosystems is one of scaling. Unlike physical hydraulic models where principles of similitude between models and prototypes are well known, no such principles of scaling have been established for biological systems. Selected biological effects of proposed water resources projects are subject to physical experiments, but simulation of any large-scale ecosystem is likely to be more effectively done using mathematical models.

At the time of passage of much of the environmental legislation reviewed in the previous sections of this chapter, modeling methods for conducting assessments either did not exist or had not been developed to the level at which they could be widely and confidently used in practice. For instance, when Congress passed NEPA, it recognized that existing methods of analysis were insufficient. In addition to NEPA's other requirements, language in it directed federal agencies 'to identify and develop methods and procedures . . . to insure that (previously) unquantified environmental amenities and values may be given appropriate consideration in decision making along with economic and technical considerations'.

In 1980 the EPA promulgated its second version of Section 404(b) (1) guidelines for permitting dredge and fill permits in wetlands. Those guidelines included the use of compensatory mitigation as a permissible action USACE could use to minimize adverse effects of development in wetlands.

With the guidelines came the need for techniques to determine the extent of adverse effects and what would constitute adequate compensation. Few were available at the time.

Some provisions of the CWA could only be implemented with the establishment of quantifiable relationships between wastewater effluents and water quality in receiving streams, lakes and estuaries. Even in relatively simple cases where mandated minimum treatment techniques were sufficient to satisfy water quality standards, water quality models had to be used to demonstrate that assessment. For more complex stream segments where minimum treatment requirements would be insufficient to satisfy water quality standards, states were required to establish total maximum daily loads (TMDLs) that segments could sustain without violation of water quality standards. Only simulation or lengthy and costly on-site field experiments can determine relationships between allowable loads and ambient water quality attained. Although water quality simulation models are subject to error, design of wastewater treatment plants on the basis of field experiments would have an unacceptably high cost. The simplest such model relating discharges of biochemically oxidizable wastes and oxygen balances in streams was first published in the 1920s (Streeter and Phelps, 1925), but that model was largely confined to textbooks until the 1960s.

Estimation of actual loads on streams is relatively easy and precise for municipal and industrial sources discharged through one or a small number of pipes subject to routine monitoring. Far more difficult is the problem of estimating loads from row cropping, animal agriculture and forestry, where sources are diffuse and run-off is subject to large temporal and spatial variability associated with precipitation events. Models that incorporate information about land use, land cover, management practices, soils, slopes, stream density, precipitation and other factors are often necessary to estimate loads from those sources. The earliest of those models were not developed until the early 1970s.

Environmental and ecosystem restoration projects placed an even greater demand on USACE and other federal agencies. These projects put the agencies squarely in the business of predicting responses of ecological systems to projects specifically designed to alter existing conditions, a very demanding task.

Most, if not all, predictive models of environmental systems have as their outputs indicators of the level of individual physical variables or chemical or biological species at a given time and location. For even a modestly complex system, the number of variables or species may be quite large and the times and locations at which the variables and species are to be predicted may be enormous. To avoid being overwhelmed by the sheer volume of predicted outcomes, it is desirable to find integrated measures that summarize outcomes comprehensible to both model builders and the general public. Considerable effort has been spent to develop approaches that support that goal.

It has also been argued that assessments of ecological systems based on individual species are less informative than those based on measures of ecological communities. That argument is based on the view that ecological health is reflected not only by the numbers of individuals of any given species but also by the diversity of species and their relative abundance. Appropriate indices or models of ecological health are needed to assess existing systems as well as to predict future states of those systems.

State of Development

Models have been developed for a wide variety of environmental systems and components of systems. Within each type there may be hundreds of models reflecting: bases in statistical or mechanistic approaches; alternative representations of physical, chemical and biological processes and how they are included; variations in the number of spatial dimensions; how time is treated; and the use of alternative solution techniques. This section focuses on a few criteria for judging the potential utility of models, including:

- Their general state of readiness for use in the field (conceptual versus operational).
- The extent to which responsible public agencies have established continuing development, training and support activities.
- The depth of experience that accompanies their use.
- Availability of supporting databases.
- How the models treat uncertainty and the level of uncertainty associated with them.
- Cost of their calibration, verification and execution.

The first two criteria above are used here to significantly narrow the discussion to those models ready for use and supported by one or more agencies or organizations involved in water resources management. Looking only at settings frequently encountered in water resources planning imposes a further limit. These are:

- hydrologic and hydraulic systems of surface water
- groundwater quantity and quality
- watershed models for transport and delivery of pollutants to streams

- water quality for streams, lakes and estuaries
- terrestrial and aquatic ecosystems.

Hydrologic/Hydraulic Models

Hydrologic and hydraulic models focus primarily on the movement of water over and through various types of conveyances and media over time and space, addressing critical variables such as velocity, depth and mixing. There is probably little dispute that hydrologic and related hydraulic models of surface water systems are the best developed water related environmental models. Scientific investigation of hydraulic processes is centuries old (Rouse and Ince, 1957) and emergence of the science of hydrology since the mid nineteenth century is well documented. The National Research Council's (NRC) review of fundamental scientific needs in hydrology (NRC, 1991) contains a brief summary of key developments.

Simulation of large-scale river basin systems was the subject of considerable development efforts in the 1960s, especially in the work of the Harvard Water Program (Maass et al., 1962). Noteworthy among the successful application of these computer-based simulation methods was the study of the Potomac River Basin in the mid 1970s. A group from Johns Hopkins University showed, through simulation studies, that if all the various water utilities serving the metropolitan Washington, DC area cooperated during a drought, the construction of a proposed reservoir on the Potomac River would not be necessary. This resulted in a large economic and social cost savings, substantially more than the cost of all the federally funded research programs in water resources systems engineering up to that time. To facilitate continued cooperation, these utilities get together to carry out real-time drought simulation exercises each year.

Since these early years of computer modeling, USACE's Hydrologic Engineering Center (HEC) and USGS have developed and continue to support a variety of hydrologic/hydraulic models. The HEC, established in 1964, has for decades developed and presented training courses in hydrologic engineering and has produced well-known software packages. Its first packages addressed watershed hydrology, river hydraulics, reservoir analysis and stochastic stream flow generation. More recent ones are designed to provide the River Analysis System and Hydrologic Modeling System packages with an expanded array of options and interfaces (www.hec.usace.army.mil).

In addition to HEC's work, independently created generic modeling shells exist for simulating water resources systems. The AQUATOOL (Andreu et al., 1991), the RIBASIM (Delft Hydraulics (DH), 2002), the MIKE-BASIN (Danish Hydraulic Institute (DHI), 1997) and the Water Evaluation and Planning System (WEAP) (Raskin et al., 2001) are representative of interactive river-aquifer simulation shells in which the system is represented by, and drawn in as, a network of nodes and links. Each node and link require data and these data depend on what that node and link represent, as well as what the user wants to get from the output. A few of these shells include both quantity and quality variables. They are particularly user-friendly because of the interactive and adaptive process they support in defining models and managing data.

The impetus for development of the first generation of these models was the need to provide support for design and operation of large-scale river basin development projects. As environmental effects of both design and operation became more important, the models were used to enhance environmental quality in at least two ways: (1) improving operational efficiency to avoid new, potentially damaging development projects and (2) exploring how changes to system operation might affect variables such as velocity and depth at ecologically critical times of the year.

Data for river basin models are readily available from the USGS, which maintains one of the finest acquisition and dissemination networks in the world. Nonetheless, uncertainty in hydrologic aspects of river basin models is primarily caused by limitations of the data, including measurement errors at stream gages, short lengths of the historical records, spotty spatial density of stream flow gages and lack of knowledge of the effects of upstream regulation. Flows in surface water systems are highly variable and the ranges of the confidence intervals on estimates of key parameters made using historical records are inversely related to the length of record. That said, however, uncertainty surrounding the predictions of river basin management models in the USA is generally attributable to projections of inputs such as populations, technologies and prices rather than to hydrologic or hydraulic parameter errors.

Groundwater Models

Models of groundwater flow and quality have reached a high level of development but the data necessary to fully calibrate and verify those models lag behind. Hundreds of variations had been developed as early as 1980, reflecting various combinations of: the number of dimensions included, treatment of temporal variability, choice of saturated or unsaturated conditions and how solute transport is dealt with. However, only a few of them were considered usable based on judgments about general data availability, adequacy of documentation and prior experience (Bachmat et al., 1980). Since then, the USGS has developed a number of fully documented and freely available models. As of 2004 the USGSs website listed approximately 30 software packages, about half of which were models and the other half graphical interfaces, pre- and post-processors and supplementary calculations. The models cover a range of two- and three-dimensional models of groundwater flow including: heat transport; single and multiphase transport; multi-species transport in heterogeneous, variably saturated porous media; and flow-through variable density media. They also include a small number of models that couple surface water and groundwater processes.

> Data for calibrating and validating groundwater models is much less available than for their surface water cousins, in large part because of the cost of acquiring such data. Values of key parameters for groundwater models have been published at the regional scale through the USGS's Regional Aquifer System Analysis Program (water.usgs.gov/ogw/rasa/html/introduction.html), but site-specific values must be determined by field investigations. Obtaining a sufficient quantity of such data is often very expensive. (Committee on Opportunities in the Hydrologic Sciences (NRC, 1991)

The USGS has had a wide range of experiences with application of groundwater models. Several sites have been heavily instrumented to calibrate and verify those models. There is also a large body of application experience stemming from cleanup programs under the Superfund. But because those experiences are so widely distributed among consulting firms working in a wide variety of chemical and geologic settings, it is difficult to draw any general conclusions from them and there has been little effort made to synthesize the findings.

Many express concern about the funding necessary to support collection of basic data for both surface and groundwater analyses. A task force operating under authority of the Advisory Committee on Water Data, established under the Federal Advisory Committee Act, undertook an extensive review by high-level stakeholders external to the USGS in 1999 (http://pubs.usgs.gov/circ/circ1192/). The task force noted:

> Current funding for the Cooperative Water Program is not adequate to satisfy all the needs identified for additional stream flow data, regional ground-water information, updated hydrologic models and technical publications. Funding levels have not kept pace with inflation or the increased demand for the services of the program. (http://pubs.usgs.gov/circ/circ1192/html/executive.html)

A report by the NRC's Water Science and Technology Board (WSTB, 2004) makes the argument that despite repeated calls to protect and enhance key legacy monitoring systems, the downward trend in funding for those programs continues. This is reflected in programs involving monitoring of stream flow, groundwater, sediment transport, water quality and water use.

Watershed Models

For more than a century, dating to work on the rational method (where run-off is assumed to be proportional to rainfall intensity times the drainage area) by Kuichling in 1889 and Lloyd-Davies in 1906 (Bedient and Huber, 1988) various models have addressed the problem of obtaining better estimates of surface water run-off associated with precipitation events. As for other models of water resources systems, the advent of digital computers made possible the development of more detailed watershed models. The Soil Conservation Service (SCS) published its method in 1964 and Crawford and Linsley (1966) developed the Stanford Watershed Model two years later. The Stanford model was then adapted by Donigian and Crawford (1976) to include transport of selected contaminants from the land surfaces to streams. The EPA initiated a parallel model with development of its Storm Water Management Model (Metcalf and Eddy, Inc., University of Florida and Water Resources Engineers, Inc., 1971) that focused primarily on run-off from urban watersheds. The US Department of Agriculture, Agricultural Research Service (USDA-ARS), also developed a progression of watershed models with a particular emphasis on run-off of non-point source pollution from agricultural lands. The progression included the CREAMS, GLEAMS, AGNPS, SWRRB and SWAT models, moving from a field-scale, single-event model to one that considers a continuous sequence of discrete time periods at a watershed or river basin scale (Arnold et al., 1998). The Soil and Water Assessment Tool (SWAT) models daily time steps and integrates the run-off of water, nutrients and sediments from large numbers of watersheds.

Several federal agencies continue their support of watershed models. The EPA's Watershed/Water Quality Modeling Technical Support Center (WWQMTSC) continues to support BASINS, a modeling tool that includes the current version of the Hydrological Simulation Program FORTRAN (HSPF) that grew out of the Donigian and Crawford adaptation of the Stanford Watershed Model. BASINS also includes the latest version of SWAT (www.epa.gov/water/soft.html), actively supported by the USDA-ARS's Grassland, Soil and Water Research Laboratory in Temple, Texas. The HEC supports its own watershed model within its Hydrologic Modeling System.

All of the time-variant, mechanistic watershed models have extensive data requirements. The HSPF and the SWAT track several species of chemicals as they undergo transformations and are transported in surface run-off, infiltration and groundwater discharge to streams. Time steps are relatively small. With large numbers of species, large numbers of kinetic rate coefficients and transport rate coefficients, there are numerous parameters to estimate if the models are to be calibrated to field data.

One of the largest applications of the HSPF has been to the watersheds of the Chesapeake Bay, a drainage area of approximately 64 000 square miles. The watershed model estimates how much sediment and how much of the nutrient of the load of nutrients applied to lands in the watershed are delivered to the bay.

Investigators at the USGS took an alternative approach to tracking seasonal loads of nutrients from watersheds. Smith et al. (1997) developed a model they call SPARROW, using spatially referenced regressions of contaminant transport on watershed attributes. It is a non-linear regression model that includes two phases of transport and fate of nutrient loads. First, it accounts for the delivery of nutrients to streams as a function of watershed characteristics, not unlike those in the USDA's Universal Soil Loss Equation. Second, it accounts for the fate of delivered loads discharged to streams as a function of travel in streams of several orders of magnitude. Instead of integrating over many small time steps to get seasonal loads, as is the case with the HSPF and the SWAT, SPARROW attempts to estimate seasonal or annual loads directly. As a regression model, it lacks the detailed specification of processes included in other models, but it provides an explicit procedure for estimating parameters and assessing uncertainty, something lacking in those other models. The USGS has summarized several applications of the model (www.water.er.usgs.gov/nawqa/sparrow/index.html). It has also been used as part of the process of establishing a TMDL for the Neuse River Basin in North Carolina.

Water Quality Models

Improvements in water quality models have been driven by mandates of the CWA. The basic Streeter-Phelps model for dissolved oxygen (DO) was first expanded to include the process of sedimentation. Diffusion terms were added for application in estuarine systems. Additional terms were added later to account for sedimentation and the distinctions between carbonaceous and nitrogenous biochemical oxygen demand. As effluent limits on many wastewater treatment plants went beyond secondary treatment to meet instream DO and other standards, as previously shown in Figure 4.6, models expanded to include oxygen consuming nitrification processes. To address problems of eutrophication in lakes and estuaries, additional species were added to the models. Advances accounted for nitrogen and phosphorous cycles including synthesis and respiration of algae. Most advances came as extensions of mechanistic mass balance models, complete with large numbers of kinetic terms for biochemical oxidation and reduction processes. Those kinetic terms include many temperature-sensitive rate coefficients.

Not surprisingly, the EPA has supported the development and application of the water quality models. The WWQMTSC currently supports the Enhanced Stream Water Quality Model (QUAL2E), a steady-state one-dimensional model for laterally and vertically well-mixed streams that can predict up to 15 water quality variables. One version of the QUAL2E allows the user to examine uncertainty using Monte Carlo techniques. The EPA also supports WASP6, a non-steady-state model that includes most of the same constituents as QUAL2E but allows variations in lateral and vertical as well as longitudinal dimensions (www.epa.gov/waterscience/wqm/index.html#epa). Documentation for both QUAL2E and WASP6 include likely ranges for all of the kinetic and stoichiometric expressions included in the models. However, considerable knowledge and skill are required for judicious selection of specific values within those ranges for any particular application.

This class of models has been widely and relatively successfully applied to streams and rivers dominated by point sources. There is much less confidence in their applications to large, complex bodies of water, such as the Chesapeake Bay and the Great Lakes, that receive loads from both numbers of point and non-point sources. In those instances any changes in water quality have been observed over long periods of time and it is not easy to judge whether a particular model could explain why changes did or did not occur as the result of some management action. It is also true that, with a few rare exceptions, regulatory agencies have underinvested in monitoring programs supporting continued evaluation and improvement of models of particular systems. All too often water quality models have been calibrated on data from one comprehensive survey, used to support regulatory decisions and then discarded without any follow-up monitoring and model or data modification if warranted. That cycle tends to be repeated during the next round of regulatory decisions.

Terrestrial and Aquatic Ecosystem Models

Management agencies use a limited set of models to assess the effects of water resources projects on terrestrial and aquatic habitats and ecosystems. The WRC published its proposed rules for the environmental quality evaluation part of its Level C implementation studies in 1980 (WRC, 1980). These rules focused almost exclusively on 'ecosystem' habitat. Results were to be reported in acres of habitat characterized by values of an associated Habitat Suitability Index (HSI, measured on a 0–1